The Art of Grief

The Series in Death, Dying, and Bereavement
Robert A. Neimeyer, Consulting Editor

Beder — Voices of Bereavement: A Casebook for Grief Counselors
Berger — Music of the Soul: Composing Life Out of Loss
Davies — Shadows in the Sun: The Experiences of Sibling Bereavement in Childhood
Harvey — Perspectives on Loss: A Sourcebook
Katz & Johnson — When Professionals Weep: Emotional and Countertransference Responses in End-of-Life Care
Klass — The Spiritual Lives of Bereaved Parents
Jeffreys — Helping Grieving People — When Tears Are Not Enough: A Handbook for Care Providers
Leenaars — Lives and Deaths: Selections from the Works of Edwin S. Shneidman
Lester — Katie's Diary: Unlocking the Mystery of a Suicide
Martin & Doka — Men Don't Cry ... Women Do: Transcending Gender Stereotypes of Grief
Nord — Multiple AIDS-Related Loss: A Handbook for Understanding and Surviving a Perpetual Fall
Roos — Chronic Sorrow: A Living Loss
Rogers — The Art of Grief: The Use of Expressive Arts in a Grief Support Group
Rosenblatt — Parent Grief: Narratives of Loss and Relationship
Rosenblatt & Wallace — African-American Grief
Tedeschi & Calhoun — Helping Bereaved Parents: A Clinician's Guide
Silverman — Widow to Widow, Second Edition
Werth — Contemporary Perspectives on Rational Suicide

Formerly The Series in Death Education, Aging, and Health Care
Hannelore Wass, Consulting Editor

Bard — Medical Ethics in Practice
Benoliel — Death Education for the Health Professional
Bertman — Facing Death: Images, Insights, and Interventions
Brammer — How to Cope with Life Transitions: The Challenge of Personal Change
Cleiren — Bereavement and Adaptation: A Comparative Study of the Aftermath of Death
Corless & Pittman-Lindeman — AIDS: Principles, Practices, and Politics, Abridged Edition
Corless & Pittman-Lindeman — AIDS: Principles, Practices, and Politics, Reference Edition
Curran — Adolescent Suicidal Behavior
Davidson — The Hospice: Development and Administration, Second Edition
Davidson & Linnolla — Risk Factors in Youth Suicide
Degner & Beaton — Life-Death Decisions in Health Care
Doka — AIDS, Fear, and Society: Challenging the Dreaded Disease
Doty — Communication and Assertion Skills for Older Persons
Epting & Neimeyer — Personal Meanings of Death: Applications for Personal Construct Theory to Clinical Practice
Haber — Health Care for an Aging Society: Cost-Conscious Community Care and Self-Care Approaches
Hughes — Bereavement and Support: Healing in a Group Environment
Irish, Lundquist, Nelsen — Ethnic Variations in Dying, Death, and Grief: Diversity in Universality
Klass, Silverman, Nickman — Continuing Bonds: New Understanding of Grief
Lair — Counseling the Terminally Ill: Sharing the Journey
Leenaars, Maltsberger, Neimeyer — Treatment of Suicidal People
Leenaars & Wenckstern — Suicide Prevention in Schools
Leng — Psychological Care in Old Age
Leviton — Horrendous Death, Health, and Well-Being
Leviton — Horrendous Death and Health: Toward Action
Lindeman, Corby, Downing, Sanborn — Alzheimer's Day Care: A Basic Guide
Lund — Older Bereaved Spouses: Research with Practical Applications
Neimeyer — Death Anxiety Handbook: Research, Instrumentation, and Application
Papadatou & Papadatos — Children and Death
Prunkl & Berry — Death Week: Exploring the Dying Process
Ricker & Myers — Retirement Counseling: A Practical Guide for Action

Samarel — Caring for Life and Death

Sherron & Lumsden — Introduction to Educational Gerontology, Third Edition

Stillion — Death and Sexes: An Examination of Differential Longevity Attitudes, Behaviors, and Coping Skills

Stillion, McDowell, May — Suicide Across the Life Span — Premature Exits

Vachon — Occupational Stress in the Care of the Critically Ill, the Dying, and the Bereaved

Wass & Corr — Childhood and Death

Wass & Corr — Helping Children Cope with Death: Guidelines and Resources, Second Edition

Wass, Corr, Pacholski, Forfar — Death Education II: An Annotated Resource Guide

Wass & Neimeyer — Dying: Facing the Facts, Third Edition

Weenolsen — Transcendence of Loss Over the Life Span

Werth — Rational Suicide? Implications for Mental Health Professionals

The Art of Grief

The Use of Expressive Arts in a
Grief Support Group

edited by J. Earl Rogers

Routledge
Taylor & Francis Group
New York   London

We gratefully acknowledge the following contributors for granting permission to include their material in this book:

Ina Albert, Penny Allport, Sara Baker, Sandra Baughman, Nicole Burgess, Lauren B. Chandler, Janet Feldman, Laura Kiser, Judith Koeleman, Deborah Koff-Chapin, Carol McIntyre, Carole M. McNamee, Debra Mier, Hernando A. Mispireta, Thomas D. Moore, J. Earl Rogers, Janet Shaw Rogers, Sara Spaulding Phillips, Laura Thomae, Sandra M. Walsh, and Lisa Wayman

Routledge
Taylor & Francis Group
711 Third Avenue
New York, NY 10017

Routledge
Taylor & Francis Group
2 Park Square
Milton Park, Abingdon
Oxon OX14 4RN

© 2007 by Taylor & Francis Group, LLC
Routledge is an imprint of Taylor & Francis Group, an Informa business

International Standard Book Number-13: 978-0-415-95535-5 (Softcover)

Library of Congress Cataloging-in-Publication Data

The art of grief : the use of expressive arts in a grief support group / [compiled by J. Earl Rogers].
    p. cm. -- (The series in death, dying, and bereavement)
    Includes bibliographical references.
    ISBN 0-415-95535-1 (softcover)
    1. Grief. 2. Bereavement--Psychological aspects. 3. Arts--Therapeutic use. I. Rogers, J. Earl.

BF575.G7A77 2007
155.9'37--dc22

2006039080

Visit the Taylor & Francis Web site at
http://www.taylorandfrancis.com

and the Routledge Web site at
http://www.routledge.com

Dedication

To my wife, Janet
Thank you for all your support, love, and hard work
My mirror

âme et esprit unis

CONTENTS

About the Author/Editor   xiii

Contributors   xv

Series Editor's Foreword   xvii

Acknowledgments   xxi

**SECTION I   THE USE OF EXPRESSIVE ARTS IN
                A GRIEF SUPPORT GROUP**

Chapter 1   Introduction   3
                J. Earl Rogers

Chapter 2   Leading Grief Support Groups   9
                J. Earl Rogers

Chapter 3   Basics of Grief and Loss   21
                J. Earl Rogers

Chapter 4   Children and Teens   31
                J. Earl Rogers

Chapter 5   How to Use This Book   39
                J. Earl Rogers

**SECTION II   THE GRIEF SUPPORT GROUP
                CURRICULUM: EIGHT SESSIONS**

Chapter 6   Session 1: The Storytellers — Oral History and
                Introduction   49
                J. Earl Rogers

Chapter 7   Session 2: The Written Story — Creative Writing,
Journaling, and Poetry   59
J. Earl Rogers

Chapter 8   Session 3: Sandtray — An Accessible Strategy
for the Grief Process   69
J. Earl Rogers

Chapter 9   Session 4: The Body of Grief   81
J. Earl Rogers

Chapter 10 Session 5: The Art of Collage — Visions and Images 95
J. Earl Rogers

Chapter 11 Session 6: The Music   101
Nicole Burgess

Chapter 12 Session 7: Drama and Theater   115
Lauren B. Chandler

Chapter 13 Session 8: Grief and the Sacred Art of Ritual   129
Janet Shaw Rogers

SECTION III   ALTERNATIVE ART FORMS, PROGRAMS, AND STORIES OF ART AND HEALING

Chapter 14 The Painters   153
*Deborah Koff-Chapin, Carol McIntyre,
and Judith Koeleman*

Chapter 15 The Writers   189
Sara Baker and Sara Spaulding-Phillips

Chapter 16 Programs in Art   199
Debra Mier, Laura Thomae, and Carole M. McNamee

Chapter 17 Programs for Teens and Children   227
Sandra Baughman and Laura Kiser

Chapter 18 Alternative Art Forms   239
J. Earl Rogers and Janet Feldman

Chapter 19 Stories of Art, Grief, and Healing   259
*Thomas D. Moore, Sandra M. Walsh, Lisa Wayman, and
Penny Allport*

Chapter 20   Conclusion   281
                J. Earl Rogers

References   287

Index   293

ABOUT THE AUTHOR/EDITOR

J. Earl Rogers, JD, PsyD, CT, is an artist and senior clinical consultant at Comox Valley Hospice on Vancouver Island where he practices as a certified thanatologist and end-of-life counselor. Dr. Rogers also maintains a private counseling practice in Courtenay, British Columbia. He has served on the board of directors of the Association of Death Education and Counseling (ADEC) and is a member of the Society for Arts in Healthcare and several prominent U.S. and Canadian hospice associations. He has 30 years experience as a civil trial attorney, 5 years as a U.S. naval pilot, and has published in several legal journals regarding stress and the law.

CONTRIBUTORS

Ina Albert
Ina Albert Associates, LLC
Whitefish, Montana

Penny Allport
Swara Inspiritations
Richmond, British Columbia

Sara Baker, MA
Loran Smith Center for Cancer
Support
Athens, Georgia

Sandra Baughman
Arts for the Spirit Coordinator
Oakwood Healthcare System
Northville, Michigan

Nicole Burgess, Bmus, BMT, MTA
Music Therapist
Comox, British Columbia

Lauren B. Chandler, BA, MSW
Consultant and Social Worker
Dougy Center for Grieving
Children and Families
Portland, Oregon

Janet Feldman
Act ALIVE
Barrington, Rhode Island

Laura Kiser, MA, ATR, LCPC
The Children's Hospital at
Montefiore
Bronx, New York

Judith Koeleman
Artist
Campbell River, British Columbia

Deborah Koff-Chapin
Center for Touch Drawing
Langley, Washington

Carol McIntyre, MA
The Painting Place
Santa Rosa, California

Carol M. McNamee, PhD
Director, The Arts in Healthcare
Project
The Family Therapy Center of
Virginia Tech
Blacksburg, Virginia

Debra Mier, RDT, LCSW
Willow House
Northbrook, Illinois

Hernando Mispireta
Nurse
South Miami Hospital
Miami, Florida

Thomas D. Moore
Violin Professor, New World
School of the Arts
Miami, Florida

Janet Shaw Rogers
Artist
Shaw Rogers Consulting, Women
in Business
Courtenay, British Columbia

Sara Spaulding-Phillips, MA
Psychotherapist
Santa Rosa, California

Laura Thomae, Mt-BC
Coordinator of Therapeutic Arts
Keystone Hospice
Wyndmoor, Pennsylvania

Sandra M. Walsh, RN, PhD
Professor, Barry University School
of Nursing
Miami Shores, Florida

Lisa Wayman, RN, MSN
Nurse and Artist
Phoenix, Arizona

SERIES EDITOR'S FOREWORD

It was Bertha Pappenheim — the famous "Anna O." of Josef Breuer's first experiments with psychoanalysis, and a pioneer social worker in her own right — who first named psychotherapy "the talking cure." And so it is, as a legion of well-controlled studies documents. Across a surprising variety of psychotherapeutic approaches, verbal exchanges between client and therapist can be powerfully curative — except when they aren't. And when they aren't, when the resources of literal speech alone are not enough, people often find themselves reaching for other symbolic resources to express, share, and transform wordless suffering into something that can be borne, validated, even cherished as a source of growth.

Grief often occasions just such a search for meaning, and the expressive arts provide a rich panoply of possibilities for its further processing. It is this insight that has stimulated a remarkably broad-ranging exploration of artistic activities of all kinds in healthcare contexts, ranging from painting classes for seriously ill children to journaling workshops for breast cancer survivors. And it is this same recognition that has led Earl "Tio" Rogers to spend a professional lifetime delving deeply into these many traditions, seeking their relevance for bereavement support groups, as well as for his own life. Indeed, it is this "leveling of the playing field" — bridging activities that proved personally healing into teachable skills that can benefit others — that accounts for the genuineness of each of the many contributions to this volume. For group leaders and members alike, immersion in and reflection on performance, music, bodywork, painting, or creative writing offer the prospect of moving beyond grief to growth, beyond trauma to transformation.

A clear strength of this book is its remarkable comprehensiveness. Virtually every medium of artistic expression seems to be represented, nearly every vein of creativity mined for its healing potential. The engaged reader will accompany Rogers week by week through a systematic curriculum refined in the crucible of his own bereavement support group experience, as participants are gently encouraged to create a space for telling the story of their loss, to themselves in a journal, and to caring others in the safety of the group; to deepen their engagement with its plot and themes through creative writing; to give it symbolic expression using sandtray; to embody it in physical movement; to assemble it in the evocative imagery of collage; to make it audible in music; to perform it in drama; and to give it sacred validation in ritual. In chapters devoted to each of these topics, Rogers distills the essence of his decades of engagement with each expressive tradition to offer concrete advice and instructions for the use of each artistic medium, for children, teens, and adults. Although, as he repeatedly cautions, the resulting curriculum is no substitute for training in formal art therapy tailored to the needs of complex individual cases, it certainly offers an adaptable structure for grief support in a wide variety of settings, ranging from bereavement programs sponsored by hospices to similar services for patients and their families in medical settings.

A second winning feature of this book is its attention to "voices in the field" — a dozen minichapters from practitioners of a rainbow of expressive arts summarizing their methods and their impact, often sharing their own stories, as well as those of their group members to convey their healing potential. Here I found myself engaged in both familiar and novel practices: the poignancy of poetry, the strange allure of Touch Drawing, the power of performance, the mystery of mask making, and much more. In addition, these chapters conveyed the creative integration of multiple methods in programs that specialize in particular populations (children, teens) and problems (cancer, HIV/AIDS). Completing this section, readers will be moved to explore the relevance of these expressive traditions for not only their group members or patients, but also for their own self-care.

In closing, in writing and editing this book, Rogers opens a door to an expanded practice of bereavement support, one that at the same time taps the wellsprings of individual creativity and mobilizes the validation and inspiration of a caring group. Along with other recent books in the Routledge Series on Death, Dying, and Bereavement such as Joy Berger's *Music of the Soul*, Shep Jeffreys's *Helping Grieving People,* and Phyllis Silverman's *Widow-to-Widow,* Earl "Tio" Rogers's *The Art of Grief* offers practical guidance for professional therapists and bereavement support providers alike in implementing services that harvest the healing potential of both symbolic talk and action. As a tribute to the efforts of Rogers and his artistic contributors, it feels fitting to conclude with a brief poem I have penned that acknowledges their courage — a courage shared by the reader — to enter the heart of grief and loss to accompany those they serve on their travel through loss to gain. In these pages the reader should find good companionship on that journey.

Travelers
© 2006, Robert A. Neimeyer

You know the lucky thing about my hip replacement?
she asked, not waiting for the answer.
It made me think about advance directives,
my living will, how I'd like to die.

Yeah, he said, her colleague
who chatted amiably with death
each day, like two old men
playing checkers in the park.
I know what you mean.

This is how it is
with the nurses, doctors, therapists
who walk down the halls of dying
as through the home of a relative,
pausing to leaf through the *Geographic*,
or straighten a family photograph on the wall.

They have earned their ease
the hard way,
learned to reach through the bramble
to find the fruit, add weight
to the rusty pail.

They have not so much grown inured
to pain as they have learned to savor it,
taste the sweetness in the grapefruit's bite,
feel the glow of a day's hard toil.

In the end, we need them
as we need seasoned travelers
met in an unfamiliar land.
They greet us on the steep trail,
in the twisting streets, point the way
to a good *taverna*, trace the path home.
Most of all, they help us
parse the dark syllables in our hearts,
bare them,

and seek cleansing
in the gathering storm.

Robert A. Neimeyer, PhD

The University of Memphis
Series Editor

ACKNOWLEDGMENTS

Where does one begin to acknowledge all those who have made this, or any other book, happen? To name anyone is to exclude someone important. With that risk, however, I want to acknowledge some of the people who supported and contributed to the completion of this book. If I have not mentioned someone, know that your contribution was as important as everyone who was mentioned. Thank you.

First to my wife, Janet, for moral support, editing, and proofreading, and her wonderful chapter on "Grief and the Sacred Art of Ritual." My children, Joseph and Devora, busy in their own careers, who listened and urged me on when I was sure that I could not write another word. To the curriculum chapter writers, Lauren and Nicole, thank you for your work and your timeliness. For all the friends who cheered me on and read drafts and applauded each little step along the way.

The depth and richness of this book is largely due to the contributors who offered their art, their stories, and their programs using art for healing. Art is a personal process and sacred to each of us who attempt to share our creative process with others. While art can be a solitary activity, it is in the group setting that deep healing can occur. You will see that healing process in the stories shared in Part III of the book. Thank you each one of you, for your willingness to share, your openness in telling the stories, and your creative spirit: Deborah Koff-Chapin, Carol McIntyre, Judith Koeleman, Sara Baker, Sara Spaulding-Phillips, Debra Mier, Laura Thomae, Carol McNamee, Sandra Baughman, Laura Kiser, Janet Feldman, Tio (the alter ego), Sandra Walsh, Thomas D. Moore, Penny Allport, Lisa M. Wayman, Ina Albert, and Hernando A. Mispireta. Thanks to Alex and Kathleen for sharing their story of the loss of their daughter and the wonderful photographs of the rituals they used to help in the healing process.

Many of the contributors belong to the Society for Arts in Healthcare, and answered my call for stories about the use of art in groups and grief. What a wonderful forum for artists and healthcare professionals to share their work and teachings.

Bob Baugher introduced me to The Association of Death Education and Counseling (ADEC), and gave me a list of books to read, so many years ago. To all the members, friends, and colleagues of ADEC who supported, taught, and mentored me; especially, Robert Neimeyer, Tom Attig, Dick Gilbert, Linda Goldman, Donna Schuurman, Lynne DeSpelder, Lu Redmond, Delpha Camp, Ron Barrett, Alan Wolfelt, and the members of the Board of Directors with whom I was honored to serve. To every author and researcher upon whose shoulders I stand, thank you for your efforts to increase our knowledge of thanatology.

This book was a small concept based on work done with Sharon Lukert at the Zen Hospice End-of-Life Counselor training (now Metta Institute), when Dana Bliss, Behavioral Sciences Editor at Routledge, walked up at an ADEC conference and asked if I could turn the concept into a book. Thank you Dana, and all your staff, for seeing the merit in the concept of using art in a grief support group and supporting me through the process. Final edits and preparation of the resource list was done by Arran Sherbourne of Courtenay, British Columbia. The photographs in the chapter on movement were done by our friend Donna Dow also of Courtenay.

I work at a wonderful hospice in the Comox Valley on Vancouver Island with fantastic volunteers and a wonderful staff: Terri, the executive director; Monique, our administrative assistant (without whom no work would get done); Christy, our volunteer coordinator; Karen our grief counsellor; and the volunteer grief counsellors. It is a pleasure working with these people. They teach me every day the lessons of compassion and service.

I have been fortunate to have many wonderful teachers on my path whom have shared their knowledge, compassion, and experience: Robert Strock who started me on this path of being with dying, Joan Halifax of Upaya Foundation of Santa Fe, who has guided so many health care professionals to just "Be with the dying," Richard Moss, although no longer in my life, has been a great inspiration, Frank Ostaseski, and the teachers and fellow students with the Alaya Institute End-of-Life Practitioner training in Marin, California. Thank you all.

J. Earl Rogers, JD, PsyD, CT

Section I

The Use of Expressive Arts in a Grief Support Group

CHAPTER 1   J. Earl Rogers

Introduction

The loss of a loved one often leaves behind the loose ends of grief.

— **Stephen Levine**

Grief, art, and storytelling are an innate part of the human experience. Each of us will grieve, or be grieved for, in our lifetimes. Art has been a form of expression for humans since the earliest times. Our history, experiences, losses, triumphs, and the essence of our psyche have been told in stories throughout human history. Often the art and the myths found in many of our stories express that which cannot be expressed through mere words.

Grief often lies beyond words, beyond the simple explanation of our conscious minds. It is in the unconscious, in the mystery of life, that expression of the deep wounds and tragedy of loss is found. Carl Jung saw that our depth lies in the unconscious, both individually and collectively. Through archetypes we find expression of who we are and how our experiences affect our conscious lives. Death is dark to the mind. It cannot be reduced to the rational — neither thought, nor interpretation, nor even memories. It is through the expression of the inexpressible that art allows us to reach deep into our unconscious and touch this mystery.

This book is designed to touch on several types of expressive arts, from the oral story we tell of our loss to the ritual that goes beyond words. Various expressive art forms are set forth in a format that allows grief facilitators to lead grief groups even without prior experience in the specific art form. The modalities have been chosen so that experience as an artist or in a particular form is not necessarily a requirement. However, facilitators should practice with the modality to be sure it works for them and they are comfortable in the use of the art form.

The layout of the book is in the form of a grief support group curriculum with a different expressive art form used each week. The facilitator can follow the format set out for the different types of expressive arts. Or, as the facilitator or group wishes, use one or two forms to make up the support group. The book is designed to be used as a curriculum and a resource. After the curriculum there are stories of how different art forms have been used. There are also listed alternative art forms that can be used in this curriculum, such as mask making or "Touch Drawing."

Speaking or writing our stories helps us come to terms with our loss and to help reconstruct meaning in our lives. So too can other forms of creative and artistic expression tell our story of loss and suffering (Neimeyer, 2000). Many people, especially adults, are not accustomed to creative and artistic forms of expression. The modalities presented here are designed to avoid the "I can't draw" response by gradually introducing the different forms and using collage instead of drawing or painting. Any medium can serve as a path for representation of loss and grief (Neimeyer, 2000). Different painting forms are described in the later chapters after the curriculum.

Art therapy is a profession that combines therapy with the creative process to assist with individual development and concerns or conflicts (Bertman, 1999). Art therapy is practiced in many therapeutic settings such as mental health facilities, schools, hospitals, hospices, and in psychotherapy. The language of art and creative expression can speak to us in ways that words cannot speak (Malchiodi, 1998; Neimeyer, 2000). Art therapy is based on the belief that images can help us understand who we are and enhance life through self-expression (Malchiodi, 1998). Intermodal expressive therapy uses all artistic or creative modalities. The use of art therapy can tell us about the inner world of the individual through the process of creating artwork, or by analyzing the product of the artist.

In this curriculum, however, we are not attempting to use art as therapy, although that may be a result. Rather, the book offers an opportunity for members of the grief group to express their story in different ways without the analysis of the facilitator. It is a strictly personal process to allow the group members to recognize the loss, experience the feelings connected with their loss and suffering, adjust to a new world, and to help in reconstructing a new relationship with the deceased (Jeffreys, 2005; Worden, 2001).

Using oral story, poetry, collage, sandtray, physical movement, drama, music, and ritual, the members of the group will be given the opportunity to move back and forth between exploring their feelings related to the loss and to picture a restoration of orientation to the external world and adjustments required to reconnect with the new world (Neimeyer 2000; Jeffreys, 2005). The participants will keep a journal during the course to tie it all together and offer them an ability to look back and see the journey they have walked. Research has supported that writing about our suffering and trauma can have positive implications for the growth required to move through the grief and loss (Neimeyer, 2000).

To facilitate the movement through the grief process the session chapters explain the process and guidelines of each week's creative modality. The section on grief will briefly explain the various grief theories and how this creative process relates to the different models. The overall theoretical basis of the course is primarily oriented toward the reconstruction of meaning in the lives of the participants. Also, the course is primarily designed to allow the group members to tell their stories in different ways. The facilitators are present to guide, offer structure, and to be, as Shep Jeffreys says, the "Exquisite Witness" (Jeffreys, 2005, p. 22). The facilitators are the containers for the safe and protected space the participants need to visit to understand their loss in all its forms.

The final session is Ritual, which is designed to bring the course together and allow healing through creative expression and ritual. However, the chapter should be read first before beginning the course. Ritual is a behavior that gives symbolic expression to feelings, thoughts, and loss (Jeffreys 2005; Neimeyer, 2000; Rando, 1984).

Each week the group will create and experience the healing of ritual in different forms. Rituals have therapeutic properties though the power of acting out, legitimizing of emotions, physical ventilation, and bringing limits to grief by having a distinct beginning, middle, and end (Rando, 1993; Neimeyer, 2000). Chapter 5, "How to Use This Book" will discuss the details of using ritual and how each week's session will proceed.

One of the difficulties of a book that is designed for different professions and levels of experience in grief and group leadership is to make it accessible both to those who are less experienced, and, at the same time, meaningful to the professional therapist or grief counselor. With this in mind, each chapter will have a list of books at the end to assist the facilitators in the work of the grief course and to offer additional materials that support the information in the chapter.

One need not be experienced in any one of the expressive arts set out in the course. Each chapter stands alone as the art form is explained and resources offered. The facilitator will be guided through the steps of using each particular art form and given tools and resources to deepen the understanding of the form. However, one need not go beyond the covers of this book to be able to use all of the expressive arts. If, for example, one has no musical background or experience, it will still be possible to lead a session into the magic of music. Sandra Bertman's book *Grief and the Healing Arts: Creativity as Therapy* would be an excellent resource for those less experienced in expressive arts. *Art Therapy for Groups* by Marian Liebmann is an excellent source for beginning art therapy groups.

It is suggested that the facilitator leading the grief group have experience in group work. For those facilitators not as experienced in the grief process it would be helpful to have a cofacilitator experienced in grief. Chapter 2, "Leading Grief Support Groups," is designed to facilitate group leadership for those less experienced with groups. Books listed will assist in the details of leading a grief group, and each chapter describes how to lead that particular session.

Grief is a universal experience, and as such, the leader will find that her or his own grief may come up during this support group. Be ready for the emergence of past losses. Chapter 3, "Basics of Grief and Loss," is for those who do not have formal training or have limited experience in working with grief. It is important that the leader is able to be present and listen. The only true gift we have to offer is the quality of our attention.

The art forms that have been chosen are selected because one can use the form without much in the way of materials or experience. Sandtray can be as simple as bowls of sand with some rocks, shells, or other materials from nature. Collage is used instead of painting, as it is easy to assemble magazines, glue, scissors, and construction paper, and is easy to clean up.

The group sessions are set out in order to move the story of loss from the conscious mind into the unconscious and beyond words. The sequence of the forms brings the story of each person from the past to the present and allows the story to become a living, developing process in the present moment rather than a story stuck in memory and time. In chapter 3, the issue of complicated mourning is discussed, such as chronic or prolonged, delayed or inhibited, and distorted grief. In each case the facilitators will have to decide whether a particular prospective group member is appropriate for a particular group.

Art therapy is a recognized form of reaching deep feelings and emotions: "[w]hat makes mankind unique is not our ability to reason, but our use of symbols" (Siegel, cited in Malchiodi, 1998). This grief group curriculum is not designed as therapy, and is not art therapy as such. One should be experienced in counseling and grief work before using these art forms as therapy. The book is meant for a group facilitated by educators, clergy, grief counselors, hospice staff, school personnel, and other professionals who wish to guide individuals in the grief process. It is the container that one provides for creating a safe place and acting as a "Sacred" witness that will allow the individuals to find their own meaning from the work. It is the silent witness who allows us to deepen into our own inner experience. The process of writing, creating, and using ritual will allow the innate healing ability of the unconscious to come forth and comfort each of the group members (Jeffreys, 2005; Malchiodi, 1998; Neimeyer, 2000; Worden, 2000).

It is the quality of our attention that allows us to be present with the mystery of death and suffering. We can learn, through practice, to provide a calm presence during the storm of fear, pain, and loss. The guiding feature of this book and the art forms offered are to create a safe container for individuals to access their own inner symbols and meaning as they reconstruct meaning in their lives.

Group leaders should not hesitate to obtain additional professional help and guidance should they feel that members of a group need additional support beyond their capacity or experience. It is, of course, useful to use additional books and references to aid in the development of the grief group, but it is not necessary. It may be helpful to have a cofacilitator to assist during the course. It will broaden the facilitator's ability to observe the group members and offer support as necessary (Liebmann, 1986).

Enjoy the art forms and do not shy away from a particular form just because you are not experienced in that modality. Drama is a part of the cultural history of most peoples and, as Lauren Chandler describes in chapter 12, "Drama and Theater," it is not necessary to be an actor or trained in the theater. Follow the simple steps and use the exercises that are easiest for you.

Use this book as it is set out, or adapt it to your needs, experience, and the makeup of your group. Not all groups will want to move from form to form, and some may want to concentrate on one or two, such as journal writing or collage. In either case, enjoy the experience of art and individual expression.

Group work is an efficient and effective way to offer emotional support (Worden, 2001). Art and the creative process are agents of self-expression and can be transforming in nature (Bertman, 1999). Combining the support of the group and the use of physical and creative activities offer the grievers what they need most: acceptance and nonjudgmental listening (Rando, 1984). The use of creative arts in a group setting facilitates a way of comprehending some of the most complex aspects of human existence and provides a structure for our emotional chaos and a shared social setting for the construction of meaning (Neimeyer, 2000).

Remember, art and play go together and offer pleasurable and enjoyable activity with no extrinsic goals, and they are best when spontaneous and voluntary with active engagement related to what is being done (Liebmann, 1986). Chapter 17, "Programs for Teens and Children," will reinforce the idea of art and play as another way to tell our story. Each session chapter will have a section on the use of that particular modality with children and teens. While this book is written for the adult mourner, the forms suggested, particularly music, are easily adapted for children and teens.

Please approach this book with a sense of adventure and as though you are a beginner. Use your skills and training to create a safe and protected space for the mourners while allowing the spontaneous expression of their individual grief process.

Resources

Bertman, S. L. (1991). *Facing death: Images, insights, and interventions*. New York: Brunner-Routledge.

Bertman, S. L. (Ed.) (1999). *Grief and the healing arts: Creativity as therapy*. Amityville. NY: Baywood.

Jeffreys, J. S. (2005). *Helping grieving people: When tears are not enough*. New York: Brunner-Routledge.

Liebmann, M. (1986). *Art therapy for groups*. Cambridge, MA: Brookline Books.

Malchiodi, C. A. (1998). *The art therapy sourcebook*. Los Angeles: Lowell House.

Neimeyer, R. A. (2000). *Lessons of loss: A guide to coping*. Keystone Heights, FL: Psycho-Educational Resources.

Rando, T. A. (1984). *Grief, dying and death*. Champaign, IL: Research Press.

J. Earl Rogers

Leading Grief Support Groups

Support groups are a safe place for people to share the pain of grief. As such, they are a healthy, healing "workplace of mourning."

— Dr. Alan Wolfelt

☐ Introduction

Support groups are widely used for many different reasons. From the well-known 12-step recovery self-help programs for addictions to the formal psychological therapy groups, the group process has been used to assist people and support the process of personal growth and recovery from illness or injuries. People gather with others in similar situations to support and comfort each other during a difficult time. As such, each group must be a safe and supportive environment for the group members. The groups can be educational, offer psychological support, or be a place where people in similar situations or conditions share their common concerns and express feelings that others, who had not experienced loss, might not understand.

Bereavement groups are a mainstay of hospice aftercare. They offer the maximum amount of support with the minimum number of staff or volunteers. Such a group can involve a deeply personal sharing of grief and the process of mourning. Compassionate Friends offers parents who have lost a child the opportunity to meet with other bereaved parents and talk about their children and the depth of the pain of losing a child. Oftentimes parents feel that others who have not lost a child really do not understand their pain, or do not wish to hear the stories of the deaths of children. Meeting as a self-help group allows the members of Compassionate Friends the opportunity to express and share their pain and loss in a safe and understanding setting.

Hospice organizations often offer bereavement groups specific to a particular type of loss: loss through suicide, loss of a child, death of a spouse, homicide, or family members dealing with the progressive and painful life-threatening illness of a loved one through cancer or some other illness. Family members who have a loved one with a disease such as Alzheimer's can share the pain of losing a family member while the loved one is still physically well but no longer aware of the world around them.

Groups can be open or closed; that is, the group may run continuously with people coming and going, or consist of a fixed group for a certain time, such as eight weeks, with a particular theme or common interest among the group members. The curriculum set forth in this book offers a closed group for eight weeks using the theme of expressive arts to support the the members' grief process. This group may be broad enough to include people with different types of losses, or a range of ages. It may also be more specific, such as for children, teens, widows and widowers, or parents who have lost a child. The ultimate makeup of the group is for the group leaders and group to decide. Time, resources, and lack of availability of facilitators may prevent establishing specific groups in a particular community.

☐ Setting Up the Group

Often the most difficult part of running a group that will meet the needs of the members and the facilitators is the initial planning, organization, and setting up of the group. This initial stage can easily be bypassed in the interests of time and the desire to begin the group. The time spent in planning, however, will pay off during group sessions and in the way the members receive what is being offered. The skill and preparation by the group leaders will offer the members a safe and protected space to experience their individual mourning process. Preparation for how the group is to be run, what may happen, and how the materials will be presented will enable the facilitators to anticipate problems and meet in the moment strong emotions that may arise during the group sessions. Remember, the group members will continue to process what they have done in the group sessions during the week. If the facilitators anticipate this, then the check-in at the beginning of each session will allow the group to share and to comfort individual members.

Group Leader(s)

Selecting the group leaders is an important task. It is, of course, best to have experienced and trained leaders for any grief group. However, the reality often means that there is little choice in selecting a group facilitator. It sometimes becomes the case that it is the person who is willing to offer his or her time and presence for the group who becomes the facilitator. A little reading and a cofacilitator can be of great benefit to the novice group leader. Remember that this is not an art therapy course, but a grief support group. The facilitators may do nothing more than describe and lead the different art forms, prepare the setting, and make arrangements for the facility and supplies. The greatest gift group leaders can offer is the quality of their attention and the ability to be present in the moment as the members of the group experience their stories of grief and loss in different ways. Group leaders should not be afraid to seek help if they feel the need for support.

If possible have a cofacilitator to assist with the group. There are several reasons for this:

- Setting up a grief support group that uses art involves a lot of work and it is helpful to have extra hands to do this work.
- While the group leader is describing the art program for the day the coleader can observe the group members and become aware of any problems that may arise.
- It often takes two people to set up the supplies and clean up the room after the group.
- One of the cofacilitators can talk to one individual while the other is continuing with the group art project for the day.
- Cofacilitators with different personalities can add richness to the group and allow for different explanations or approaches to a particular issue. Keep in mind that the leaders do have to understand their roles, how the other leader works, and how they will work and interact together during the group.

☐ Duties of the Facilitators

The primary role or duty of a facilitator is to provide a safe place, physically and emotionally, for the participants to experience their grief and loss. A leader who is sensitive and able to listen deeply is often a crucial link in the ability of the group members to find continued meaning in their lives after the death of a love one. It is also necessary for the leader to manage the administrative details of the group and to control, so far as possible, the physical surroundings.

Purpose and Structure of the Group

The group described in this book is designed as a closed-ended eight-week art group, but there is nothing to prevent a leader from using just part of this curriculum in an open-ended group, or to extend this group to use other art forms or create an ongoing theater troupe or art group. The leader must make these decisions and be clear about the purpose for the group.

The structure of the group has been laid out in chapter 5, "How to Use This Book," but each session needs to be planned and organized. Be familiar with how each session will flow and be ready to adapt to changes in the group or outside factors (such as losing your meeting room). Flexibility becomes the watchword for facilitators both before and during the group process.

Preplanning and Organization

Physical Setting

Decide where the group will meet and whether it conforms to the needs of the art form and the age of the group members. While children and teens will be quite comfortable sitting on the floor, older adults might not adapt so well to this situation. The meeting room will have to be large enough to accommodate the participants and the art forms that will be used during the course. Be sure to check the lighting and whether air circulation is sufficient for a given number of people (especially if you are using paints). Check for tables and chairs suitable for artwork and group discussions. Is there a storage locker or room for the artwork? What else will you need to present the art program?

Group Members

Who will be in your group? According to the needs of your community or organization you may have a diverse or homogeneous group. Consider whether certain types of deaths will work with a general grief group. Parents who have lost a child or survivors of a suicide may not be comfortable with a general grief group. Consider having a separate group for these types of losses. Age can be a major factor in developing a grief group. Children and teens will often work best with peers. Adults past their teens or in their early 20s can tolerate a wider age range. It is most important to *screen* potential group members. There are some people who will not do well in a group setting, or who will disrupt the group. Some personality disorders, such as a borderline, can be very difficult to deal with. Also consider whether the loss is too recent for the individual to be able to function in a group. A group of this sort may not be appropriate for people in the acute period of grief. A homogeneous group offers the participants the opportunity to share a common type of loss and gives them the opportunity to be with others who are more likely to understand what they are experiencing. However, this may not be possible in small organizations or communities. There is much to say for diversity, but be sure that the participants can tolerate such differences. Art can be an excellent process to move beyond the differences in types of losses or ages.

Materials

Obtain all the necessary materials before the group's first session, so as to ensure that the materials are available and to have them organized to prevent last minute difficulties and panic. Go through each chapter and decide what materials you need or want, and whether they will fit your budget. As process takes place it may create alternative approaches to a particular art form or dictate the necessity to use another form than the ones suggested in the curriculum. Make sure that all the supplies are available and have coverings for the tables and floors if you are using a messy form. Decide how you will set up for each session and have extra supplies such as rags, tape, candles, matches, music (something to play the music on such as a CD player), and colored pencils and markers. Keep all the supplies in one location so that everything is ready for the beginning of the group.

Expectations and Ground Rules

What is the job description of the facilitator of this group? What are the expectations? Answer these two questions and there will be an ease in presenting the group. Make sure the facilitator's role is understood and what the program is offering to the prospective group members. Clarify any uncertain issues before the group starts. If no one knows exactly what is expected then write a "job description" of the role being played by the facilitator, and what the group will be doing. Is this a support group? Is there an expectation that there will be group "therapy" involved? So far as possible anticipate problems and unstated expectations. What are the specific responsibilities of the group leader? By answering these questions the group will move more smoothly and the job of the facilitator will be more satisfying. Ground rules are important not only for the smooth running of the group but for the creation of a safe environment for the group members. Consider some of these ideas as possible ground rules for the group:

- Group members may share as much or as little as they wish about their experience
- Group members get equal time so that no one monopolizes the time for speaking
- There should be no advice given by group members, unless an individual specifically asks for advice
- Confidentiality is important, and what is said in the group stays in the group
- Members are expected to attend all sessions and be on time
- Only one person at a time speaks and there are to be no interruptions while someone is speaking
- Time limits will be respected

Other rules may need to be established as the group develops. For example, the group may decide that there is to be no talking during the art making session, or that there is to be no smoking. General rules of social behavior and responsibility of the group members for cleanup may apply as the group wishes.

Leadership Roles during the Group

The group leader must plan and organize each session. During the sessions the leader facilitates the schedule of the day and insures that everyone who wants to speak is heard. Time schedules are important if the group is to have an opening section, completion of the art form, and a closing section. In each chapter session a general plan is offered along with a timetable for the activity. In chapter 5, "How to Use This Book," a general format for each session is offered.

Especially in the first session, it is important to have a check-in or warm-up phase. This will help ensure a safe environment and ease anxiety. It will also allow the members to share their ongoing story of loss and healing. Opening and closing rituals create a quiet space of reflection and room for spiritual healing.

While it is important to keep the schedule, and to ensure that everyone who wants to share can do so, it is equally important not to control the group to the point where members do not feel ownership of the group. It is certainly a fine line between moving the group along and running the group as a dictator. The group has an interest in the group process and sometimes it is best to let the group dynamic take charge of the direction. There is a time for firmness, but it can be done with gentleness and understanding.

The group members will watch the facilitators, so modeling deep listening, openness, and caring will serve to help the group achieve its purpose. There will be difficulties that come up during the group. It is the ability of the facilitator to listen deeply and guide the group with gentleness that will resolve any destructive behaviors that occur during the group sessions. Be willing to listen to conflicts in the group and not take anything personally.

Many strong emotions may come up in a grief group, especially one using an art form that brings up unconscious material. Do not avoid strong emotions from the group nor ignore your own feelings. As a grief group progresses our own losses and unattended grief will emerge. There is no need to hide behind the safety of being the group leader to avoid natural feelings. At the same time, as facilitators we don't want the strength of our own material and history to be a surprise to us that causes us to fall apart. This is another advantage of having a cofacilitator: Let your emotions be present but not overwhelming.

Individual participants will bring their own history and behaviors to the group. You will meet challenging participants no matter how well you screen. Your ability to meet the needs of these challenging members will be a result of building a caring and trusting relationship between yourself and the group from the very first session. Some of the possible situations that may arise are:

Comparison Grieving

Especially in mixed groups, but even in homogenous groups, some members will feel that their loss is greater than any other losses. A parent who has lost a child may feel that it is a greater loss than a widow who has lost a spouse of many years. Meet this situation directly and immediately. One possible response is to say, "We all have losses and each is important to us, we are not here to compare, but to share."

Spontaneous Nonrequested Advice Giver

Each group will have someone who finds it easier to give advice than be present for their own deep grief and emotions. Gently remind the group that advice is not to be offered unless someone asks specifically for advice. If unasked for advice giving continues, take the advice giver aside at the break and ask the person not to offer advice because each person needs to find his or her own way through the grief.

Should, Must, Have To

More than an advice giver, the person who offers advice in a moralistic manner, leading with "must," "should," or "have to," tends to lead to resentment in the group. While often well intended, this preacher tells other people what they must or should do. A gentle comment that each person must find his or her own way through grief or deal with their own issues is helpful. Ask the moralist to speak about himself, or suggest, when appropriate, that he or she might say, "This is how I would feel about the situation."

Faith

Many people have strong religious faith, but sometimes people will spend so much time talking about their version of God, or their beliefs, that others in the group who do not share such strong beliefs become uncomfortable or resentful. This person uses faith so much that at times it can appear as though the person has no problems or grief. Suggest that each person needs to find his or her own path, and that strong faith does not prevent feeling grief or having to work through the mourning process.

The Talker

Some people will talk every chance they get and soon overpower the group and prevent deep sharing, or will create resentment and anger amongst the group members. Remind the talker that everyone gets equal time and that sharing must be limited so that all members get to speak. The sooner the facilitator intervenes in this type of situation the easier it will be to maintain the ground rules. Curb the talker at the first opportunity by reminding the group of the equal time rule. A variant of the "talker" is the one who also interrupts other group members or the leader.

Again remind the person of the ground rules that each person gets to share without interruption, and the importance of listening to each other. In all cases, when attempting to enforce the group ground rules maintain a gentle and kind manner, and speak with good humor. People avoid the pain of loss in many different ways and a gentle reminder of the purpose of the group will often suffice. If the behavior continues, talk with that person one on one.

The Challenger

This will be the most difficult one for the group leader as the challenger will often attack whatever the group leader suggests or find fault with the leader's words or actions. Do not get defensive! Listen, and then repeat back what the challenger has said, and move on with the group. If the challenger's behavior persists, ask for an alternative suggestion (although this can be a dangerous opening that allows the challenger to take over the group). If the challenger attempts to attack or continues in attempts to undermine what the leader is doing, ask if he or she wants to talk about it further with you after the group. There is no need to get in a discussion during the group. Most people will respect a leader who listens to criticism without getting defensive. Certainly, criticism can challenge our self-esteem and we often want to defend ourselves or prove our competence. Remember it is not about you but the way the challenger meets his or her own inner needs. Listen and gently move on with the group.

Small Talk (Idle Chitchat)

Most people tend to deflect deep feelings of loss, fear, or anxiety. One way to do this is to socialize with other group members on unrelated and minor matters so as to defuse the group energy. The chitchatterer wants to keep the group from getting too serious about anything. This can grossly interfere with the art process and certainly with the ability of the group members from "getting into" their story or artwork. Gently ask the chitchatterer what he or she is feeling at the moment and whether the person is having a difficult time with feelings of loss or grief.

Speaking for the Group

This person purports to speak for the group by using "We think…." Resentment can build in the group because not everyone feels the same way, but people don't want to speak up and challenge the self-appointed leader. Ask the speaker if he or she is speaking for the entire group, or ask if everyone feels the same way as the speaker. Be gentle in the intervention but meet it early and directly. It may be nothing more than a bad style of speaking and totally unconscious.

☐ Dangerous Situations or Alerts for Referral

Some situations call for action and referral to outside help. This is not a group therapy setting, but a support group using art to help deal with grief, so it is inappropriate to attempt to counsel or do therapy in the session. Certain behavior or talk can suggest that a referral for counseling or crisis intervention is appropriate.

Anyone who shows up with alcohol on his or her breath or shows a pattern of alcohol or drug abuse probably should not be in the group and may be more appropriately referred to a drug or alcohol recovery program. Being under the influence of anything tends to prevent the feelings of grief from being felt, and will interfere with the group process.

Excessive anger or rage, especially directed to others in the group, is a warning sign that perhaps outside counseling would be appropriate. If the rage or extreme anger is disrupting the group or others feel in danger, then it would be appropriate to ask the person to leave the group and seek individual help. Always have referral sources available to give to people who may not be appropriate for the group.

A group member who is not eating or not getting enough sleep, or is not handling other self-care issues, might need additional individual help or counseling outside of the group. A group member who self-harms or harms others definitely needs a referral to an appropriate agency or counselor qualified to deal with such situations.

If one of the group members does not appear to change at all in her or his mourning behaviors over several months it may be an indication of a need for individual bereavement counseling. One feature of complicated mourning is a sense of being stuck over time. Refer to chapter 3, "Basics of Grief and Loss," for a more complete explanation of complicated mourning.

It is a major red flag when there is an expression of suicidal intent from a group member. While all talk of wanting to die or suicide must be taken seriously, not all expressions of not wanting to live mean the person is suicidal. Ask if the person just feels as though he or she doesn't care if they live or if the individual really wants to kill themselves. Don't be afraid to ask the question. If in doubt, refer the person to appropriate health care providers or therapists. There are a few indicators that may provide more information than just asking if the person wants to kill him- or herself and whether the individual has a plan. Many people in deep grief find it difficult to want to go on with life, but have no intention of killing themselves. If, however, they say they want to die and have a specific plan for how to do it, immediately refer them to an appropriate agency or the local crisis team or the police.

Suicide risk factors for certain groups are higher:

- High-risk groups include people with mental illness, males, youth, elderly, or a person with a long term painful illness.
- Historical factors to consider are whether the person has had a prior suicide attempt, a family history of suicide, or a childhood or adult history of abuse, trauma, or neglect.
- Consider current risk factors. Is there a current mental illness or active addiction? Is the person experiencing symptoms of anxiety, panic, or agitation? Is the person socially isolated or have a rigid style of thinking (black or white type thinking)? Has the individual been recently exposed to another person's death by suicide?
- Are there currently present thoughts of suicide, is the individual considering suicide, and are the thoughts frequent, specific, and persistent? Does the person have a plan and the apparent ability to carry out the plan?

These areas are red flags for the facilitator and signal the need for outside assistance or referral to qualified therapists or agencies. These suggested warning signs are not complete and the leaders must be alert for problems that cannot be handled within the support group format. It is part of the planning process to have a list of appropriate agencies and therapists for referral and assistance.

☐ Session Plans

In chapter 5, "How to Use this Book," there is a sample outline for the group sessions. In addition, each chapter outlines what is necessary for the particular session, the timing, and the materials needed. It is strongly suggested that you have a check-in time at the beginning of each session as well as a check-out time before the end of the session. This allows the participants an opportunity to express what is going on for them, to ease anxiety, and bring the group together. Ritual and meditation or a few minutes of silence at the beginning of the session can deepen the group experience and allow the participants to let go of the outside world for a couple of hours. This also serves as the platform leading into the art form of the session.

Leading a group can be a rewarding and fun experience. Preplanning serves to lessen anxiety and provides a smooth and free flowing session. Relax and be willing to go with the flow of the group. There is much freedom in being able to adapt to the moment and to be flexible.

Resources

Liebmann, M. (1986). *Art therapy for groups: A handbook of themes, games and exercises*. Cambridge, MA: Brookline Books.

Wolfelt, A. (1994). *How to start and lead a bereavement support group*. Written for Batesville Management Services.

Worden, J. W. (2001). *Grief counseling and grief therapy* (3rd ed.). New York: Springer.

J. Earl Rogers

Basics of Grief and Loss

We all grieve when someone we love dies, but if we are to heal, we must also mourn.

— Dr. Alan Wolfelt

Bereavement care is often approached in our society in a manner where grief is assessed, diagnosed, and then treated. It is sometimes approached as a problem that needs a cure. But grief is inherent in living — a part of our human experience. It does not need to be "fixed," "treated," or ignored. Grief needs to be lived as a normal emotional response to loss. It will be unique to each of us and there is no "normal" timetable to "complete" the process.

Grief takes many forms according to our personal makeup, our relationship to what has been lost or the person who has died, and how the loss has affected the meaning in our lives. Unfortunately, all too often, our society dictates that for successful mourning we must disengage from the deceased and "let go." We are told that we need to "move on" and "accept" the death of a loved one. These terms, however, seem to limit the process of grief, and the cultural need for "closure" denies any form of continued relationship with the person who died.

There are no set stages or tasks that need to be worked through or accomplished. We merely need to live the experience (Schuurman, 2003).

That experience will greatly differ, from the loss of a distant relative who was expected to die to the loss of a child. The depth of meaning and degree of loss is not comparable. Both are a loss, and both will in a greater or lesser degree affect the meaning of our lives. And, both are a part of life.

Long-term grief over the loss of a mate after a lifetime together, or the choiceless pain from the loss of a child (whether born or unborn), is a part of life. These are not losses to "get over." All too often our modern understanding of grief pathologizes extreme grief or cultural differences in grief experiences.

As family, friends, and caregivers the only gift we have to offer those who are grieving is the quality of our attention. There are times when the additional support of counseling, grief support groups, and extra help and support from friends and family is needed and necessary. But the process is essentially a spiritual one, requiring contemplation and turning inward. There is nothing to fix. No one is sick. There is nothing to be done but to live. We are all fellow travelers in the journey into grief and the willingness to be present in that journey will allow us to go on until we too, die.

It is expected that facilitators leading this grief support group have some experience and training in grief and loss. Most local hospices have bereavement support personnel who can offer training or assist in setting up a grief group. In addition to having a trained co-facilitator, J. Shep Jeffreys' book, *Helping Grieving People: When Tears Are Not Enough,* offers an excellent basis for understanding all types of deaths, grief responses, and grief theories (2005). Additional books and resources are listed at the end of this chapter.

It is the goal of care providers to accept the grieving person at whatever level of emotional expression the grieving person is willing to express (Jeffreys, 2005). Grief can come in many forms and from many experiences. While this book and the proposed curriculum is directed toward grief from the death of someone close to us, it must be acknowledged that grief can come from many different losses, such as divorce, moving, job loss, changing schools, or severe chronic or terminal illness. Change creates loss and grief is how we react. Grief is the internal reaction to loss and mourning is the process or outward manifestation of grief. When one is in mourning or grieving over a death it is said that the person is bereaved. To describe the process of reacting to loss it is often useful for experts to attempt to understand and explain the reaction and process of dealing with loss by the use of models and theories. However, it is for us to be with the feelings (Schuurman, 2003).

Grief is a universal experience and comes from both the tangible and intangible losses of life. Our grief response is an attempt to restore that which is lost and to recreate meaning in our lives (Jeffreys, 2005). Grief is also a universal internal response involving physical, psychological, social, and spiritual aspects of our being. People may say things such as: *I'm feeling lost, I feel empty, I hurt everywhere, I can't think, It feels as though I have a hole in my heart, I feel as though I am going crazy,* or *nothing makes sense,* in order to explain what they are feeling. They may have responses such as anger, sadness, emptiness, despair, loneliness, hopelessness, relief, and much more. These responses may have no particular order or logical relationship, and the feelings may come all at once in an inexplicable ball of raw emotion. You may hear complaints of fatigue, exhaustion, lack of energy, pain, or inability to sleep. All of these symptoms may be the way the body and mind deals with the shock and seeks release of the energy of grief. Bereaved people often find themselves questioning their beliefs in God and their assumptions about life. Art and storytelling are ways people can come to an understanding of what has happened in their life and the creative acts are often enough to enable grieving and to stimulate the search for meaning and initiate change (Bertman, 1999). Often words are not enough.

The point of this curriculum is to offer the participants an opportunity to tell their story in several different ways, using different aspects of their emotional, physical, social, and spiritual being. During the use of the different expressive arts the participant can touch the meaning the deceased had in their lives and perhaps reconstruct new meaning in their lives and a new ongoing relationship with the deceased. However, the process will be very different for each person and deeply personal.

☐ Factors Affecting Grief

Many factors affect one's grief and the mourning process. The characteristics and meaning of the lost relationship will influence the response to the loss, as will the personal characteristics of the individual mourner (Jeffreys, 2005). Some of the characteristics and meanings of the lost relationship might be:

- The quality of the relationship
- The type of relationship
- The role the deceased played in the bereaved's life
- Any unfinished business between the deceased and the bereaved
- Secondary losses arising from the death, such as finances
- The personal characteristics of the deceased

Personal characteristics of the bereaved also affect how the person will respond to a particular loss. Individual coping behaviors, personality, and state of mental health will affect their response and ability to deal with loss. Other factors in the individual's makeup that affect the grief response might be:

- The level of maturity and intelligence
- Past experience with loss and death
- Cultural, ethnic, social, and religious background
- Age and sex

The circumstances of the death will affect the mourner:

- How the person died — such as illness, accident, or suicide
- Whether the death was expected
- Long illness prior to the death
- Legal issues such as lawsuits, criminal trial, or probate fights

Social factors of the family and the bereaved will affect how they express their mourning (Rando, 1984):

- Social support systems
- Social and cultural background
- Socioeconomic, educational, and occupational background
- Funeral rituals

Physical health can also affect how one is affected by loss:

- Drugs and sedatives or alcohol use by the bereaved
- Nutrition can affect how much energy one has to deal with the stress of loss and one's mental state
- Rest and sleep are important to be able to maintain coping behaviors during the mourning period
- Exercise assists the body in responding to the demands of stress due to one's grief

Lack of social recognition of the significance of the loss can prevent open mourning and disenfranchise the grief. Situations such as suicide, AIDS, miscarriage, abortion, or criminal behavior can lead to the lack of social support and acknowledgment of loss. Also, losses in relationships not socially sanctioned such as an extramarital affair, a gay relationship, or the loss of a former spouse may not receive social support or understanding (Jeffreys, 2005).

☐ Grief Theories

While it is not the intent of this course to interpret, analyze, or conduct therapy it may be useful for the facilitators to have some idea of the different models or theories used by professional thanatologists. Remember however, that grief does not come in a clear package neatly fitting into one of these theories or models. Allow the process of each participant to come out in its own unique way, and just be present in the moment for the individual and collective manifestation of grief.

1. John Bowlby, Attachment Theory: We form bonds from birth and the breaking of those bonds or attachments causes grief. The four components of grief are (Jeffreys, 2005; Rando, 1984):

   a. Psychological: emotional and cognitive disturbances;
   b. Physical: health and physical symptoms;
   c. Social: relationships, society, and attitudes toward grief;
   d. Spiritual: faith, life beliefs, and philosophy.

Bowlby proposes four phases of grief:

   a. Numbing
   b. Yearning and searching
   c. Disorganization and despair
   d. Reorganization (a new definition of self)

2. William Worden's (2001) four tasks of mourning are:

   a. To accept the reality of the loss
   b. To work through the pain of grief
   c. To adjust to the new environment after loss
   d. To emotionally relocate the deceased or other changed condition and move on with life

3. Therese A. Rando's (1984, 1993, 2000) phases and processes of mourning include three broad periods or phases with six processes (the six R's):

   a. Avoidance — recognizing the loss (to acknowledge and understand)
   b. Confrontation — reacting to the separation, loss, and secondary losses
      - Recollecting and reexperiencing the deceased in the relationship
      - Relinquishing the old attachments, including preloss assumptions

    c. Accommodation
- Readjusting to move adaptively into the new world without forgetting the old attachment and revision of assumptions.
- Reinvesting energy from the prior bond into other relationships

4. Margaret Strolbe's dual process model (Jeffreys, 2005; Neimeyer, 2000):

    a. Loss-oriented focus (express feelings of grief)

    b. Restoration-oriented focus (behavior that reorganizes the self in light of the loss)

5. Thomas Attig's (1996, 2000) theory of relearning the world: To help the grieving person relearn the world and "make sense" of the post-loss world. The bonds with the deceased continue but in a new way.

6. Robert Neimeyer's (2000) meaning reconstruction: The bereaved person relearns the assumptive world and seeks meaning in a changed world

These are just six of many theories or models of how to understand and explain grief. Grief theory has changed over the years. Elisabeth Kübler-Ross was one of the first to articulate the process of loss with her stage theory for people at the end of life. Many have used her stages to explain the grief process. The unfortunate aspect of her stages was that people interpreted them to be a fixed and certain process that each person must go through or they have not died or grieved properly and thus have failed the process. (Jeffreys, 2005; Neimeyer, 2000; Schuurman, 2003).

Dennis Klass (1996, 1999), in talking about parents who have lost a child, suggests there are continuing bonds of such relationships whereby the parents find a new inner representation to revise the inner image and find equilibrium in the new world reality. This then allows reestablishment of both inner and outer social equilibrium (Jeffreys, 2005). Alan Wolfelt speaks about the need for mourning: to acknowledge the reality of death, embrace the pain of the loss, remember the person who died, develop a new self-identity, search for meaning, and receive ongoing support from others (1997; Jeffreys, 2005).

In the various weekly sessions with each new expressive art there may be discussion on reconstruction of meaning (Neimeyer, 2000), and relearning the world as the bonds with the deceased continue in a new way (Attig, 2000; Jeffreys, 2005). However, whatever model you choose, remember they are just models and the most important thing is to offer your attention to each individual where they are in their grieving process at each particular moment. What grievers need most is acceptance and nonjudgmental listening (Rando, 1984).

☐ Complicated Mourning

Complicated mourning is grief that has escalated to problematic proportions (Jeffreys, 2005). It becomes extreme in one of several dimensions of typical grief:

- severity of symptoms
- duration of symptoms
- level of dysfunction (socially, occupationally, or activities of daily living)

According to Therese Rando (1993) a person suffering a more complicated grief process seeks to avoid aspects of the loss, its pain, and the full realization of its implications. Or, they hold onto and avoid relinquishing the lost loved one. There are no specific criteria for complicated mourning and the distinction between "typical" and complicated mourning is not clear. Rather the symptoms of complicated mourning appear along a continuum and levels of dysfunction and severity of symptoms can be used as markers (Jeffreys, 2005).

Some of the factors that might lead to a complicated mourning process include the nature of the death, the relationship with the deceased, or the psychological characteristics of the grieving person. Social issues may also increase the risk of a complicated course of grief. Additionally, certain types of death may be a predisposing risk factor, such as:

- sudden
- violent, suicide or homicide
- multiple deaths
- catastrophic disaster, such as earthquakes, airline crashes, or hurricanes
- death viewed as preventable
- lack of a body
- death of a child (or a death out of expected time)
- witnessing a violent death
- following a very long illness where the bereaved was a caregiver

The nature of the relationship between the deceased and the bereaved may contribute to a more difficult grief process. For example: where there is unfinished business between the two, a past history of sexual/physical abuse, or overidentification with the deceased.

The psychological characteristics of the grieving person may also contribute to a difficult course:

- dependent personality
- personality disorders (e.g. borderline personality)
- severely limited ability to express feelings
- inadequate nurturing as a child
- substance abuse
- life crisis and multiple losses

Social issues associated with the death where the loss is stigmatized, or the grief is disenfranchised, or the bereaved is socially isolated can also contribute to the risk factors associated with complicated mourning. Psychiatric disorders associated with complicated grief are severe affective disorders, demoralization (inability to cope), or an adjustment disorder in response to a stressor (Jeffreys, 2005; Rando, 1993).

The length of time of the mourning process or strong reactions should not by itself tempt us to pathologize the grieving process as though it were an illness. However, reorganization of one's life after a major loss may warrant additional support and assistance through the mourning process (Neimeyer, 2000). Some conditions may contribute to complications and suggest the need for professional help: substantial guilt, suicidal thoughts, extreme hopelessness, prolonged agitation or depression, substantial physical symptoms, persistent functional impairment in the ability to work or accomplish routine tasks required for daily living, or substance abuse (Neimeyer, 2000).

Look to the nature and severity of symptoms to determine the presence of complicated mourning. Time in and of itself is not an indicator because the time it takes for our grief varies for many reasons. But if it is an unusual length of time, is coupled with profound and widespread dysfunction, or severe symptoms one should look for issues of complicated mourning (Jeffreys, 2005; Neimeyer, 2000; Rando, 1993).

☐ Ritual and Art in the Grief Process

The last session of the grief curriculum, Ritual, deals in detail with the use of ritual in grief and loss. Each chapter has a brief suggested ritual that could be performed each week. It is suggested that the reader refer to and read the last chapter in the curriculum, chapter 13, before proceeding with the grief support group. Almost all societies have some form of funerary ritual. Rituals can confirm and reinforce the reality of the death, acknowledge and express feelings of loss, and offer a vehicle for expressing feelings. Such end-of-life rituals stimulate recollection of the deceased, assist in beginning to accommodate the changed relationship to the deceased, allow for input from the community, and offer social benefits such as support during the grieving period and reintegrating the bereaved back into the community (Rando, 1984).

Formal and informal rituals can give meaning to the transition from life to death as well as other transitions in life (Neimeyer, 2000). Ritual can be a safe container for our grief (Jeffreys, 2005). It is not the end of the journey, nor does it mean that we have to let go of our loved one or our feelings. It is a symbolic act to express our feelings and speak the inexplicable: a way of comprehending one of the most complex aspects of our existence.

Our openness, as facilitators, to the creative acts of the members of the group is often enough to enable grieving, to stimulate the search for meaning, and to initiate change (Bertman, 1999). Whether adults or children are involved, the techniques in this book can be liberating and enabling. The spoken or written word has great power in helping us recreate meaning in our lives. However, it is not the only path in reconstruction of meaning: for many people symbolic forms of artistic expression can be significant in speaking of their loss and possibilities for the future (Neimeyer, 2000).

Grief is both a private and public expression of our losses and our relationship to that which we have lost. The path of each member of the group will be deeply personal. At the same time, by speaking, writing, and using images and movement in a group it will become a public statement of the individual's grief. Not to be analyzed, studied, or explained, but to be seen, and acknowledged.

Resources

Jeffreys, J. S. (2005). *Helping grieving people: When tears are not enough.* New York: Brunner-Routledge.

Levine, S. (2005). *Unattended sorrow.* Emmaus, PA: Rodale.

Lewin, M. (Ed.). *Buddhist reflections on death, dying and bereavement.* Newport, Isle of Wight: Buddhist Hospice Trust.

Neimeyer, R. A. (2000). *Lessons of loss: A guide to coping.* Keystone Heights, FL: PsychoEducational Resources.

Wolfelt, A. D. (1997). *The journey through grief.* Fort Collins, CO: Companion Press.

CHAPTER J. Earl Rogers

Children and Teens

There are thousands of children who know death far beyond the
knowledge adults have ... those little children [are] the wisest of
teachers.

— Elisabeth Kübler-Ross

Children and teens are often the forgotten mourners. They can get lost
in the grief of the adults around them or missed by the myths of society
that children don't know what is going on, or in the case of teens that they
don't care. This book is written for adults, but the beauty of art is that
the forms can be adapted to the needs of any audience (Bertman, 1991).
Each chapter in this book will contain a section on how the particular
expressive form can be used with children and teens. Specific exercises or
alternative modalities will be offered for use with younger groups where
appropriate. In part III, chapter 19, Penny Allport tells the tale of being
introduced to a cemetery exercise by her seventh-grade teacher, Mr. Reid.
Many years later as an adult she was introduced to the Mexican Day of the
Dead traditions. She then brings what she has learned to North America
and uses the Day of the Dead ritual with teen girls. There are many doors
into the minds of children and teens, and ritual and activities are wonderful ways to activate their innate curiosity.

It is important for anyone leading a group to have experience with
group facilitation. For teens and children it is even more important to

understand how they respond on developmental levels as well as having experience in working with children and teens who are grieving. This chapter is directed to those who have less experience with teens and children in grief. Resources are offered at the end of the chapter to enable facilitators to gain more information and knowledge about working with teens and children as well as learning how youth grieve.

All children understand loss. They may not understand death, but they do react to loss (Grollman 1995). Alan Wolfelt (1983) believes that if a child is old enough to love, the child is old enough to grieve (Goldman, 2000). Children grieve differently from adults according to their developmental level. If we understand the developmental level of each child, which may not be the same as chronological age, we may better understand the grieving process of that particular child. Not having the same tools for expression and understanding, children use behavior to communicate their pain, confusion, and needs. Regression to an earlier stage of development may be due in part to the need to create safety for themselves during the chaos of grief. The familiarity of a known earlier age and behaviors may give them the ability to deal with their grief (Goldman, 2000; Grollman, 1995; Jeffreys, 2005).

Often adults are uncomfortable dealing with the emotions and sadness of grieving children. Yet, it is from the behavior of the adults around them that children and teens learn about mourning behavior and what is expected (Grollman, 1995). Silence from adults does not take away the pain children feel after a loss. In fact it increases their sense of isolation and abandonment. Children are all too aware of the reality of death. How they perceive death depends on their age, development level, and life experience (Goldman, 2000; Grollman, 1995).

Linda Goldman (2000) points out that today's children are grieving children. Through TV the violence of war, terrorism, guns, murder, and suicide are all brought into our homes. Children experience constant losses of many different types. By acknowledging their losses we can affirm their reality. Children and teens escape and deny just as do adults. Often, children work through grief in the form of play (Grollman, 1995). For children the process of art making is a way to gain symbolic control over the experience of loss and death. Art is a way for them to establish an inner sense of security and safety (Malchiodi, 1998).

It is not just parents who have the responsibility for helping children and teens through the grief process, but teachers, clergy, and other caring professionals. Grief is a part of the lives of children today. In a school of 6000 students, an average of four will die each year (Goldman, 2000). Twenty percent of children will lose a parent by the end of high school. We can help children through the hazy maze of grief by being honest with our own feelings, and acknowledging the losses of the children, whether through death, divorce, moving, or the loss of an important object. Through deep listening we validate the feelings of loss and become an active participant in sharing the loss.

Students spend an average of six hours a day in school (Dougy Center, 1998). That places a great burden on teachers in addition to their often hectic schedule (Goldman, 2000). It has become the schools, where children spend most of their time that have become the place where we must often go to support them in their grief and loss. I was asked to visit a middle school after the death of a well-known student from a sudden illness. We offered two grief groups during the day once a week for four weeks. The first day in both groups it was fairly easy. The students spoke of their relationship with Sean (not his name) and their feelings about the memorial service and how they got the news. The second week was a different matter. The students came into the room and we waited for them to begin to talk. Rather than leading the conversation Cheryl, the other adult, a school counselor, and I sat and waited. On the table, as had been the case the week before, were colored pens, markers, and paper. After a while one of the boys said, "This feels really weird just sitting here." Without comment the other facilitator just reached out and picked up a colored marker and began to draw. Soon everyone in the room was drawing. My scribbles seemed somehow meager compared to the drawings of these middle school children. The voice of my childhood fourth-grade teacher came back to me from the shadows of my mind: "You just can't draw." I have been an artist for over 10 years and still the belief that I am not an artist follows me. After a while, sitting in silence and drawing, one of the other boys said, "What do you think of reincarnation?" The conversation was off and we all sat there together drawing and talking about death and whether there was life after death, forgetting that one of the facilitators couldn't draw.

For teachers and school counselors there are some wonderful books on grief and loss published by the Dougy Center in Portland, Oregon. The books and address are listed at the end of this chapter. Linda Goldman has written books that will be of great assistance to school staff. Like it or not school is the place where children and teens often go for help and support in the face of grief and loss.

Grief is a natural reaction to loss and each child's experience is different. There is no right or wrong way to grieve. There are, however, coping behaviors that are less effective than others. Every death is different and the grieving process is influenced by many factors:

- The child's social system
- Nature of the death
- The status or relationship between the child and the deceased

- Emotional/developmental age of the child
- Community and cultural views on the death. (Dougy Center, 1998)

It is suggested that there are no stages in grief. No linear or progressive tasks or processes in grief. Feelings and emotions may arise in no logical order or perhaps all at once. The loss forces children into a new world from which they will never return. Through their process of mourning and grieving they will recreate meaning in their lives (Neimeyer, 2000). Art and play are two of the ways children and teens can recreate meaning. Children love to express memories through art work (Goldman, 2000). Letter writing, poetry, biographical writing, creative fiction, collage, drama, and music are all forms of art that children and teens can use to explain what they are feeling and thinking. Music is a resource to explore feelings, with drums, bells, or recorded music. Feelings can be projected into music through body movement and dance. Doing so is very freeing for children and teens (Goldman, 2000).

☐ Developmental Levels

Developmental levels do not necessarily correlate to exact age so the following age groupings are general in nature and offered as guidelines.

Under 2 years

Infants and toddlers respond to the emotional reactions of the parents and adults around them. They can't understand death but can and do react to loss and the changes in the family and emotional climate.

Ages 3 to 5

These children are very concrete and egocentric. Death is experienced as a loss of love and protection. There may be a feeling of abandonment with the loss of a parent. The mourning behaviors may be intermittent, and children may exhibit regressive behaviors. Death is more like going on a trip or going to sleep. It is irreversible and it is difficult for these children to understand the finality of death. It becomes important to all children between infancy and about 5 years of age to keep consistent schedules and routines. They may need constant repetition of the facts of the death, and continued reassurances about the future and their safety. Since they tend to connect the death with whatever event preceded it, or with what they are told about what happened, they may confuse death with sleep, or going to the hospital, or being sick. Simple, honest, age appropriate answers are best.

Ages 5 to 8

These children are better able to understand death. They may use denial to avoid the reality or magical thinking to explain the death. The grieving may be more internal. They often ask a lot of questions, especially about the "gory" details. The mix of both concrete thinking and magical thinking may bring on confusion. They are beginning to understand the finality of death but do not understand that it happens to everybody. Thus, for these children the idea of life after death may be a contradiction because their linear thoughts would see death as the end of life. Information and explanations should be accurate and literal with no euphemisms. Again, honesty and age appropriate information should be the rule and only as much information as the child requests should be given. They need help expressing anger and they need to know that it is OK to be angry. The use of dolls, puppets, toys, or props may help them work out their understanding and feelings about death and the secondary losses that so often accompany a death in the family.

Ages 9 to 12

While this age group has the intellectual capacity to understand the finality of loss, and will use less denial, they may still have levels of magical thinking. These children have become less egocentric and more aware of the feelings of others. Peers are becoming important and talking to other bereaved preteens may help. This group does not want to be singled out for special considerations, especially in front of their peers. They have a strong need to feel "normal." Death is seen more clinically and they can view death as part of life. As they transition from concrete to more abstract thinking they can understand the universality and certainty of death, even though it may feel removed from them in time. They will struggle with the understanding that death can happen to anyone. This age group may have anxiety and general fearfulness but at the same time attempt to cover up emotions so as to appear "normal." Preteens require accurate information about the death and opportunities to ask their own questions. It is important to answer their questions without judgment and reassure them about their own future, such as who would take care of them if the other parent died. If they wish they should be included in adult activities such as the funeral or other death rituals. Include them in the family discussions. Keeping a journal may be of assistance. And, some preteens may want to produce some type of theater in the form of skits to demonstrate what has happened to their world.

Teens

This is a broad age group and differs greatly between the early and late teens. Overall there is a conflict between the drive toward autonomy and desire to be with the family in a time of crisis. Teens need involvement with their peers. Bereavement groups may give the opportunity to release anger, sadness, fear, and guilt with other bereaved teens without the fear of judgment by parents or other adults. Peer conformity is most important, yet teens need the support and understanding of their parents and family.

Teens are often preoccupied with their personal burdens and developmental changes and may not see situations in the same way as an adult would do. Young teens need to achieve emotional separation from parents. Midteens are striving toward competency, mastery, and control. In the late teens they begin to seek to establish intimacy and commitment.

Most teens will respond to adults who choose to be companions on the grief journey rather than direct it. They often feel vulnerable and resist sharing because it magnifies their feelings. While teens experience a wide range of emotions they may show few outward signs. Boys often resist sadness, and the risk of aggravated grief reaction is high because it is not "cool" to cry or seem vulnerable. Girls may have difficulty expressing anger (though always be careful with such gender generalizations). Most children and teens respond well to peer support groups. Kids can help each other and share a common experience.

For all ages it is important to listen. Deep listening requires an adult to not just listen, but to reflect back and perhaps paraphrase what has been said. Honesty is most important if one is to keep the trust of children and teens. Age appropriate answers coupled with the opportunity for children and teens to make choices help them through the grief process. Whatever the age, consistent routines and boundaries are important. Structure and routine provide a degree of safety and reassurance.

Journaling, letters to the deceased, creative writing, drawing, collage, puppets, sandtray, music, and some form of theater allow the expression of feelings and an outlet for the energy of the emotions arising from grief. In chapter 17, Sandra Baughman and Laura Kiser describe other programs for children and teens ranging from bereavement camps to art programs.

Resources

Buscaglia, L. (1982). *The fall of Freddie the leaf*: Thorofare, NJ: Charles B. Slack.

Dougy Center, Portland, Oregon, The National Center for Grieving Children and Families. P.O. Box 86852, Portland, OR 97286, phone 503-775-5683. http://www.dougy.org. [The Dougy Center has published a number of books to help children, teens, families, and schools with dying, death, and bereavement.]

Dougy Center. (1999a). *Helping teens cope with death*. Portland, OR.

Dougy Center. (1999b). *Thirty-five ways to help a grieving child*. Portland, OR.

Dougy Center. (2000). *When death impacts your school*. Portland, OR.

Dougy Center. (2003). *Helping the grieving student: A guide for teachers*. Portland, OR.

Goldman, L. (2000). *Life and loss: A guide to help grieving children* (2nd ed.). New York: Taylor & Francis. [This is a wonderful resource for being with grieving children. It has a section for teachers and a long list of references for different types of loss and different ages. There is a list of community resources and support groups. Ms. Goldman has worked as an elementary school teacher and is the author of several books on death and dying for children and their families.]

Grollman, E. A. (1995). *Bereaved children and teens*. Boston: Beacon Press. [This is a classic book for helping grieving children and teens, but more importantly it helps parents, teachers, and health care providers to understand the needs of these "forgotten mourners." Written in a friendly, accessible manner it comforts adults in dealing with children's sadness and helps them with how to begin the conversation.]

Jeffreys, J. S. (2005). *Helping grieving people: When tears are not enough*. New York: Brunner-Routledge. [Chapter 4 offers a concise and readable section on the grief of children and adolescents. This book is an excellent resource for all aspects of grief and loss.]

Wolfelt, A. D. (2001). *Healing your grieving heart for teens*. Fort Collins, CO: Companion Press. [A wonderful story of the life of a leaf will help children of all ages in coming to understand the cycle of life. Parents will enjoy reading this story to their children.]

CHAPTER 5   J. Earl Rogers

How to Use This Book

Since grief is not a cerebral problem but a subjective experience, we understand grief only and entirely as we filter and interpret it through our own experience. Initially it captures us, but we can capture it back and reshape it: and the expressive arts and therapies function beautifully as vehicles to help us reshape grief.

— **Sandra Bertman**

Use this book in any way that works for you, the facilitator, and your group. The book is designed as a sequential series of sessions, each of which uses a different art or expressive modality to create a curriculum for a grief support group. The grief course is set up for an eight-week session. However, you may want to extend some of the sessions to two or three on the same modality. Not a lot can be done with drama and theater in one two-hour session. Lauren Chandler set up her chapter so that it could be the basis of extended sessions or an ongoing theater group.

In similar groups people wanted to stay with the journaling and writing aspect of the arts. An entire group could be devoted to the journaling process. If you have an expertise in an expressive modality, such as painting or authentic movement, you may want to devote more time to your specialty and substitute it for one of the modalities offered in this book. Please let this book be a guide and companion, not a director.

The book has been written on two levels: first to be a complete manual and curriculum standing alone for facilitators leading grief support groups, second, to be a workbook for those leading grief groups that may or may not use art as the main feature. For art therapists the book is a resource to use as an adjunct to their work. However, this book is not designed to be used for art therapy. This is a book for grief support groups. Leaders may be hospice professionals or trained volunteers, therapists, counselors, ministers and clergy, teachers, or school counselors. Anyone with experience in leading groups and in the grief process who wishes to lead a grief support group will be able to use this book as a guide and resource.

It is a good idea to begin reading this book by exploring chapter 13, "Grief and the Sacred Art of Ritual." Janet Shaw Rogers has set forth a number of rituals which can be used at the opening and closing of each session. The chapters on drama and music work well into other sessions, especially for teens and children. These chapters may offer guidance in setting up other sessions, how to approach the overall course, and how to end the course. Each chapter is designed to build on the one before, so that by the time the reader gets to drama and ritual the group members will have told their stories in several different ways using different aspects of themselves. In part III additional modalities and programs are described by artists and health care professionals, including painting, writing, bereavement camps, and programs for teens and children.

☐ Leading Groups

It is assumed that facilitators using this book will have experience in setting up and leading groups. As already noted in an earlier chapter, it is recommended that those who are inexperienced in leading groups get a cofacilitator who is familiar with leading support groups. For those who have some experience but feel the need for additional help, chapter 2, "Leading Grief Support Groups," offers suggestions along with a list of resources.

Teens probably do not want to be in a group with younger children. It is usually best to have a homogenous age range in your group. You may also want to consider the types of deaths that have occurred within your group. Parents who have lost a child often do not want to hear about other people's losses and sometimes feel different or separate from other types of grievers who have not lost a child. Suicide survivors have very different issues from other types of death and can have difficulty assimilating into a general grief group. In each case you will have to decide, based on community resources, whether you can separate different types of losses into specific groups.

☐ Sample Format for Group Sessions

Each facilitator and each group will dictate how the group sessions develop. However, this guide will be followed in the chapters on each expressive art form. The format can easily be adapted to individual needs and conditions.

1. **Opening:** Allow a period of quiet time for reflection, meditation, or just to bring each person's presence into the energy of the group. You may want to light a candle, use music, or ring a bell to signal the beginning and ending of this opening ritual. Allow 2 to 5 minutes for this quiet time.

2. **Check-in**: This is a time for the participants to check in with the group as to how they are doing, what has been going on during the past week, and generally how the group is doing. The group members' journals are the connection from week to week and people may want to read from the journal or just talk about how the week has been for them. Make it clear at the first session that while it is important for each person to be heard, it is not necessary to speak. It is also important that no one person take over the group with lengthy speeches. This section may last 15 to 20 minutes according to the size of the group and the issues that have come up. Keep in mind the time necessary to complete the expressive art of the day.

3. **Main activity:** The different modalities will take different amounts of time to complete and each chapter sets out the ideal time for the art form. Generally allow about an hour to an hour and half for the activity. The sessions are suggested to last about 2 hours. If the group wants to do more on a particular expressive modality just modify the group to add on an extra session or eliminate a particular art form. It is not unreasonable for the group to concentrate on two or three modalities.

4. **Closing:** Allow time for the group to come together, check in, and talk about the experience of the art form. This may take as long as half an hour. The sessions on the various art forms have built into their structure about 10 to 15 minutes for closing. However, a facilitator's experience with a group will allow him or her to know whether the specific group requires more time to close a session. Again, allow a period of quiet time for reflection or meditation at the end of the talking. Give assignments if necessary for the next week's session. These assignments might include, for example, bringing magazines for the collage or ritual items and objects for the sandtray session.

Ritual is an important part of the group grief process. You may want to include some of the rituals explained in the chapter on ritual during the group sessions. The final session is designed for a ritual, both individual and for the group. You may also want to include food and time to talk in the last session to bring closure for the group.

☐ Individual Sessions

Session 1: Introduction, Chapter 6

The grief course is introduced, the ground rules are set, and group members are able to get to know each other. This session is also the first time people will tell the story of their grief and loss. The oral story is an important part of our human history and an important way for people to come to an understanding of how the loss has affected their life. Lauren Chandler has an excellent exercise in chapter 12, session 7 in the course, "Drama and Theater," on getting to know each other. All you need is a beanbag, or a couple of Beanie Babies to toss back and forth while people get to know the names of the other group members.

The use of the journal will be introduced in the first session. The journal will tie the sessions together from week to week, and be a road map of where the group members have traveled during their journey of grief.

One of the ways to honor the story of each member, and to be sure each person is heard, is to use the Counsel Process, described in Janet Shaw Rogers's chapter on "Grief and the Sacred Art of Ritual" (the final session). This process can be used for introductions of each person and their story, as well as the weekly check-in.

We are all subject to the experience of grief, and throughout human history storytelling and art have spoken and symbolized this experience. We begin the grief support course with the oral story, the first of different ways our story will be told throughout the eight weeks of the grief support course.

Session 2: The Written Word, Chapter 7

Our story is continued via the written word. The members will learn more about the journal writing process and be introduced to creative writing. Using the narrative story form, fiction, or Haiku poetry, the group members will have the opportunity to write their story. Writing in a creative manner allows for a deepening of the story and understanding of their grief. Different details may come out during the writing, and the story of loss becomes the pathway to new meaning.

Be sure to allow time for the members to read their stories. No one is required to read, but hearing the story read out loud to others can make the reality of the death more present in this moment and offers a way, in the future, to keep ongoing ties to the deceased.

Session 3: Sandtray, Chapter 8

Observing the observer is one of the unique aspects of the sandtray experience. As with dream work, the unconscious speaks to us in symbolic ways when we place small objects in a tray of sand. However, while doing the sandtray we are awake watching our own process unfold. This is the first of the symbolic modalities and can offer an insight into our unconscious grief process. Several methods of using sand are presented so the facilitator can make best use of materials available.

The sandtray process is explained in chapter 8 as well as how to select and present the miniature objects that will be placed in the sand to tell the story. This is the first movement out of the cognitive process of the grief story and into the realms of physical activity and the unconscious world of symbols. Sand can have a grounding effect on people as they touch the earth. The small archetypal figures become the symbols by which the unconscious tells the story. In grief and loss it is always about the story.

Session 4: Physical Movement, Chapter 9

The grounding element at the midpoint of the grief support group curriculum is physical movement. The body will tell its own story as the group members move through the various exercises. Getting in touch with our bodies and what emotions might be held in various parts of the body is an important step in relearning the new world which has been created by the death of our loved one. The gentle physical movements suggested in this chapter will awaken the body, and then allow the mind and body to relax. The facilitators are invited to use physical practices in which they are trained, such as yoga, dance, continuum movement, or martial arts, such as tai chi or qi qong. The purpose of this session is to move out of the head and into the body. Physical movement will also serve to loosen up the group and prepare for the sessions on music, drama, and ritual.

Session 5: The Art of Collage, Chapter 10

Using magazines, photos, fabric, and objects, the group will be led into the world of art making without having to think about whether they can paint or draw. By cutting and pasting, group members put together pictures, words, and objects together on a piece of heavy paper or cardboard to tell, yet again, the ongoing story of loss and memories in a new and changing world.

Collage is much neater and involves less clean-up than painting. It takes fewer supplies and allows images to be used that individuals might have difficulty creating on their own. No one has ever said, "I can't cut and paste." So often, especially as adults, we are afraid to draw or paint because we feel we can't, or aren't artists. Collage eliminates this fear factor.

However, once again, if the facilitator is trained in drawing or painting and feels comfortable leading a group into the world of visual arts, then his or her expertise can be substituted in the session. Three artists share their style of painting with groups in part III: Deborah Koff-Chapin with Touch Drawing and Carol McIntyre with the Painting Experience, "Painting the Dragon," and Judith Koeleman with group painting. Painting can be a very therapeutic practice and is often used in art therapy. Remember that this course is not designed as art therapy, but may lead into that area with a qualified therapist.

Session 6: Music, Chapter 11

Nicole Burgess outlines how music may be effective in relieving anxiety, reinforcing feelings of identity and self-concept, and providing one more way for emotional expression of the story. The session on music will lead the facilitators through the life review process by way of music, combining music and art through mandalas, and involve the group members in either songs or drumming. The leaders will be able to follow the exercises outlined in the chapter whether or not they have a musical background, to benefit the bereaved through song and meaningful music for their life review. Music may be one of the best modalities for teens. The use of music for various populations is presented.

The exercises and ideas presented in this chapter may be appropriate during the course as background music and ritual. The participants are invited to bring their own music that is meaningful to them. This session paves the way into drama and theater and provides further openings for the last session on Ritual.

Session 7: Drama and Theater, Chapter 12

Lauren Chandler tells her tale of how without being a theater-trained person, she was able to move through the fears of performance to leading bereaved teen groups in public performance. The chapter outlines the steps necessary to deal with resistance to speaking in front of a group or bigger audience. Through the exercises the group will be able to act out the story, both individually and as a group. The chapter is designed so as to allow facilitators to open this session to an entire group program for teens and adults.

As the grief group sessions proceed, the facilitator can begin to plan, along with the group members, how the session on theater might be presented. Written stories can turn into a script for the members, or a theme that has come up with the group may be the starting point for a play or drama scene. The session may evolve into additional sessions building a story of grief and loss for the community.

Session 8: Ritual, Chapter 13

Using individual and group rituals Janet Shaw Rogers explains how ritual can be a safe container for the darkness that often comes with grief. The chapter offers suggestions for each individual to prepare and set up a personal ritual to honor or memorialize their deceased loved one. The group will use ritual to tell the collective stories and to bring closure to the end of the bereavement group sessions. Each person is a spiritual being in his or her own way, and it is ritual that brings our spiritual questions into the light.

The entire last session is devoted to Ritual so as to allow, as far as possible, not only an honoring of the deceased but of each member of the group. Bonds have formed and for a short time a community has been created. Food has long been a group ritual to bring individuals into community. Consider using food not only as a way to honor what has happened over the previous weeks, but to allow a social lightness to enter the group as they say good-bye to each other and the process each has just gone through during the grief course.

Each of facilitator has a unique background and life experiences and it is anticipated that each will bring these talents and understandings into the grief group sessions and adapt the curriculum to fit his or her special way of leading and facilitating. Group leaders should use this book as a guide and supportive tool. It is the intent of the book to allow enough flexibility so that the program fits each group leader's abilities and the needs of his or her group. Enjoy making art!

Resources

Liebmann, M. (1986). *Art therapy for groups*. Cambridge, MA: Brookline Books. [This handbook of themes, games, and exercises begins with a wonderful explanation of how to form an art therapy group and gives detailed explanation of what can go wrong, types of groups, the use of art in a group and how to run a group.]

Malchiodi, C. A. (1998). *The art therapy sourcebook*. Los Angeles: Lowell House. [Ms. Malchiodi believes that the creative process of art making is healing and life enhancing. She offers explanations of art therapy and guidelines for various art forms.]

Section **II**

The Grief Support Group Curriculum

Eight Sessions

J. Earl Rogers

Session 1

The Storytellers — Oral History and Introduction

In the public telling of our tales we seek help in finding answers, or at least permission to share the burning questions.

— Robert Neimeyer

☐ Introduction

Human beings are storytellers. Long before we told our stories via paintings on the walls of caves, we sat together telling each other the stories of the day. The oral tradition continues to this day — the myths of each culture and the tales of our families are shared in groups and around the dinner table or on special holidays. In this first session of the grief support group we will use the story to lead us into our own grief and prepare the ground for the weeks to come. Introductions among the members, the telling of the story of their loss, and the beginning of the grief journal will be the focus of this first session.

Activities and expressive arts are suggested each week. However, facilitators should not feel bound by the curriculum presented in the chapter. Instead, they should use the guidance of the group and their own experience and training to follow the natural path for the group they have brought together. This first week is designed for the members of the group to get to know each other and to share, so far as each individual wishes, their stories of loss and how and why they came to the group. Introductions are best done slowly and gently, letting the personality of the group form organically as each member shares who they are and what brings them into the group. The stories can come out after introductions when there is a bit more of a feeling of safety in the group. This first week is designed to create a safe and protective space where feelings and emotions are welcome and tears are a loving guest.

This is the time to begin the process of modeling the "exquisite" or sacred witness (Jeffreys, 2005). The stories that will unfold during the weeks to follow are sacred and need to be observed as sacred ritual by the facilitator and cofacilitator and the members of the group. What happens this first week will set the tone for openness and safe sharing of the story as it unfolds in different forms over the weeks ahead.

☐ Week 1 Curriculum

Activities

	Estimated Time Required
1. Brief personal introduction to the group	10 minutes
Facilitator's name	
Background (who you are)	
Reason for the group	
How the course will unfold	
Ground rules	
Confidentiality	
Physical setting (bathrooms, etc.)	
Not talking while someone else is sharing	
2. Introductions by group members	5 minutes each
Name	30 minutes to
Reason for coming	60 minutes
Break (optional — participants may want to have snacks)	
3. Opening ritual (this may be done just after facilitator's introduction and before the group begins)	5 minutes
4. Introduction to journaling	5 to 10 minutes

5. The stories   Variable
                                                  amount of
                                                  time

Note that the stories may have come out during introductions or the facilitator may have to prompt the group to tell something about the loss that they have not told before. Invite detail in the stories and ask questions.

6. Closing: Allow time for closing remarks and ritual. Don't just blow out the candles. Take a moment to remember the names of the ones who have died, and to honor the courage of the group in coming. Make any announcements that are important for the following week, such as what to bring next time and any changes in location or times.

Materials Needed

- Several boxes of tissues around the room (supply every week)
- Attractive notebooks or journals if people have not brought their own (pens should also be available)
- Candles for ritual and some type of cloth or small table to act as an altar or centerpiece for the candle and any photos people bring

☐ Ritual

The opening ritual on the first day can take place after people have had the opportunity to introduce themselves and gain a bit of comfort in the group. However, the facilitator may find it more appropriate to open with the ritual. It is important to feel into the best time for an opening ritual. The first ritual is designed to be simple and nonthreatening: a simple candle lit to honor those we have lost or wish to remember. People may be invited to speak the names of their loved one as the candle is lit. An alternative would be to have a candle for each person in the group and have each one come to the center and light a candle for their loved one. Flowers and an attractive piece of cloth may add to the ritual. Invite people to bring in objects or photographs for the following weeks. If the facilitator has had a prescreening meeting with prospective group members, then suggest at that meeting that they bring a photo or meaningful object to share with the group. Allow a few minutes for silence after the candle(s) is lit for people to be with their own thoughts. Future sessions will allow more time for silence and meditation or contemplation. It is suggested that facilitators read chapter 13, the final session, by Janet Shaw Rogers before beginning the course.

☐ Oral Stories

The spoken word has great power in helping us understand and deal with our loss. It is one of many ways to tell the stories about ourselves and our lost loved one, as the group will discover in the coming weeks. However, the spoken story is the most common way to express our feelings, thoughts, experiences, and relationship to our lost loved one. Many people are quite comfortable speaking in a group and will be willing to tell about their loss. Others, more introverted, may hold back and not easily share. There is no requirement in this group for people to share, or to share more than they are comfortable with in the group. Ensure that each person has the opportunity and time to share as much or little as they need.

Our grief is all about the story: the story of loss, of moments from the past, both sad and pleasing, of the good and not so good parts of our relationship with our deceased loved one, the details of our lives, and the life of the one who has died. At first the story may just be the facts of the accident, the illness, or the death. Gradually we paint in the details of feelings, history, trauma, frustrations, anger, laughter, and other losses. In the telling and retelling of our story we begin the reconstruction of meaning in our lives (Neimeyer, 2000).

What grievers need most is to be heard in a nonjudgmental way with acceptance of who they are and how they are grieving (Rando, 1984). Understand that the greatest gift any of us has to offer is the quality of our attention. This is a time for stories not for advice. Make sure that the group understands that each person has his or her own process and that listening and speaking from the heart constitutes a gift to themselves and the other members of the group. We cannot fix or take away the pain of loss. Allow the grievers space to cry, talk, repeat, cry, repeat, and talk. It is sometimes difficult in a group to allow enough time for all this to happen, and the facilitator will need to keep one eye on the clock and remind the group that there must be enough time for all to speak. Remind them that there will be time enough to tell the details of their loss during the ensuing weeks.

It is difficult for some people to speak in a group. Questions may prompt more depth into the story. "What did you do after … ?" "How did you find out about … ?" "When did … happen?" "What was the most difficult feeling for you?" "Where were you when … ?" "What other losses have occurred as a result of the death?" Questions that are open and require more than a "yes" or "no" answer are most likely to bring out the details of the story.

☐ Children and Teens

Writing may be difficult for younger children, and allowing them to draw, glue images or photos, or color in the journal may be a way for them to express what they cannot speak or write. The journal may become a memory book (Goldman, 2000). It is not necessary to create the journal in any particular way. For teens the journal may become much more than just a feeling or memory journal. They may use it to find their place in the world by asking questions that may have no answers.

If children have difficulty getting started in their writing, suggesting some of the following may be helpful:

- Write about a favorite memory
- What does the group member miss most about the person who died
- Write letters to the loved one who died
- Write a good-bye letter
- Tell a story (whether truth or fiction)

Remember, for middle school and teens confidentiality is a major factor. Make sure they know that what they say and write will not be disclosed unless they so choose. The only exception would be in cases of child abuse or if they are in danger, to themselves or from/to others.

☐ Journaling

Speaking all the feelings one has, especially feelings judged as wrong or bad, such as relief at the death, anger at the dead person, resentments against other family members, and the like, can be difficult for many people. Some feelings or events are very difficult to express or disclose to others. Journals provide the outlet for feelings, events, and memories that people may not wish to express to the group. Journals range from writing down the facts of each day to the creative feeling journals where one writes, paints, draws, and puts together collages of images and themes that allow the communication of feelings through visual forms (Malchiodi, 1998).

Research shows that writing about personal trauma and loss can help one's mental and physical health (Neimeyer, 2000). The journal for this course is not only a daily ritual for the participants but a travel guide to show them where they have been and point to where they may be going. Through the journal the writers can see how far they have come and perhaps have some insight into the journey of grief. Robert Neimeyer (2000) suggests certain guidelines about writing a journal of grief and loss:

- Write about difficult losses, or events that are traumatic or difficult to share with others. Write about upsetting events or feelings. Significant events tend to be more beneficial to the writer and the more details that are included the deeper the personal understanding.
- Share with your journal those aspects of the loss or experience which you have discussed the least, or have not yet told anyone else about. What have you not told anyone? Even if the writing is never shared with another, the seeing of one's thoughts and feelings in writing is good for personal self-esteem and recovery.
- Write about your deepest feelings and thoughts. Write about events in detail and then how you feel about those events. What were your reactions, both external and internal. Was there a difference?
- Don't worry about spelling, grammar, penmanship, errors in facts, dates, or events. What is important is your relationship with the material you are writing about. Neatness does not count. Just let the pen flow with what ever comes without editing or judging.
- Write for at least 15 minutes a day during the course. Going over the loss seems to promote new meaning in participants' lives in ways that just one telling of a story does not offer. Bring in other losses that come to mind as you write. Don't limit the writing to just one style of expression or one story. If you feel blocked and can't seem to write, just write about not being able to write. Whatever comes up in your mind should be recorded: keep writing!
- Keeping a journal of feelings and stories of loss can be difficult and even painful. Allow some time or activity for yourself after you write in your journal. Let the material sit in your mind for a few minutes before resuming your daily activity. Quiet time before engaging in "normal" activities allows you to quiet your mind and emotions before having to function in the outer world.

Writing in the journal does not have to be limited to the emotions and experiences of loss. Planning, writing down dreams, and notes that arise out of the grief course are all ways to use the journal as a personal map of the group member's journey through grief and life. Drawings, pictures, collages, or scribbles may be used to express emotions that cannot be expressed in words or to add to the visual expression of the journal.

One final note on journaling: Remind group members to keep their journals safe and confidential. Knowing that no one has access to the journal allows for more room to discuss those things that are deeply personal, traumatic, or shameful. While the journal may be a good jumping off place for sharing at the beginning of each session, there are some things we do not wish to share.

Journaling Example

Journaling can be a path into our grief that otherwise lies dormant in our psyches. Ina Albert could not touch the deep grief following the death of her mother. The only memory was that of an old woman lying in bed. It took her journal to lead her onto the path of mourning.

Reach Out and Touch Someone

Ina Albert

In the days before cell phones, "Reach out and touch someone." was AT&T's slogan to encourage long distance calls to keep families together even though they lived far apart. In this particular instance, my brother and I just didn't connect. I lived in Chicago; he lived in Maryland and there was no bridging the distance.

"Where have you been," he shouted over the phone from Maryland. "I've been trying to get you for three days! Mom died on Tuesday and now it's Friday. The nursing home didn't know how to get hold of you, so they called me."

There was a pause. My voice was stuck in my throat, my emotions were lodged in my diaphragm, and my temper was about to explode as soon as I could get my mouth to work.

"I'm married to a rabbi, you ninny, and it was Rosh Hashanah. For the past three days we've been in synagogue. You remember — that place where Mom and Dad took us every Jewish New Year." My voice leaked sarcasm like an old oil drum.

Again a pause. Maybe he's regrouping, I thought.

"Mom died on Tuesday," he groped, "and I didn't know what to do. You have all the papers, her will, and everything. And I didn't know what to say to Dad. Her body's got to be shipped to Philadelphia for the burial, the funeral parlor had instructions but I didn't know if there was any money to pay for it. I was so frustrated. Sorry."

For 10 years, I had taken responsibility for my parents. At first, I tried to manage things from Florida, but finally moved them from Philadelphia to Miami's Jewish Home and Hospital where I was working at the time.

Mom had Alzheimer's disease and Dad suffered with eschemia, a heart condition, and constant bouts of depression. In Miami, they lived on the hospital grounds; he in an apartment and she in the nursing home. Dad spent every day by her bedside, feeding her, dressing her, coaxing her to smile, and talking to her about all the things they would do together when she got well.

To handle the situation, I dressed myself in a thick coat of emotional armor and moved through our visits like a zombie, buying clothes for them, taking Dad to dinner, and talking to doctors, care managers, and administrators.

Nine months prior to this phone call, I was married and moved to Chicago. By that time, my emotions were buried so deep that I was completely unaware of them. "There's nothing more I can do," I told my husband. Things would play themselves out in their own good time. The armor seemed to be in place permanently.

Now the end had come for Mom and that was a blessing for everyone but Dad. He still waited by her bedside waiting for her. Now, finally, the end-of-life details had to be handled.

"I'll take care of the arrangements," my husband volunteered. "Just give me the necessary papers. Just sit down here and I'll tell you when I need you."

Who better to do this than a rabbi? I thought.

So I sat at the window of our downtown Chicago apartment staring out at Lake Michigan. It was a fall day and the trees were turning color in Lincoln Park twenty-four floors below. The life force of summer was retreating and soon the leaves would fall to the ground and crumble to dust.

I sat in that chair for hours rocking back and forth. The strange body language of sorrow took over my body without my consent and refused to let go.

"It's six o'clock, honey," said my husband. "Are you going to sit there rocking all night? You've been there for hours."

"I didn't realize," I said, "time is standing still. I'm not feeling anything."

And that's what it was. I went through the motions of arranging for an autopsy, sending on the information to the undertakers in Philadelphia to arrange for a graveside ceremony, and made reservations to fly from Chicago to Philadelphia. We would stay with my friend Betty in Center City.

Calls had to be made to relatives and friends. My sister-in-law ordered food for the reception after the funeral, and Rabbi Allen would perform the funeral service.

I even had enough presence to compose a eulogy to Mom that I read at graveside. Everything was handled. Again, I was an efficient zombie going through the motions.

It was not until after we returned to Chicago that I felt any emotion. Only when I sat at my desk to write personal notes to friends and relatives did the armor begin to crumble and morph into a catharsis of tears.

It was a dreary Chicago day. A lake wind, the kind that blows right through you, was howling around our apartment building. I picked up a pen and started to write — "She was only a skeleton in the bed. Only a murmur of human breath was left, like a shadow that passes so swiftly that you are not sure you've seen it. That's what she was all those years — a shadow, not my mother. But she was my mother, a degraded, absent, odorous, unresponsive blank of a person. And at the end, all that was left was the odor."

As I wrote, the tears fell. They wet the page like the rain drops splashing the window, running down the pane.

I don't know how long I wrote or how long I cried, but when it ended, I was in a different place — vulnerable and exhausted, yet relaxed and calm. The urgency of being responsible was gone. In its place was a simple appreciation for having known this elegant woman in her best days. Gratitude for her love, for the home she made for us, for her ambitions for us, for her support during the hard times in our lives, for the pride she took in her grandchildren.

Several hours later, after a nap and a martini, I reached for the phone to call my brother.

"Joel, I just wanted to say hello and tell you that Mom was really quite a lady, and something tells me that our memories of her will help us reach out and touch one another again."

It was years later that I realized that sharing the value of journaling with people suffering from illness and stress gave them a voice in their healing process — that writing about what you feel helps you feel better — that true healing happens when pain is released. I shared that discovery in our book *Write Your Self Well … Journal Your Self to Health*" and continue to shed my emotional armor every time I journal. It was Mom's gift to me.

Ina Albert, MA, is a health care communications consultant. She has developed and facilitated workshops for health care providers for many years. She and Zoe Keithley, MATW, coauthored *Write Yourself Well … Journal Your Self to Health* (2003), a book about journaling and its health benefits.

Resources

Albert, I., & Keithley, Z. (2003). *Write your self well ... journal your self to health.* Whitefish, MT: Mountain Greenery.

Albery, S. W. (1996). *Writing from your life: Telling your soul's story, a journey of self-discovery for women.* New York: Treacher Putnam.

Flynn, N., & M. Erickson (2000). *Teen talk, a grief support group for teenagers.* Grief-Works: A Bereavement Resource, 3718 Rodesco Dr. S.E. Puyallup, WA 98374-1761, USA. (800) 850-9420; e-mail griefworks@yahoo.com

Ganim, B., & Fox, S. (1999). *Visual journaling: Going deeper than words.* New York: Quest Books.

Neimeyer, R. A. (2000). *Lessons of loss: A guide to coping.* Keystone Heights, FL: PsychoEducational Resources.

CHAPTER   J. Earl Rogers

Session 2

The Written Story — Creative Writing, Journaling, and Poetry

> This [book] is my attempt to make sense of the period that followed [the death of my husband], weeks and then months that cut loose any fixed idea I had ever had about death, about illness, about probability and luck, about good fortune and bad....
>
> — **Joan Didion**, *The Year of Magical Thinking*

☐ Introduction

Creative writing and journaling is a good way to begin to tell the daily events following the death of our loved one. It can be a doorway into alternative endings to the story we don't want to have to tell ourselves: that our loved one has died. Gently we move into creative ways of telling our stories, writing down the details of each moment so we won't forget. The written story has a different texture from the telling of our story of loss and grief. For weeks and months we will be unable to express all of our feelings and memories in a coherent fashion. But gradually a whole picture will slowly emerge: fuzzy at first, perhaps unintelligible to anyone else. Sitting before our journals blankness faces us from the page and from our minds, and then we write a word, a feeling, a thought, and gradually a sentence, fragment though it may be, and then several thoughts, memories, or feelings emerge one after the other.

Many authors have written the stories of their losses in their journals. Joan Didion tells the story of the sudden death of her husband of nearly 40 years in *The Year of Magical Thinking*; C. S. Lewis describes the loss of his wife in *A Grief Observed*; and Isabel Allende the story of the illness and death of her daughter in *Paula*. It is not important that we write well, that our sentences make no sense to anyone but our selves, or that anyone else ever reads our stories. It is the process of writing that heals, and allows us to look at that which we wish to ignore and change back to the world that existed before the death that has arrived uninvited in our lives.

Today we will write in a creative manner our stories, our fantasies, our fears, and our wishes that things were other than they are now. We can write the biography of our lost loved one, or tell a story of an event that occurred many years before the death, or write a short piece of poetry. Once we start, the story will tell itself almost without our conscious intent. Let the magic of the written word heal our wounded soul.

☐ Week 2 Curriculum

Activities

	Estimated Time Required

1. Opening ritual (see chapter 13)
    Light a candle for those we have lost
    Place ritual objects on altar
	5 minutes

2. Check-in (using journals)	3 to 5 minutes each
3. Writing exercise	30 to 50 minutes
4. Closing	5 to 10 minutes

Materials Needed

Pens, paper, and journals (colored pens and markers optional)

☐ Creative Writing

Often the first response to the idea of creative writing is "I can't write" Joel Saltzman (1993) says in *"If You Can Talk, You Can Write."* The second response is "I don't know what to write." Julia Cameron, in *The Artist's Way* (1992), tells of using the "morning pages," or for our purposes, the mourning pages. Each day, using the Artist's Way, one writes three hand-written pages. It matters not what is written, whether it makes sense, or is nothing more than a rambling list of complaints, pain, worries, and fears; the point is to write. The same is true for this week's curriculum: write. There is no inner critic telling us we can't write, because it doesn't matter what we write. The writings don't have to be shared, although time will be made available for those who wish to read to the group the written story of their grief. As with the journal, spelling, grammar, punctuation, and story line do not matter. Neatness does not count. It only matters that we find a new way to express our loss and life.

Ms. Cameron's book on creativity sounds much like grief theory, or an 11-week grief support group: recovering a sense of safety, identity, power, integrity, possibility, abundance, connection, strength, compassion, self-protection, autonomy, and faith. Her book on creativity is a guide for people to find the spiritual basis of their own creativity. And, here, we offer people an opportunity to find new meaning in life after a major loss through creative acts — not to create art, but to create the story of their lives. "How?" we ask. Hal Zina Bennett says, *"Write from the Heart"* (1995).

Creative Writing Exercise

Begin with a 5- or 10-minute write. Tell the participants to just write for 10 minutes. Do not let the pen lift off the page, keep writing no matter what, even if it is about how they can't think of what to write. Let the participants write about whatever comes to their mind; it may not be directly related to their loss and grief. It can be a story about their loved one, a fictional version of something that happened in the past, or will in the future. It may be the beginning of a biography of their lost loved one, or their family. Fantasy is a wonderful way to enter into our unconscious and may lead to observations of our selves not easily seen by our conscious mind. It does not matter whether what we write is true or accurate. The writing can be about feelings, events, or our fears and wishes.

Writing can be very difficult for some people. They can't get started, or they can't decide what to write about. Use what are called "jump-off lines" to start the process. A jump-off line is merely a few words that may start a sentence or line of thought. People can choose to use the line or come up with their own.

Examples may be:

- The last time …
- I remember the first time we …
- What I don't want to say is …
- I have something to say …
- What I miss most is …
- I want to tell you about the time …

After the group has written for 10 minutes ask who would like to read their stories. Some people are uncomfortable reading what they have written, but at least some of the people should be encouraged to read out loud, because it is very powerful and releasing for many people. The written word has a different impact from when we tell our story orally. If there is not enough time for a 10-minute writing session, then use 5 minutes. The point is to get the group to start writing. They may even wish to continue the writing for the rest of the meetings. Some groups have found that writing is the only thing they want to do.

As with the journal tell the participants not to edit, judge, or be concerned with grammar, spelling, punctuation, accuracy, or content. Write from a place of deep feelings and emotions. What stands out in their minds at this moment? What is most difficult to write about (Neimeyer, 2000)? Our handwriting, whether neat or illegible, is not important. But have the group use pens or pencils not computers. A computer interferes not only with the group, but also with the inner process of our grief. It places an electronic machine between us and our thoughts and feelings.

If people are really stuck, tell them to talk to the page (Saltzman, 1993). Tell participants to write as they talk — nothing fancy, nothing that "sounds" like writing. It is the power of seeing and hearing our words that carries the healing effect of writing. Make up stuff. What we write doesn't have to be true. But even in fiction the writer enters into the story and tells a bit of truth about himself or herself.

Biographies

Another exercise that may be important to people is to tell the life story of the person who died (Neimeyer, 2000). A biography can allow us to learn more about and tell the story of our loved one in a more detailed manner. While we cannot write the biography of someone in 10 minutes, we can start the story and then go back later and fill in the facts and details. The story of our loved one's life is a way to honor them and give us perspective on the person and their loss. Robert Neimeyer outlines the general idea of how to write a biography in his book *Lessons of Loss* (2000). Whatever approach one uses, the biography can be a wonderful and powerful journey into our understanding of the person we have lost, and how that loss has affected our life.

Poetry

Many people easily write in a poetic style. That is not easy for me. I am much more comfortable writing in a talking narrative style. While I struggle with this my son and daughter easily write poetry. I think that I only remember the lectures of teachers talking about rhyme and different forms of "formal" poetry. There must be some special way to write to make "real" poetry, I think. Whatever the reason, I always end up staring at the blank page when asked to write poetry. That was true until I encountered Haiku. It has a form that I understand and it is short enough that I don't get overwhelmed with the process.

Haiku comes to us from Japan but has been adapted to the English language to become the American style of Haiku. It is a short poem, usually just three lines, and generally has a line of five syllables, then a line of seven syllables, and the last line, again, five syllables. Traditionally there is a nature feature or theme in this style of poetry, and one or two images. I wrote this Haiku many years after my father died:

> Father carries son
> The winter snows come to us
> Son carries father

It follows Haiku form only in that there are three lines with 5, 7, 5 sounds or syllables and does have a seasonal or nature aspect to tie the two images together. Otherwise it is my version of Haiku. It was the expression of how the cycle of life and the death of my father came together in my understanding.

Another feature of Haiku is that it is to take place in the present moment. It is an expression of feeling experienced in the moment. Bruce Ross has an excellent book, *How to Haiku* (2002), which explains the details of Haiku poetry. It is so simple to look at and yet complex to do well. However, it is easy to begin and is easily done by beginners as well as those who have practiced the form for many years. Don't try to sound "poetic" or dramatic. Avoid rhyme and other rules or forms learned in school and keep it simple. A simple moment of awareness or expression of feeling is called for in the Haiku. The writer should do what delights or surprises her in the moment. It does not have to be serious, in fact humor or joy can be a spontaneous expression of the moment as well as a philosophical insight into death and meaning in one's life.

The shortness of the form will allow the group to write many different Haiku during the session. It can be an experience where the members of the group, after grasping the basic idea, popcorn out to the group their current attempt. Thus the group becomes, by both writing and speaking at the same time, an expression of feelings in the moment.

☐ Children and Teens

Teens have little trouble writing poetry or in creative writing. However, children often have difficulty writing in an unstructured manner and Haiku may be too complex. Letters to loved ones are a useful tool that can help the child work through his or her thoughts and feelings with regard to the person who has died.

> Letter writing is a wonderful grief resolution for people from 3 years to 103. It allows the expression of feelings and the ability to have an ongoing, ever-present internal relationship with a loved one that can continue to grow and develop. (Goldman, 2000, p. 66)

Drawing may be a more appropriate method for younger children to express and tell their story. Words and drawings work well together, such as "Me and Mom in Heaven," the words which accompanied a drawing of the little girl and her mom in Linda Goldman's book *Life and Loss* (p. 64). Drawing may bring out conversation for teens and allow expression for children. It is usually a good idea to have colored pens and markers and an abundant supply of paper for both these groups. Music for teens is often a must. Teens don't sit still well. Whether it is homework, or writing in a grief group, they usually seem more comfortable with loud music to accompany their thoughts. In chapter 11, Nicole Burgess offers some suggestions for music for children and teens.

Since we are suggesting drama/theater in chapter 12, it might be a useful writing project for the teens to begin to write a play about loss. This project can go on during the course of the group and result in an amazing experience around loss. Lauren Chandler has several suggestions for teens using theater. In chapter 15, Sara Baker, "Woven Dialog," and Sara Spaulding Phillips, "Fierce Living," describe how they use creative writing in groups.

In 1999 my wife and I were the primary caregivers for our friend Heather. After she died I wrote the following in a writing class based on the jump-off line: I remember …

☐ Heather's Story

I remember the first time I met Heather, or rather, I remember seeing her guitar case sitting in the living room of our condo in Pacific Palisades. Each week the guitar case would show up at our house with a tall, almost skinny, dishwater blond — I didn't see the guitar or hear her sing for several years.

Janet, my new Canadian wife, and Heather met at massage school in Santa Monica. Heather had spotted Janet's Canadian accent the first day of class. She had lived in the same Southern Ontario town as Janet's brother and sister. Each week ,Janet and Heather would get together to practice massage on each other. I would get home from work on Tuesday afternoons and there would be the guitar case sitting at the end of the sofa with teacups on the table.

A year after Janet and Heather met, Heather moved to Calistoga in the Napa Valley. She had been offered a massage practice in St. Helena a few miles south of Calistoga. First Janet, and then the two of us, made trips to visit Heather, once or twice a year, then gradually several times a year for a week or more. Heather and I became friends on our own — we cooked the same way, drove and gave directions the same way — she became my sister. For two months in 1994, I stayed next door to Heather, house-sitting for Jerry and Loma, the couple whose guesthouse Heather rented.

Ostensibly I was there to write my dissertation in the quiet and solitude of January and February in Dutch Henry Canyon. Heather spent her days writing her music, which had become the driving force in her life — one album already on tape and a CD in the works. However, instead of writing the dissertation I wrote short stories. We each wrote by day and cooked and shared our day's work each night: she sang to me, I read to her as we ate.

The CD came out a couple of years later — but it was not enough. Spirit told her to go on the road: NOW! In July 1998 she said goodbye to all her friends in the Napa Valley and she and Francis (whom she had met four years before and was now her life partner), despite his fears and doubts, went on the road for a concert tour. In early December of 1998 they passed through Los Angeles and stayed with us for a few days.

She arrived weak and exhausted beyond fatigue and unable to move or walk without extreme pain. Doctors told her it was a virus affecting the nerves. She lay on our sofa all weekend. She sang to us and looked forward to getting back on her concert tour. We left for Australia for two months a few days later.

In February, a few days after our return to the United States we decided to catch up on our e-mail. There were a flurry of notes from Frances and other friends of Heather. She had stage 4 metastasized breast cancer. The doctors gave her three months to live. They had given up on traditional medicine and stopped the chemotherapy and radiation. They were going to use alternative means.

Over the next six months, Janet alone or the two of us, made several trips from LA to the Napa Valley in order to share in caretaking duties. Usually Janet did the hands-on work and I cooked for Heather, Frances, and whichever caretakers or family were present. Since Heather's family lived in the east her care became the responsibility of her community of friends. A schedule was set up and each of us took turns.

Heather and Frances had little money and moved several times in the next few months staying with friends. In May Janet and I decided it was time to move from LA. After years of looking during the downturn in the LA real estate prices, the market had turned and we sold our home the first week, and had 60 days to find a place in the Napa Valley and move. There was nothing: nothing to buy, nothing to rent. Finally at the last minute we rented a small apartment in the downstairs of a friend's home. Ken lived in Dutch Henry Canyon about a quarter mile down the road and next door to the couple who owned the guesthouse where Heather had lived and where we had spent so much wonderful time over the years.

The week we moved in, Loma, our friend who owned the guesthouse, offered Heather and Frances her place in the canyon and they moved in. Over the next six months we became the major caregivers for Heather. It took a community to care for her. She was bedridden and Frances could not do everything. Again Janet did hands on and I cooked. After celebrating four birthdays, Thanksgiving, Christmas, and New Year's Eve together, Heather could no longer go on. Finally she asked for morphine and to let go of this life. She died six days later on January 17, 2000.

On New Year's Eve Heather sang to a gathering of 30 friends and family from her bed. Flat on her back she sang like an angel. It was her last concert.

Janet couldn't be there that last week because her father was dying at home in Canada. Dave died 10 days after Heather on January 27.

Both died at home surrounded by family, friends, and love: Two deaths, two different funerals, both at home.

Heather wanted to stay at home for three days before the memorial service, then to be cremated. We opened the windows after she died and placed her on dry ice, wrapped her in cloth and flowers, and sang to her around the clock. We painted her cardboard coffin to celebrate her life and art. Family and friends each painted whatever it was that spoke of their relationship with Heather. The day after the memorial a small group of us took her to Santa Rosa to be cremated. Forty-nine days later we spread her ashes in the Pacific. I remember her guitar case in our living room. I remember her salads. I remember her voice. I remember my friend.

☐ Notes for Next Week

In the next session we will be using various forms of sandtray. The facilitator may want to ask the group to bring articles from nature, such as rocks, shells, small stones, feathers, driftwood pieces, leaves, or pinecones. According to the form of sandtray used, members should be asked to bring small objects such as toys, animals, cars, small dolls, human figures, military figures, and meaningful objects. Boats, ladders, bridges, artificial trees, such as one might find for electric train sets, are also possible choices to bring for the sandtray.

Resources

Bennett, H. Z. (1995). *Write from the heart*. Mill Valley, CA: Nataraj.

Cameron, J. (1992). *The artist's way*. New York: G.P. Putnam's Sons.

Davis, M. (1999). Against daily insignificance: Writing through grief. In *Grief and the healing arts* (p. 303). Amityville, NY: Baywood.

De Spelder, L. A., & Strickland, A. L. (2002). Telling the story: Narrative approaches. In *The last dance: Encountering death and dying* (6th ed., p. 242). San Francisco: McGraw-Hill.

Goldman, L. (2000). *Life and loss* (2nd ed.), Philadelphia: Taylor & Francis.

Ross, B. (2002). *How to haiku; a writer's guide to haiku and related forms*. Boston: Tuttle.

Saltzman, J. (1993). *If you can talk, you can write*. New York: Warner Books.

CHAPTER **8**   J. Earl Rogers

Session 3

Sandtray — An Accessible Strategy for the Grief Process

In grief we access parts of ourselves that were somehow unavailable to us in the past.

— **Frank Ostaseski**

☐ Introduction

The use of sand as a medium for creating a sacred space has a long history, from the sand mandalas of Buddhist monks, to the sand drawings of the Navahos in which images are created with sand to invoke the healing powers of the universe, to the use of Sandplay in psychotherapy. It is a process that can be as simple or complex as the group facilitator wishes.

I was introduced to sandtray by Joan Halifax at a "Being with Dying" workshop for health care professionals at Upaya in Santa Fe, New Mexico. I was taken by the magic of the figures and objects in the small room where the sandtray materials were kept. A doorway to the archetypal and mythological world had been opened for me. I stood transfixed and in awe. I did a sandtray with several witnesses and was amazed at what occurred as I arranged the figures and objects in the sand. This was followed by a year's study on Sandplay with Harriet Friedman in Los Angeles. During this time I realized that I wanted to include this process in my work with those who were grieving and dying.

I invite readers to see into the magic and mystery of the sandtray process, and suggest that it is a strategy and tool that may assist the grief process. I have used sandtray with families who have lost a child and have found that it enables the parents to create a story about the death and their relationship to the deceased child. This often paves the way for deeper insights and expressions of grief. In one instance, a man in his late 50s had lost his son in an automobile accident. The driver had been the son's friend and was drunk. As the grieving father placed the objects in the tray a pattern developed. On one side of the sandtray were all the rescuers, a lifeboat, divers, firemen, police officers, and on the other was an overturned car with the expanse of empty sand in between. As the father sat there looking at the scene in the sand, tears formed in his eyes, and he said, "I'm still trying to rescue him." We held each other and cried. He finally knew what he was attempting to hold away from his conscious mind: that he was supposed to rescue his son but he could not and would never be able to rescue him. A sense of relief formed in his face and he said that perhaps now he could begin to really understand his loss.

The following pages contain a brief explanation of sandtray and Sandplay, the process of using sandtray, various methods or approaches, and how to set up a sandtray for individuals and groups. Books are listed to assist the facilitator in expanding the use of the sandtray in the grief process.

This process of using sand as a method of telling the story can be as simple as having bowls of sand in which to place the hands and just feel the sand and earth element. It can be expanded to include objects from nature, or the addition of archetypal figures. Whether simple or more involved it is a process that allows the unconscious to come forth without words.

☐ Week 3 Curriculum

Activities

	Estimated Time Required
1. Opening ritual or meditation	5 minutes
2. Check-in with journal or the object each person brought this week	3 to 5 minutes each
3. Sandtray exercise (select the one that best suits the situation)	40 minutes
4. Closing ritual and comments	5 to 10 minutes

Materials Needed

Trays or bowls for clean soft sand, objects, and materials for the sandtray story as described below.

Begin the session, as usual, with a meditation, ritual, or a few quiet moments for the group to become present for the session. Check in with the participants as to how they are doing, or what has come up for them in the past week. Members of the group may wish to read from their journals. It is the journal that ties the various expressive arts together to form a container for each person's unfolding story. If you have asked the group members to bring a special object/s for the sandtray you might ask them to tell about the object and why they brought it for the group.

Explain the sandtray process that the group is going to use (taken from one of the models below), and the basic rules for how the session is going to proceed. Unless a group sandtray is planned, divide the group into pairs and give each pair a sandtray. If there are not enough trays of sand, or conditions prevent the use of sand, pillowcases, large pieces of firm paper, cardboard, or areas marked out on the floor with tape, string, or ribbon can be used. Ask the participants to create a picture of their story with the objects at hand. Do not evaluate the trays. Let conversation come naturally and invite each participant to tell the story if they wish.

Allow about 10 to 20 minutes, according to how many objects are available and the complexity your materials allow. Then let the person who did the tray share with the observer how the experience felt. Reverse the roles and have the second member of the pair do his or her own tray, followed by the same conversation. The observers will dismantle the tray before proceeding with their own turn. If there is to be a group tray, divide the members into two groups, one to observe and one to participate. Whether in pairs or groups there will always be an observer to hold the attention and sacred space.

☐ Sandtray and Sandplay

Sandtray, the generic term, is the use of miniature objects, archetypal figures, toys, rocks, shells, and other items from nature and the man-made world placed in a container of sand. It can be a group or individual process based on the experience, training, and philosophy of the group leader. Sandtray can be done without sand using any flat surface or piece of cloth. Pieces of firm paper or cardboard can define the space, as can pieces of string or ribbon. The sand alone may be enough of a form, allowing the participants to just feel the sand through their fingers.

FIGURE 8.1 Harriett Friedman's Sandplay™ room, Los Angeles, CA. (Photo courtesy of Earl Rogers.)

FIGURE 8.2 Sandplay™ shelf. (Photo courtesy of Earl Rogers.)

Sandplay™ is a Jungian oriented technique developed by Dora Kalff and based in part on Margaret Lowenfeld's *World Technique*. It is more specific and structured than sandtray. In Sandplay, a term trademarked by the Sandplay Therapists of America, it is recommended that two trays of sand be used, one dry and one with moist sand to which water can be added (Figure 8.1). The Sandplay trays are 28½″ by 19½″ and 3″ deep. The bottom and sides of the tray are painted blue to give the impression of

FIGURE 8.3   Sandtray collection. (Photo courtesy of Earl Rogers.)

FIGURE 8.4   Close-up of portable sandtray collection. (Photo courtesy of Earl Rogers.)

water or sky. (Rogers-Mitchell & Friedman, 1994; Weinrib, 1983). Sandplay therapists will have a vast array of figures and objects (Figure 8.2).

Smaller and more portable versions can be used where the objects can easily be transported to the bedside or other setting (Figures 8.3 and 8.4).

In this session we will use the broadest interpretation of sandtray to allow it to fit into the facilitator's experience and practice. The unconscious uses symbols (Jung,1964), and the symbols of the sandtray figures and objects allow the inner state to manifest in a similar manner to dreams. However, with sandtray the participant is both the observer and the observed of his or her own unconscious experience. The sandtray can give space and value to the unconscious and irrational, which are often unrecognized and unacknowledged sides of our psyche (Mitchell & Friedman, 1994). The sandtray offers a nonverbal picture of emotions that may not otherwise be expressed. A basic postulate of sandtray is that, given the proper condition, it enables the unconscious to heal itself. Sandtray allows the individual to reconnect to forgotten or repressed aspects of the psyche. It allows expression of that which is beyond words (Bradway & McCoard, 1997; Weinrib, 1983).

☐ Alternative Forms Can Easily Be Adapted to Materials at Hand

Darcy Nichols, RN, M.Ed., at King's University College, London, Ontario, Canada, uses soft sand in deep bowls or containers with few objects. The feeling of the sand can become sacred, as the story unfolds in a new way. The bowls ideally should have sloped sides so that the participants can easily get their hands into the sand. The participant, with one or two observers, then places his or her hands into the sand and allows the sand to flow out as with water. The grounding feeling of the soft sand allows the participant to connect with the earth and to feelings that may still be unconscious. Let the participant move his or her hands in the sand and speak if feelings or words come to mind. As always, the observers are there to listen and attend to what is happening in the moment. Observers, by their quiet attention, allow a safe and contained space in which a deep exploration and sharing can happen. (Association of Death Education and Counseling, National Conference. [2005]. *When Words Fail: Expressing the Inexpressible Through the Use of the Sand Tray*).

Marion Weber and Rachel Naomi Remen, MD, use the group sandtray as a multimodal educational experience. One of the methods used at Commonweal, a retreat center north of San Francisco, CA, is a round table about 5' in diameter. It has depth to hold the sand. Objects line the shelves around the room containing the table, and the larger group is divided into two groups: one to participate in the placing of the objects and one to observe. After the first group has completed their sandtray, the second group will dismantle the table tray and then select the objects for their own process. This table will accommodate four to eight people. Sticks or pieces of doweling are used to divide the tray into sections to accommodate each person. After the members of the group have completed their individual section, the dividers are removed to show the group experience (Weber & Remen, 1993).

The Process of Using Objects and Sandtrays

Use as little instruction and introduction as possible. Divide the group into two or three people. Let one person at a time create his or her sandtray with the other(s) as observer(s). Invite the participants to touch and play with the sand and let them know what is available, such as rocks, candles, matches, and the like, objects which may not be immediately obvious. Then allow the participants to choose the pieces they wish to use in their trays. Tell them to recount a story in the sand using the objects available to do so. Have the observer(s) take the tray apart for the next person to proceed.

Let the process unfold and let the observers provide the sacred witness to the participant's expression of his or her experience. It is the witness to the process who provides the space for the healing of the unconscious. The only gift we have to offer is the quality of our attention. While Sandplay can be a diagnostic and therapeutic tool, in this context sandtray is designed to be a tool for the participant to allow expression of grief and a healing of the wounds of loss. Interpretation can be counterproductive and intrude on the very personal process of grief, both conscious and unconscious (Rogers & Friedman, 1994; Weinrib, 1983).

The less said the better. The fewer instructions and rules the better. Don't interpret, evaluate, or diagnose. Listen and observe. Ask a few questions about the story that is presented in the sand: for example, "Is there a story?" "What does this bring up?" Or, as you point to a piece, "What does this piece feel like to you?" When the participants are the observers, a few such instructions may be of guidance and avoid the observers' unintentional intrusion into the story.

When introducing the sandtray convey respect for the process with openness and a nonjudgmental attitude. Be nondirective even when making specific suggestions about the use of the tray. We want to touch a healing level in the psyche, and just allowing time to "be with the scene" may allow the participant to deepen in the healing process.

Do not allow the participants to remove the figures after the picture has been completed. Let the observers clean up the sandtray and replace the objects and figures after the participant has left the area. This allows the process to remain fresh in the person's mind and keeps the process sacred.

☐ Children and Teens

Children will, of course, be at different developmental levels, and that needs to be taken into consideration when putting the group together and during the process. With children, the play is confined to the sandtray container. It is best to use the "third person" perspective when speaking of the tray. Usually the children do not connect themselves with the figures in the tray as adults may do (Boik & Goodwin 2000). Teens can sometimes relate the figures to themselves according to their age and developmental level.

We are attempting to offer a free and protected space (Weinrib, 1983). Sandtray can be a powerful tool for healing and great attention needs to be paid to the children or teens. Children work through their grief through their play and sandtray offers even more opportunity to work out grief, anger, frustration, magical thinking, and adaptation. This is a nonverbal, nonrational form and allows the unconscious to do its healing work (Bradway & McCoard, 1997). Remember, however, unless you are a trained Sandplay therapist do not attempt to do therapy with sandtray, which is one of many *art* modalities whereby children or teens can tell their story in another form.

The selection of pieces will change with the age of the children. In most cases a selection of toys, rocks, and objects can be anything the child's imagination says it is. Include appropriate toys for boys and girls. Children will play out war and caregiving in their sandtray. Include toy soldiers, cowboys and Indians, farm animals, wild animals, cars, dolls, people, and beads. Small trees or bushes can be included and fences are important for the children to be able to make barriers (Rogers-Mitchell & Friedman, 1994). Children may not be able to verbalize what is in their tray (Boik & Goodwin, 2000), and teens may not want to speak about the tray. Let them be because the grief work is done through the process of creating the tray. While small plastic toys aid the children in creating their "world," stones and items from nature will do just fine.

☐ Selection and Purchase of Pieces

Selection, purchase, and obtaining of pieces are an individual choice and at the same time should offer as much opportunity as possible for others to relate to the pieces. Use a cross-section of external and internal worlds. Take symbols from both the real and the imaginary worlds. Use the natural world: wood, leaves, branches, shells, and rocks that you may come

FIGURE 8.5   Assorted objects from the sandtray collection. (Photo courtesy of Earl Rogers.)

across in your daily life. You may ask the participants to bring their own objects the preceding week. Ask the members of the group to bring objects that are important to them: rocks, shells, toys, items that carry memories of the deceased loved one, and other objects from nature or from their homes that are meaningful.

Use the human world of work, play, religion, war, and mechanical things such as cars, boats, airplanes, and machinery. Use toy people of different races and occupations (Figure 8.5). Fantasy and archetypal pieces as well as realistic representations aid the participants in presenting their inner world (Boik & Goodwin, 2000; Bradway & McCoard, 1997; Cirlot, 1971; Rogers & Friedman, 1994).

If the facilitator is purchasing figures and objects, it is important to attempt to find items that are of good quality and that will appeal to both the aesthetic and creative aspects of the people who will be using the sandtray. The facilitator needs to be creative in the selection and listen to his or her own inner voice. The selection is an individual process and can be a fun and rewarding experience if we let our inner child play rather than the therapist or professional part of us.

Objects can be obtained easily in the world around us. Objects can also be purchased from a supplier specializing in sandtray products, or in antique shops, toy stores, garage sales, and secondhand shops. Objects can come from the ocean, lakes, rivers, mountains, and deserts. Our children's old toys (or our own) can be a wonderful way to personalize the collection. Color, shape, and tactile qualities are important. If an object doesn't appeal to the facilitator, then it should be excluded from the collection. We need to use both our cognitive analysis as well as our intuitive process to select what belongs in our collection.

The bowls or trays can be anything that will hold the sand and are big enough to hold a number of objects or figures. Garden bowls made of plastic with sloped sides work well. Shallow plastic sweater trays, aluminum cooking trays, or plastic dish trays will all work. Trays should be at least 3" deep.

☐ Conclusion

The core of sandtray work with the grieving is the quiet presence of another person who is fully present and attentive: a sacred witness if you will. To be with another in such a sacred manner is to listen with one's heart, suspending judgment, beliefs, and assumptions. To "Be With" as a sacred witness is to be fully present to the other person: open, authentic, caring, accepting, understanding, and compassionate. Sandtray allows that process to deepen and birth new understanding and healing.

Bring the session to a close after all participants have had the opportunity to create a sandtray and be an observer. Gather the group together and invite discussion about what happened during the course of the session. All are welcome to share and none need share. As with the other expressive arts, sessions allow a few minutes of quiet before ending. Music may be an excellent way of ending the session with a minimum of ordinary chitchat. Help the participants to keep the feelings and energy of the session, but be sure to check in to see if any need some extra help before leaving.

☐ Notes for Next Week

Remind the participants to wear loose comfortable clothing for the next session because they will be doing physical movement.

Resources

Boik, B. L., & Goodwin, E. A. (2000). *Sandplay therapy: A step-by-step manual for psychotherapists of diverse orientations.* New York: W.W. Norton. [This may be the best book for the beginner.]

Bradway, K., & McCord, B. (1997). *Sandplay — Silent workshop of the psyche.* New York: Routledge.

Cirlot, J. E. (1971). *A dictionary of symbols.* (Trans. Jack Sage. New York: Routledge & Kegan Paul.)

Jung, C. G. (1964). *Man and his symbols.* NY: Doubleday.

Rogers-Mitchell, R., & Friedman, H. S. (1997). *Sandplay — Past, present and future.* New York: Routledge.

Weinrib, E. L. (1983). *Images of the self.* Boston, MA: Sigo Press.

Weber, M., & Remen, R. N. (1993). The sand way, Parts I & II. *Atlantis,* March and April.

CHAPTER 9

J. Earl Rogers

Session 4

The Body of Grief

The Dance

There are times when I would choose to dance
Breaking the plodding rhythm of my grief
Catching a moment to breathe "free"
And celebrate who you were
But there are those who would misconstrue my dance
Determining that I have "healed"
I dance in the privacy of my mind.

— Susan, 1998 (a bereaved Mom; with permission)

☐ Introduction

Using various forms of movement this session will address the issues of
the body and attempt to tell the story of grief and loss through the body.
Whether it is through dance, yoga postures, gentle breath exercises, or just
physical movements, the activity will allow the group members the opportunity to move out of their heads and into their bodies. At a minimum this
session of physical movement will facilitate deep relaxation, concentration, and mental recovery. Specific exercises and physical movements will
be offered, or the facilitator can use a different form of movement, such as

yoga or dance, with which they are experienced. At the end of the session a guided meditation or visualization is offered to deepen the experience of letting the body tell its own story.

Grief involves more than just emotional work. It affects us on all levels: psychological, social, physical, and spiritual (Jeffreys, 2005; Neimeyer, 2000; Rando, 1984). Most grief theory books address the physical components of grief but do not discuss, beyond suggesting exercise, actual ways to deal with the physical aspects of our grief reaction. Physical symptoms of grief can include sleep problems, exhaustion, lack of strength, lack of energy, restlessness, shortness of breath, gastrointestinal disturbances, loss of weight, loss of sexual desire, and possible heart palpitations and anxiety. In this session we will look at ways to discharge the energy of physical symptoms and offer a short series of simple exercises to lessen the impact of these physical reactions.

Stress studies have for many years made it clear that psychosocial stress can effect pathological changes in our bodies (Stoyva & Anderson, 1982). Our thoughts and feelings can produce alterations in body structure and function (Zegan, 1982). In his work at the University of Massachusetts Dr. Jon Kabat-Zinn uses yoga, meditation, and breathing exercises to lessen the impact of stress and to strengthen the heart and mind (Kabat-Zinn, 1990). The stress of our grief affects our bodies just as physical pain and distress affects our mood and psychological outlook. Our mind and body do not act in isolation but are interconnected (Stoyva & Anderson, 1982). Research, both in western medicine and in Yogic traditions, shows that physical activity can reduce tensions, lessen anxiety, externalize aggression, and relieve depression (Rando, 1994; Saraswati, 1986).

On a practical level, physical activity and awareness of our body during times of stress can inform us of unattended grief and emotions as well as tell our story of grief and loss in a new way. Yoga, qi qong, tai chi, walking, swimming, gentle stretching, dance, and soft sports all serve to support our bodies, minds, and spirits. While only a person trained in yoga, qi-qong, or dance can properly lead such activities, with guidance and gentleness anyone can use gentle stretches to aid the body and loosen tight and shielded muscles. Judith Lasater, PhD (1995), uses the ancient practices of yoga to provide support and relaxation during times of illness and stress. More advanced books on yoga by B. K. S. Iyengar (1979) and Dr. Swami Karmananda Saraswati (2005) provide instruction on how to use the yoga postures (asanas) to improve health and release tensions in the body (Iyengar, 1979; Saraswati, 1986). These practices should only be done with a qualified teacher. But for facilitators trained in yoga the books may advance understanding of the Yogic management of common diseases and how to deepen the mind and body connection to aid in treatment of physical symptoms from the grief reaction.

The suggested activities for "The Body of Grief" are simple and easy for all levels. A suggested exercise uses basic movement, stretching, breathing, and relaxation techniques. If facilitators are experienced in other areas they should substitute their own experience and knowledge for this session. However, it is important for the overall experience of the grief course to have sessions using movement to get the people up and moving and out of their heads. The use of the body can free up emotions and feelings that are sometimes not able to be spoken.

☐ Week 4 Curriculum

Activities

	Estimated Time Required
1. Opening ritual or meditation	5 minutes
2. Check-in (using journals or objects for the altar)	2 to 5 minutes each
3. Physical movement	30 to 40 minutes
4. Closing	10 minutes

☐ Simple Exercises to Do Each Day

By doing these simple exercises we bring more oxygen into our bodies, allow the muscle groups to stretch and relax, and move our spinal columns by lengthening, twisting, and strengthening. This movement will allow the body to feel freer and for the blood and oxygen to flow into and through our system more easily. During the stressful times of grief and loss not only is it important to exercise, but also to eat properly, get adequate rest, and have quiet time to ourselves for contemplation and to help adjust to the world without our loved one. The following is a brief exercise developed to help with stretching, getting the body moving, opening the system for more oxygen, and moving our energy to help clear and quiet the mind.

Start the Energy Moving

1. Rub the hands together until they create heat, and then hold the palms over the eyes for a few seconds and pull the hands away from the eyes while the eyes open wide. Repeat twice.
2. Rub the hands together again then rub over the face as though washing.
3. With the knuckles of the thumb or first finger, rub around the eyes on the orbit or bones around the eyes (8 times).
4. Then, again with the knuckles of the thumb or first finger, rub the sides of the nose (8 times up and down — helps clear the sinuses).
5. Continue with the knuckles, rub the temples in a circular motion (8 times, then reverse direction).
6. Rub the backs of the ears with the thumbs (8 times).
7. Gently pull the ear lobes (8 times).
8. Place the palms over the ears with the fingers extending over the back of the head, and tap the back of the head and pull the hands quickly away from the ears (repeat 4 times).
9. With the thumb and first finger of either hand rub the area just below the jaw, where the lymph glands are located, gently from the back of the jaw forward toward the chin (8 times).
10. In the same manner, rub the throat on either side of the larynx from top to bottom (8 times).
11. Seated or standing, pat the area around the kidneys with the backs of the hands.
12. Pat with hands down the outside of your legs from hip to ankle. Repeat.
13. Pat one knee and then rub it. Then reverse and pat and rub the other knee.
14. Pat the left shoulder, then rub it, and then rub/pat the other shoulder.
15. With both hands rub in a clockwise motion the upper chest (8 times).
16. Then move down to the upper belly, or diaphragm, and again rub in a circular motion (8 times).
17. Lastly, move to the lower belly and rub in the same manner (8 times).

This exercise will get the energy in your body moving, increase the blood flow, move the lymph system, and increase your available oxygen. Now that the body is awake we can begin to stretch and move.

FIGURE 9.1   Neutral spine. (Photo courtesy of Donna Dow.)

Stretching and Body Awareness

1. Neutral Spine (Figure 9.1)
   - Sit straight up in a firm chair
   - Pressing heels lightly into the floor
   - Connecting to the body core
     - Navel moves back to spine
     - Spine comes forward to navel
     - Breathe in and out gently
2. Lengthening and Rounding (Figure 9.2)
   - Spine lengthening/arms lifting up, breathe in
   - Arms lowering and spine shortening, rounding the back toward the chair, exhale breath
3. Twist (Figure 9.3)
   - Press heels and sitbones down
   - Upper body faces forward
   - Place left hand behind and down onto the seat of the chair
   - Bring right arm across front of body and hold the arm or back of chair (or leg)

FIGURE 9.2   Lengthening and Rounding. (Photo courtesy of Donna Dow.)

FIGURE 9.3   Twisted (Photo courtesy of Donna Dow.)

FIGURE 9.4   Forward bend. (Photo courtesy of Donna Dow.)

- Breathing in and out, initiate a twist from the body core (lower belly), not from shoulders and head
- Let head look over left shoulder with soft eyes. Repeat on the other side

4. Neutral to Forward Bend, and Back to Neutral (Figure 9.4)
  - Press sitbones and heels down
  - Allow upper body to come forward over legs
  - Keep navel moving toward spine and spine to navel
  - Let upper body soften
  - As the person lifts up — keep core (belly) active to protect low back. Repeat

5. Lengthening Spine and Stretching Hamstrings (Figure 9.5)
  - Hold back of chair with both hands shoulderwidth apart
  - Walk legs away from chair so back is flat and legs are under the hips
  - Contract thighs (to lift kneecaps)
  - Press heels down into floor
  - Press hands down on chair, or into wall
  - Shoulders move *toward* hips
  - Hips move *away* from head
  - Work the body core (navel and spine come together). *Note*: The head should *not* drop below the chest, rather lengthen crown of head toward chair or wall and keep head in line with spine. Lengthen spine

6. Balance (Figure 9.6)
  - Looking forward let the eyes softly focus on the horizon level
  - Firmly root right leg

FIGURE 9.5 Lengthening the spine. (Photo courtesy of Donna Dow.)

FIGURE 9.6 Balance. (Photo courtesy of Donna Dow.)

- Lift left foot up to knee or groin of opposite leg and rest left foot against right leg (at knee or groin)
- Once legs are rooted, lift arms above head and join palms and fingers pointing to ceiling (balance permitting)
- Breathe in and out for three breaths and lower arms and leg (repeat on other side)
- Use the chair or wall to support yourself if balance is difficult

Centering with Breath

"Closing out the world and going in"

1. Finger Positions on Face and Head (Figure 9.7)
   - Pinky fingers to lower nostril
   - Thumbs to close ears
   - Third fingers inside eye socket (upper inside corner)
   - Second fingers on forehead above eyebrows
   - Index fingers on temple at hairline

2. Breathing and Body Position
   - Low soft hum in throat
   - Spine lengthened

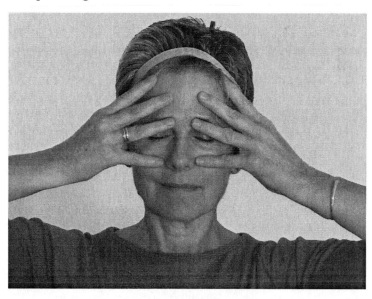

FIGURE 9.7   Centering with breath. (Photo courtesy of Donna Dow.)

- Lower belly active
- Breathing in (through nostrils) — breath comes to back of throat with humming sound
- Breathing out (through nostrils) — breath leaves with humming sound (repeat until arms begin to tire)
- When done, sit quietly with arms at side and hands on thighs breathing normally (breathe deep into the belly, into the ribs and under the collar bones). Breathe in, feel the body rising, lifting, and expanding. Exhaling, drop shoulders, elbows, breastbone, buttock bones, thigh bones, and wrists and let go.

The breathing is designed to close out the world, relax the mind and body, and allow us to feel deeply into this moment. As in the stretches we want to activate the core of the body. That is the area just below the navel, between the navel and the spine. It is the area where all movement begins and ends. It is the center of balance and grounding.

☐ Meditation and Visualization

Meditation is not a complicated process. It is merely sitting quietly and noticing what comes into our awareness. Not judging or being attached to thoughts or sounds or feelings, but noticing them, and keeping our awareness there until something else becomes prominent in our awareness.

Meditation has been used for stress reduction programs at the University of Massachusetts for the treatment of anxiety disorders (Kabat-Zinn, 1992). Follow-up studies have concluded that an intensive time-limited group stress reduction program based upon mindful meditation can have long-term benefits (Miller, Fletcher, & Kabat-Zinn, 1995). Meditation has also been used to treat chronic pain (Kabat-Zinn et al., 1987). Most religions have some aspect of quiet contemplation or meditation. Christian centering prayer and Buddhist insight meditation both direct the mind to this moment and to quiet the busy mind so as to attend to the divine. There are many schools and forms of meditation, and people study for years to become adept. However, for our purposes meditation or contemplation is a time to just be aware of our feelings and to have a quiet moment with our loved one.

It sometimes helps to have something to focus on when beginning. One can observe the breath as it come in and out. Just be aware of the breath as it flows past the nostrils. One may focus on an object such as a flower, a piece of art, or music. Just take a few minutes to sit quietly and breathe. Each day after you do the exercises set forth above take a few minutes to sit quietly and notice what has come up for you. Sitting, breathing, and offering ourselves the gift of our own presence may be a life-changing practice.

After the physical exercises have the group sit quietly and allow their eyes to close. If some people cannot close their eyes, have them look down at the floor at a 45-degree angle and soften their focus. After a few minutes guide them through a relaxing guided visualization. If the facilitator is not practiced in guided visualization she or he might want to read the following visualization which is designed to relax the body and mind. Alternatively you might want to use some of the music suggested in chapter 11 on music by Nicole Burgess.

☐ Relaxation

The following is a suggested list of things to say when guiding visualization.

In a soft voice, speak slowly and avoid using the same word over and over, such as *relax*.

- Breathing in, become aware of your breath. As you breathe out, let your belly soften.
- Bring your attention to your head and let the skin around your skull soften. Feel the tension in your face soften and let the muscles of your jaw relax, and let your jaw open slightly. As you breathe in soften your eyes. As you breathe out soften the neck.
- Allow the neck to relax. Let tension flow from your throat. Feel the shoulders drop and release. Breathe into any tension in your back, and on the out breath let the tension release. Feel the muscles down your spine and let them relax.
- All the way down the spine, let the muscles soften. Feel the tension release and soften. Allow the belly to be soft. Breathe into each area of your spine and ribs and feel them expand and relax.
- Bring your attention to the bones of your pelvis and hips and feel them move down into the chair. Breathe in and soften, breathe out and let go.
- Notice the bones of your thighs and let them drop into the chair. Let your leg bones be heavy and the muscles of your thighs soften and release.
- Feel the muscles let go as you breathe down into your calves. Your feet feel heavy on the floor. Breathe into your feet and let go of all the tension held in the feet.

- Breathe now into any areas of your body where you have pain or tension. Breathe in and become aware of the pain and tension. Breathe out and let the tension and pain fade into softness. (Pause for a bit)
- Where is the pain of your loss? What part of your body hurts from the pain of loss and grief? And, with the greatest gentleness, breathe into that pain of loss and grief. Gently, gently, go slowly now, and again breathe into the pain. Soften into your loss and allow it to be with you: in a gentle way. Feel your body as your mind wants to harden against the pain. Breathe again into the pain and again soften against what the mind wants to avoid. (Pause)
- Gently breathe until I ring the bell. Just be with what comes into your mind, and then let it go. (Pause)
- (ring a soft bell) Gently allow your mind to come back into the room, and when you are ready slowly open your eyes.

There are many tapes and CD's on guided visualization and these are available at most book stores. Steven Levine offers guided meditations in several of his books and tapes. The idea is to allow the body to relax and for the participants to feel where in their body they have put the pain of grief.

☐ Alternative Exercises

Use exercise 2 or 3 from chapter 12. Lauren Chandler, in her chapter on drama and theater, offers excellent exercises that can get the group to work together and increase awareness and trust.

The following exercise only take a few minutes and can increase trust, bring awareness to how the body moves, and keeps the attention of the members in the moment.

Divide the group into pairs, with one in each pair to go first. Have the person going first place their index finger on the back of the hand of their partner, and then close their eyes. The partner leading then begins to move the hand in slow and gradually larger movements. The pair is to maintain contact between the finger and the back of the hand at all times. Without opening the eyes the first partner follows the hand of the other. The partner with the back of the hand leads the first person in a safe manner, avoiding other pairs and objects in the room. After a few minutes have the pairs stop, and without talking change roles. Now the first person leads the other in the same manner. After both people have had the opportunity to lead and to follow stop the process. Ask the group to share, quietly, with their partner how the exercise felt to them and what happened during the exercise. Group sharing may follow, time permitting.

☐ Dance and Movement to Music

There are many forms of dance, and facilitators trained in a particular form of dance should please use it for the movement session of the group. But facilitators don't need to be trained dancers or teachers to put on music and let the group move to the beat. Use some of the suggestions Nicole Burgess offers in chapter 11. Be sure to vary the music and the beat of the selections. Start with slow rhythmic music, generally avoiding songs with words. As people get used to moving, up the beat and increase the tempo of the music. Alternate between smooth and sudden sharp rhythms.

☐ Children and Teens

There are books, listed in the resources, for meditation and yoga for children. Teens may have more difficulty with the meditation but give it a try. Always rely on music or drawing as a backup for teens and children. It allows them to not feel foolish or silly, and still brings up matters that are on their minds. Rather than a guided meditation on relaxation try a story that uses the imagination of the group members. "Feelings can be projected into the music through body movement and dance" (Goldman, 2000, p. 98). Using music that is current and age appropriate for the group can create movement in a natural manner. Formal exercises sometimes make children and teens feel awkward, which may cause them to resist.

☐ Closing

Using a closing ritual, have a check-in with the group to see how the experience of the movement felt. Make sure there is time to deal with any issues that may have come up for the group members. Remember, physical movement and guided meditation can be quite powerful.

☐ Notes for Next Week

Advise the group that they will want to bring magazines, cloth, paper, or photos (that can be cut up or pasted onto heavy paper) for the following week. The next session will be collage.

Resources

Goldman, L. (2000). *Life and loss*. Philadelphia, PA: Accelerated Development.

Lasater, J. (1995). *Relax and renew*. Berkeley, CA: Rodmell Press.

Liebmann, M. (1986). *Art therapy for groups: A handbook of themes, games and exercises*. Cambridge, MA: Brookline Books.

Rozman, D. (1994). *Meditating with children* (2nd ed.).. Boulder Creek, CA: Planetary.

Stewart, M., & Phillips, K. (1992). *Yoga for children*. New York: Simon & Schuster.

 J. Earl Rogers

Session 5

The Art of Collage — Visions and Images

The artist is often surprised himself at the shapes of his own creation.

— Joan Miró

☐ Introduction

The largest collage I know of is a tower of found objects built slowly over the years. It rises high over the one-story modest homes that surround the towers and the small house of its builder. He is dead now, but his collage of things found around him and his neighborhood still stands and has become a monument to the creative urge that lies within each of us. The Watts Towers speak of all the different ways we create meaning and beauty in our lives.

What is collage? It is a putting together of images, objects, words, and bits of cloth or paper to tell a story, create an image, or express a feeling. Artists call it a mixed medium. In the early 1900s, Pablo Picasso and Georges Braque made collages from rubbish. German painter Kurt Schwitters worked with trash from his home (Jung, 1964). Spanish painter Joan Miro wandered along the beach every day to collect things and then assembled them into compositions that surprised him even as he worked on the collage (Jung, 1964).

Collage is a collection of everyday things, images, photos, junk, objects, and drawing or painting put together to create something more than the objects themselves. The collage becomes a symbolic expression of our story, our view of life, or a moment in time. What has meaning for one may not for another. What is trash for one is a component for the creation of art for someone else. Everything can go into a collage; there are no lines, hues, or forms that need to be followed. Collecting objects and images and placing them on a board can be much less daunting than drawing or painting (Liebmann, 1986).

Using magazines, photos, and objects, the group will be led into the world of art without having to think about whether they can paint or draw. By cutting and pasting, the pictures, words, and objects are put together on a piece of cardboard or firm paper, to tell, yet again, the ongoing story of loss and memories in a new and changing world.

☐ Week 5 Curriculum

Activities

	Estimated Time Required
1. Opening Ritual or meditation	5 to 10 minutes
2. Check-in (using journals)	2 to 3 minutes each
3. Collage activity (include time to share the collages, which may be part of the ritual)	1 hour
4. Closing (check-in and ritual)	5 to 10 minutes

Materials Needed

1. Scissors (at least one pair for two people)
2. Magazines and photos (that can be cut up and glued)
3. Colored paper (different weights, from tissue to construction paper)
4. Fabrics, and other objects that can be glued onto the posterboard
5. Natural objects (leaves, shells, small branches)
6. Junk materials (broken china or plastic toys, buttons, stickers, and ribbons)
7. Felt markers, crayons, or colored pens and pencils

8. Firm construction board or heavy paper on which to glue the images and objects (size is a matter of choice, but 18" × 24" gives enough room for images and objects; 12" × 9" can also be used, especially if more than one exercise is being done). White is the best color, especially if the whole page is to be covered. However, sometimes the color of the background adds to the collage. It might be well to give the group some options on the color of the background.

9. Glue (different types of adhesives such as glue sticks, white school glue, rubbery emulsion for cloth, and a glue gun for objects). Glue sticks are excellent and easy to use, especially for children.

10. Extra paper for lying on the floor to put the glue on the back of the images or objects before placing on the collage board.

☐ Types of Collage

Have the members *tell the story of their loss* using images and words from magazines, photographs, and objects.

Telling the Story of the Loss

Let the images select themselves as the group members look through the magazines and other materials. Allow the process of selection of materials and images to occur with little thought beyond the idea of telling a story about the death of their loved one. Let go and let the images take over and follow where they lead. Rational thought does not apply here; let the collage create itself.

The story may be a narrative, a collection of memories, or a memorial to the deceased. The collage may be the beginning of a book telling the life story of the one who died and his or her family. Instead of a story, the collage may be an expression of feelings and emotions that create a tapestry of what has happened to the individual since the death. It may also be the beginning of creating new meaning in the person's life.

One of the advantages of using images and pictures is that it may be easier to choose angry images than it would be to paint such feelings. The use of pictures from a magazine tends to distance the person from uncomfortable or unacceptable feelings. The "angry" images may, but do not have to, relate to the person who chooses them. This form may give the individual more room to express that which is unconscious or not yet ready to be spoken.

Pictures of Opposites

Have the participants select images that are pleasing and that they are attracted to. Place these images on one side of the collage board. Then have the group select images that they don't like, or even hate, or that repel them in some way. Glue these negative images on the other side of the collage board. During the sharing of the collages the group members can tell why they are drawn to certain images and dislike others. This telling of opposites allows the mind to grasp the idea that we may have opposing emotions about the person who died. This feeling of opposites gives permission to hold the memory of the deceased even though there are aspects of the one who died that are or were hurtful, or still hold difficult and painful memories.

Creating a Vision

After a death grieving people sometimes find it difficult to find meaning in their lives (Neimeyer, 2000). They can be lost as to how to proceed with their lives and even the thought of the future is more than they can tolerate. Often it is difficult to understand how to keep the memory of their loved one alive and ongoing (Attig, 2000). In creating a vision of how they would like the future to look, and how they wish to remember their loved one, the bereaved begins the long slow process of making meaning in a new life and connection with the one who has died.

Henry David Thoreau said, "If one advances confidently in the direction of his dreams and endeavors to live the life which he has imagined, he will meet success unexpected in common hours." The Vision collage may be the start of how one wishes to live one's life from this point forward. In her book *Visioning*, Lucia Capacchione, PhD (2000), uses collage for creating vision in designing one's life. As one would put a puzzle together we start with the edges and move toward the center. Or, perhaps, use or create a central image that offers a creative-self symbol, and place it in the center of the collage board and move out into the empty space.

After creating the Vision collage, place it in a location where it can be seen everyday. In that way, we can allow the images to lead us into the life we have envisioned.

Using images, pieces of junk, scraps, and pictures cut from magazines is a far less threatening first step than actually creating images and pictures using drawing or painting. Collage reduces the performance anxiety of painting and drawing when one does not consider oneself an "artist" (Liebmann, 1986).

Another possibility for the creation of the collage is to cut the collage boards into circles in order to create a mandala, a part of most religions and a symbol of the cycles of life. Stained glass windows in the great churches and cathedrals, sand paintings of Buddhist monks and Navaho, and the intricate Celtic mandalas all use the circle as symbol and form (Davis, 1994). The word *mandala* comes from the Sanskrit and means holy or magical circle. The three principles of order in a mandala are the center, the radiation from the center, and the periphery of the circle. These sacred circles have been used in all religions and cultures (Copony, 1989).

Suggest to the participants that they may want to continue working on the collage after this session. The collage can be an ongoing process leading into mystery and discovery. Also, in the last session, Ritual, Janet Shaw Rogers suggests using the collages of the group to create a living mandala as part of the final ritual.

☐ Children and Teens

Children take to collage and cutting and gluing with ease and excitement. Teens, once again may have the feeling that it is a "childish" thing to do. Children, depending on the developmental stage, may use the collage to create a memory board, a photo album (make sure their parents want to give up the photos the children bring to the group), or a picture of what has happened in their life. Cutting and pasting may allow the child to express feelings that might not normally come up. They will approach the project as play. Remember children process life events through play (Goldman, 2000). The collage may be a path for the child to share about how the death has affected them.

If teens are reluctant to participate it is always appropriate to fall back on drawing and music. However, the idea of a mandala, after it is explained to them, is often intriguing and offers them an "adult" approach to tell their story of grief. Pictures of mandalas from different traditions may excite interest in the project. Teens don't like to be singled out and so the invitation to share the collage (or mandala) is best made in a general non-threatening manner. And, while they don't like to be singled out, they often love to be in the spotlight. Explaining the symbols may be an easier way for them to move into the story of their grief and loss.

☐ Notes for Next Week

The next session is music and the participants may want to bring music that has meaning for them. This is especially true for teens and children. If they have drums or other instruments that will fit into the anticipated program invite them to bring them along.

Resources

Capacchione, L. (2000). *Visioning*. New York: Tarcher/Putnam.
Copony, H. (1989). *Mystery of mandalas*. Wheaton, IL: Theosophical Publishing House.
Liebmann, M. (1986). *Art therapy for groups*. Newton, MA: Brookline Books.

CHAPTER 11   Nicole Burgess

Session 6

The Music

> The music soars within the little lark,
> And the lark soars.
>
> — **Elizabeth Barrett Browning**

☐ Introduction

When working through the grief process, music can be an important and healing companion throughout the journey. Music can be effective in relieving anxiety, reinforcing feelings of identity and self-concept, and promoting relaxation while providing both a source of comfort and an opportunity for self-expression.

☐ Week 6 Curriculum

Song

Song is an element of music that can be especially beneficial when working with bereavement care groups. For most people, songs play a role in connecting a person with either significant times in their lives, their culture, a biographical period in their life or, in the case of song lyrics, they may act as a means to personally express feelings. The melody or rhythm of a song can either connect a person with an emotion or transport them from one feeling to another. Throughout our lives we all have songs that play a role in our journey. They may be a children's lullaby or nursery rhyme, a favorite song shared between friends, a song of significant religious meaning or for those who play an instrument or sing in choirs, it may connect them with a performance. Whatever the significance, songs are an important vehicle for expression of thoughts, feelings, and emotions. The following exercises provide a means of expressing oneself through song.

Exercise: Life Review through Song

1. Begin with a discussion about significant songs in people's lives. Examples of significant songs may include the following: a song danced to at a wedding, a lullaby sung to a child, a piece of music that may be used to relax, or simply a song that was sung on long family car trips. These significant songs create a musical story that is a reflection of people's lives.
2. Encourage each group member to create a list and gather easily available recordings of significant music/songs from their life. Each list may be as short as three songs but could be as long as 10 or 20.
3. Have each person in the group share a song or a piece of music that is significant to them and if possible play a recording. Perhaps someone may even want to sing or hum their song. Allow time for the participant to reflect on the significance of their selection.

This exercise is appropriate for both teens and adults. It is important to remember, however, that many people feel an intense connection with song and may therefore find sharing their songs very difficult. For those people, it may be helpful to ask them to share the reasons for choosing songs (but not to play them) or to ask them to share only one of their songs from their song biography. For others, simply taking part in the activity without sharing with the group may be most appropriate.

This activity may also be adapted for use in children's bereavement groups. Adaptations may include the following: completing the activity as a group by asking participants to suggest their favorite songs and possibly share why they chose their selections; or completing the activity as a group, but creating the song review with a theme such as "songs that make you happy" or "songs that are in your family."

Materials Needed

Pens, paper, stereo, and music recordings provided by group participants.

Song Writing

The process of coupling one's words with music often results in a very personal and meaningful experience. Just as certain songs are especially significant to some, creating one's own song is often a powerful form of expression.

Materials Needed

Pens, paper, recording of a familiar song (if needed by group).

Exercise: Song Writing

1. Songs, like poetry, provide a vehicle for expression. Depending on musical background, it is easier for some to create melodies to fit song lyrics. For those with little or no music background it is still possible to create a song that is meaningful to them. By borrowing an existing melody a person can use this as a blueprint to create their song lyrics. The song may be one of significance, a personal favorite, or just one whose melody is familiar.
2. Once each participant has chosen the song, he or she can then move toward changing the lyrics or melody to reflect something of personal significance. All of the words may be changed or just a few, but in this way the songs become personal to each participant. If comfortable, participants may want to share their song with the group.

This activity is appropriate for both teens and adults. It can be adapted for children by making it simpler. Choose a song that is universally known to most children such as "Twinkle Twinkle" or a popular children's song of the day. Alternatively, if none of these seem appropriate to your group, bring in a recording of a song that would be appropriate so all members of the group can become familiar with the music. Then provide copies of the song but with words or sections made blank so that the group members can fill in these sections. For example, if one were to take the opening of the song "What a Wonderful World," instead of writing "I see trees of green, red roses too — I see them bloom for me and you," you may provide the outline of "I see _____ and _____ too. I see them here for me and you and I think to myself what a wonderful world." Another alternative

for children may be using an existing song that has spaces for lyric improvisation such as "Down by the Bay" or the "Quartermaster Store." Again
these songs can be based on themes such as family or feelings. For example, if using the song the "Quartermaster Store" and using the theme of
feelings, you may sing something such as, "I feel happy, happy when I'm
with my Daddy in the store, in the store." Alternatively, if using family as
a theme one may sing, "There was granny, granny eating cotton candy in
the store, in the store etc." Again with any age group remember that songs
are often very personal and you may meet resistance. Allow each person
to participate in any way he or she feels comfortable and allow sharing of
the song to be optional.

☐ Music for Relaxation

Music is often useful when paired with relaxation techniques. It helps to
distract from pain, transport the mind to another place, conjure healing or
helpful images, and provide a vehicle for escape.

When setting up a room for any relaxation exercise, the participants'
comfort is very important to its success. Making sure the environmental
factors such as room temperature, lighting level, and physical comfort are
taken care of will help with this. First, make sure that the room temperature is comfortable, keeping in mind elements such as cold air vents or
open windows. If possible, lower your lighting level a little, but not so
much that your participants will be tempted to immediately fall asleep. If
participants are lying on the floor make sure they are not directly under
lights that will glare in their eyes. Finally, whether sitting or lying down,
make sure participants have the physical things they need to stay comfortable. These may include blankets or floor mats to either cushion them
from a hard floor or simply to keep them warm.

Below is a list of music that may be a useful pairing with simple relaxation techniques. However, whether you use one of these or your own
there are several elements to consider, the first of which is the volume or
dynamic range of the piece. Unless specifically scripted to coincide with
the music, the music should not offer any abrupt changes such as a loud
orchestral section that will hinder the participant from relaxing fully. As
with the volume, although the melody need not be monotonous, it should
not surprise too often. This is also the case with harmony. While there may
be some tension within the chords and harmonies, make sure they resolve
and are generally pleasing to the ear. Consider the tempo of the piece too.
You do not want the pace to be too fast, but make sure that it is not so static
that it becomes boring or monotonous. As you can see, choosing music is

often difficult when working with a group because there are so many factors such as musical tastes, culture, and preferences at play.

Always ask your group for feedback and remember to never play a piece of music for your group unless you have become familiar with it first. It is helpful to use music that does not contain lyrics because they are most often a hindrance to participants when trying to relax. In addition, it is confusing if you are reading a script to the group because lyrics will make it more difficult for participants to concentrate on your words. Finally, if lyrics are used one must make sure that they are appropriate to the entire group.

Relaxation scripts are widely available and incorporate many different styles and lengths. Choose one that feels right for you and remember to read it in a slow, natural, and clear manner. Be sure to read through it ahead of time and adjust any phrases that seem awkward or unnatural to you.

Music Examples for Relaxation Exercise

1. *Simple Fare*, Nancy McMaster
2. *Song of the Stars*, Rita Costanzi (harp)
3. *Quiet Heart*, Richard Warner
4. Enya
5. *The Winding Path*, Kevin Kern.
6. *Harp*, Kim Robertson
7. *Spa*, Hennie Bekker
8. *Graceful Passages*, Stillwater and Malkin
9. *Celtic Harp of Dreams*, Lori Pappajohn
10. *Rosa Mystica*, Therese Schroeder-Sheker
11. *Soothing Massage, Solitude's Collection* (Nature's Spa series)
12. *Secret of the Panpipes*, Midori (Andean)
13. *Temple in the Forest*
14. *Healing*, Anugama
15. *Afterglow*, Tillman and Hoppi
16. Mozart, *Clarinet Concerto*, KV622: Adagio
17. Albinoni, *Oboe Concert*, Op. 9/2:
18. *Enchanted Meadow: Stress Relief*, Guy Maeda (piano)
19. J.S. Bach, *Goldberg Variations, Aria*
21. *Essential Bach*
22. *Meditations for a Quiet Dawn*, Nimbus Records
23. *Meditations at Sunset*, Nimbus Records
24. *Flute for Relaxation*, J. Galway
25. *A Childhood Remembered*, Narada Artists
26. *Relax with the Classics*, Lind Institute

Sample Relaxation Script

- Take a moment to make yourself comfortable. Check in with your body to find any spots that may need adjusting and take the time to do so. Close your eyes and allow yourself to breathe naturally. Now pay attention to the inhale and exhale of your breath, counting the number of seconds it takes to inhale and then slowly exhale, working toward your exhale being twice as long as your inhale. So inhale 1, 2, 3, 4 and exhale 1, 2, 3, 4, 5, 6, 7, 8. Take some time now to inhale and exhale.
- Now choose a color that you find nurturing and relaxing and imagine it forming a beautiful ball lightly hovering above you. Again concentrate on your breath and slowly inhale that beautiful color, allowing it to fill all the parts of your head. Allow that color to release any tension in your forehead, your face, and your jaw. Feel your tongue rest gently behind your top front teeth, making sure that your jaw is not tight. Again, take a breath and allow that beautiful color to fill and relax any other areas in your head. This time when you breathe in that gorgeous color, feel it travel down to your neck and shoulder releasing any tension and allow yourself to fill with deep relaxation and comfort. Now the relaxation travels down your arms all the way to your fingers making them feel weightless, almost like they could float away.
- That beautiful ball of color is lightly hovering above your chest. Take the time to breathe in that color so that it fills your chest, all the way down to the bottom of your stomach. Take some time to breathe now, allowing each breath to take you deeper and deeper into relaxation.
- That beautiful ball of color now travels down to rest above your hips, allowing that relaxation to travel through your hips and buttocks all the way to your thighs. If you find any areas of discomfort, breathe in the beautiful color and allow the tension to drift away. Continue to breathe deeply, allowing the relaxation and comfort to travel down your legs and all the way down to your toes, gently breathing deeper and deeper into relaxation. That beautiful color should fill your entire body now, making it feel weightless and relaxed. As you are breathing, take a moment to check in with your body and find any little spots where tension needs to be released, all the while breathing in that beautiful color from the ball that is gently floating above you. Take some time now to breathe and enjoy the feeling of deep relaxation.
- When you are ready, allow yourself to become aware of your surroundings. As you become aware of the sounds and the physical

things around you, keep the feeling of relaxation and comfort with you as you continue to relax and breathe.

☐ Music and Art

The word *mandala* comes from a Sanskrit word meaning whole circle or wheel. Most often in a circular form, it is believed that the circle represents balance, harmony, and symmetry and is often able to balance many elements together. It is also believed that mandalas should be in this circular form as the symmetry of a circle is found throughout nature as in the sun, moon, or even the shape of flowers. Mandalas are found in the Buddhist and Hindu religion and are used in ceremonies to aid in meditation and to help people on their journey toward enlightenment ("How Does Music Therapy Work?," 2005).

When choosing music to pair with mandalas, use similar guidelines as outlined when pairing music with the relaxation exercise. Do, however, allow a little more liberty surrounding melody and harmony. This activity is appropriate for children, teens, and adults, so be sure to choose music that works well with your particular group. It is important to stress that there is no right and wrong with this activity and the purpose is not to create a perfect work of art. Instead the purpose is to enjoy the process of expressing oneself without self-judgment or judgment from others. (Please see mandala illustration below by Sara Newman.)

Exercise: Mandalas

Materials Needed

Stereo, music recordings, paper, pastels, or other drawing materials. (Optional materials such as fabrics or buttons and glue to add to the drawings.)

1. Provide each group participant with paper and drawing materials. You may want to have circles drawn on each person's page.
2. Allow each person to draw independently while listening to the selected music. Remind each participant not to judge their drawing skills because there can be no mistakes in their work. Drawings can be abstract or symbolic and do not have to be literal or photographic.

FIGURE 11.1 Mandala. (Photo courtesy of Sara Newman.)

3. Once each person completes his or her drawing, invite participants to explain the significance of their mandala. Some may want to share their drawings without explanation or others may simply want to participate in the drawing exercise.

☐ Active Music Making

Active music making rather than passive listening provides many benefits. Through active music making, group members are given more opportunities for self-expression. By actively making music with others, participants gain a greater support and connection to the group. Self-esteem is often increased as participants take ownership of the music they have created. Physically, participants also gain from actively participating in music making. For example, by singing, group members must take deep regular breaths. This deep breathing often results in lowered stress levels.

Drumming and Leading a Group

Drumming is a wonderful solo or group activity that connects the mind, body, and spirit. It is also appropriate for groups of adults, teens, or children. For some it is a deeply meditative experience, for others it is a cathartic release, and for others still it is a means of expressing oneself while having a lot of fun. Rhythm is all around us in our daily lives; in fact even before we were born we encountered the rhythm of our mother's heartbeat. For this reason, many people find drumming and rhythm therapy an intensely healing process.

Methods of Starting Your Drum Improvisation

1. Make your voice and/or body rhythmical so you can hear/see the beat. Try using a phrase such as: "one, two, let's all play" or "OK, let's drum." If you are clapping your hands along with your phrase it should fit nicely into four claps (i.e., 4/4 time).
Or
2. Start by playing a simple steady beat, and invite the group to join as the members are ready. Remember, the simpler your rhythm the easier it is for the group to join you.

Methods of Stopping Your Drumming Group

1. Get the group's attention (hand in the air, make eye contact). Once you have the group's attention, show an exaggerated final beat.
Or
2. Get the group's attention. Once you have their attention, count down (4, 3, 2, 1).
Or
3. Do a gradual stop and allow the group to fade out naturally. Reminder, in most cases you will have to make the group quieter first so they become aware that it is time to stop.

Ways to Improvise

- play your name
- slow heartbeat

- call and response — use simple rhythms, rests, physical cues, pairing with words
- play the rhythm of favorite foods (kids)
- dynamics — loud/soft
- tempo — fast/slow
- general group improvisation — don't try and shape it, just see where the music takes you
- taking solos
- vocal rhythm improvisation
- gradual start/stop — remember with this kind you must have a strong beat to start, so either start it yourself, or choose someone who can keep and sustain a strong beat/pulse
- playing to music
- sing and drum together
- adding other percussion instruments

Making a Drum Ensemble

In order to have a richer sounding group, you need to have drums of various shapes and sizes. Adding other types of percussion instruments made out of wood, metal, and skins produces even more texture to your sound.

Making Instruments

Making instruments is easier then you might think. Drums can be made easily from water cooler bottles (your local company will usually donate them). Cut a hole in the bottle where the spout is, decorate the outside, making sure to leave the bottom of the jug undecorated as this will be your drum head. The outside of the drum can be decorated with acrylic paints, fabric, or paper collage. You can also make different-sounding drums by cutting the drum in half and fitting the two sides together. Once you change the size of the drum, you change the sound.

Shakers are easily made by filling film canisters or other containers with different-sized peas and beans.

Smaller plastic water bottles with ridges can be used to make a guiro instrument. The sound is created by running a mallet along the ridges.

Mallets or beaters are made by attaching a small rubber ball to a piece of dowel. Cover the ball with a square of felt or soft fabric and secure with a ribbon or string.

Exercise: Drumming Affirmations

1. Ask each group member to create his or her own affirmations. An affirmation is a positive thought and may include an accomplishment the person is proud of, an emotional state that he or she has strived for, or an outcome the person would like to occur. Examples may include: "I am a wonderful mother" or "I will be calm and grounded" or "everything will be all right."
2. Ask each group member to play the rhythm of the words from the person's affirmation on his or her drum.
3. Each person joins into the drum circle continuously repeating the rhythm of the affirmation on his or her drum while at the same time repeating it either out loud or silently.
4. When you feel the exercise has been completed, either quiet your group using the techniques discussed in the previous section, or allow the drumming to quiet down naturally.

Exercise: Improvised Drumming

1. This is a much less structured approach to a drum circle. Once a steady beat is established by either the group leader or someone else in the group, allow each person to add in his or her own sounds to the circle.
2. Allow the rhythms to develop and grow. You may want to add other rhythmic instruments such as bells, woodblocks, shakers, or even the voice.
3. This is a free activity, so allow it to end naturally when the group members are ready.

Exercise: Chanting

1. Using the example given below as a guide, have the group make up its own chant. This can be done either as a large group, or depending on the group size, small groups work well also. Some may even want to make up their own individual chants.
2. Practice singing the new chants as a large group.
3. If participants are comfortable try singing together while standing in a circle to allow the sound to come together for everyone to hear.
4. If group members are willing, repeat the chant many times, each time singing specifically to one individual in the group. Continue until all group members have been included.

FIGURE 11.2 Chant by Nicole Burgess.

5. Once all group members have been recognized, return to the chant and slowly let the chant move toward silence.
6. Debrief by discussing the meaning each person took from the experience and what the lyrics and the chant means to her/him.

Exercise: Group Singing

1. Create a collection of songs the group is familiar with. These may include: campfire songs, songs with special meanings or significance, or even family car songs. See list below for songs that are familiar to most people.
2. If possible hire or bring in a volunteer to play piano or guitar for your group singing session.
3. Supply the words (and music if your group is musically knowledgeable) so that each person can participate.

☐ A Few Suggestions of Well-Known Songs

For Adults

Yellow Submarine
Get By With a Little Help From My Friends and most other Beatles songs
Stand By Me
Lean on Me
Many Van Morrison songs
This Land Is Your Land
You Are My Sunshine
Many religious hymns (if appropriate to your group)

Children's Songs

Twinkle Twinkle
Old MacDonald
Happy and You Know It
Quartermaster Store
Skinnamarink Song and other songs by Sharon, Lois, and Bram
Going to the Zoo
Rooster Song
Down By the Bay

Nicole Burgess, BMus, BMT, MTA, is a music therapist in private practice living in the Comox Valley, British Columbia. She studied piano and
music composition at the University of Victoria before completing her
music therapy degree at Capilano College in Vancouver, BC. In addition
to her music therapy training, Nicole has studied rhythm therapy and
drumming with Barry Bernstein and Arthur Hull and has completed the
Drum Circle Facilitation training with the New Rhythms Foundation in
California. Within her practice, Nicole works in complex and palliative
care; in dementia care; with chronic pain and brain injury groups; and
with children and adults with developmental disabilities.

Resources

Art of Asia: Mandala teacher's guide. (n.d.). Retrieved July 15, 2005, from http://
www.artsmia.org/
How does music therapy work? Music therapy in palliative care. (n.d.). Retrieved July 9,
2005, from http://www.mtabc.com/index.htm

Lauren B. Chandler

Session 7

Drama and Theater

> *Illness as a descent of the soul into the underworld* is a metaphor that brings to the intuitive mind and knowing heart a depth of understanding that cannot be grasped consciously otherwise.

> —**Jean Shinoda Bolen**, *Close to the Bone*

☐ Introduction

When I was 12, my mother died of leukemia. I did not have adequate support to deal with the loss at that time and as a preteen I was difficult for others to reach. Support groups were not offered at my school, and I knew no one else who had experienced a similar loss. No one in my life discussed my mom, and I did not feel I had permission to mention her or my feelings about losing her.

Twelve years later, Lola Broomberg, the founder and director of a theater troupe for teenagers who had experienced the death of a family member, invited me to a rehearsal. The theater troupe was sponsored by the local hospital's grief support program, Courageous Kids.

All of the teens were screened by the staff at Courageous Kids, who got to know them during weekly support groups. The teens selected for the troupe had all come to a place in their healing in which they felt they received what they needed from the weekly support groups but still wanted to stay connected to peers who had a family member die. In the theater troupe, participants created and performed an original production about death and grief in the lives of youth and toured it in local middle and high schools. The performers engaged and educated the audience by sharing stories about the day of the death, anecdotes about going back to school, original poetry and music inspired by their feelings, and honest appraisals of what they have found helpful and challenging since the death.

As I watched the teens rehearse, I was awestruck by their conscious-ness and courage to express their feelings. They shared their views on how to treat someone who is grieving and spoke the truth about their own experiences — a truth that I had wanted to speak so long ago when it seemed as though no one knew how to listen. The director and the teens eagerly encouraged me to join them in the troupe, despite the age gap. I began participating both as a peer who had lost a parent and as a mentor who helped guide and support them in facing their own losses. That gave me a unique perspective and credibility with the teens.

The following year, I became the director of the troupe. I was very intimidated by the idea of being a director, considering I had no training in theater. Because of the theatrical nature of the program, the term *direc-tor* was adopted early on in the program. However, I considered my role to be as a facilitator. (It is not a prerequisite to have had a significant death in order to be a good facilitator, although it may help to form a connection with the group.) My job was to simply encourage the participants to share their stories. I wanted them to take the lead and did not want to tell them what to do, or direct them. I was excited about the prospect of helping to make it possible for them to share their stories. I knew firsthand how powerful it was for me and my teen "peers," and also saw the audiences' overwhelmingly positive response. I dove in, determined to provide a space for the teens to explore their feelings, bond with each other, play and have fun, create some skits, and perhaps if they chose to, develop a performance to share with audiences.

☐ Foundation of Theory

I investigated drama therapy. According to the National Association of Drama Therapy:

> Drama therapy is the intentional use of drama and/or theater pro-cesses to achieve therapeutic goals. Drama therapy is active and experiential This approach can provide the context for participants to tell their stories, set goals, and solve problems, express feelings, or achieve catharsis. Through drama, the depth and breadth of inner experience can be actively explored and interpersonal relationship skills can be enhanced. Participants can expand their repertoire of dramatic roles to find that their own life roles have been strength-ened. (http://www.nadt.org /faqs.html)

My role in leading the theater troupe was not as a drama therapist, which would involve years of education, training, and experience. However, I did use dramatic techniques to evoke some of the outcomes listed above.

In the prologue to her book, *Acting For Real*, Renee Emunah, a leader in drama therapy states:

> The use of drama as therapy fosters liberation, expansion and perspective. Drama therapy invites us to uncover and integrate dormant aspects of ourselves, to stretch our conception of who we are, and to experience our intrinsic connection with others. (1994, p. xvii)

Together, individuals can use drama to explore their feelings and personal experiences. In a death denying culture, the troupe served as a safe space for participants to be seen and heard and for their feelings to be normalized and validated. They felt empowered by being around peers who shared similar experiences.

Additionally, I reviewed literature about narrative therapy, bereavement, and Erik Erikson's developmental theory. The use of theater and drama can serve the same purpose as narrative therapy — the externalization of a narrative. A narrative, or story, may be about the person who died, the story of the death, or the aftermath of the death. Drama can be a vehicle to help people tell their stories because it can provide a form or shape for feelings and events that may not have been previously articulated. This may be a way to find meaning in the loss and integrate the story into the bigger picture of one's life.

In *Narrative Therapy in Practice: The Archaeology of Hope*, Gerald Monk (1997) writes that the counselor of narrative therapy will "take up the investigative, exploratory, archaeological position" (p. 25). This was the approach I took as a facilitator. My position was one of curiosity and interest as I sought to draw out the participants and provide room for their process to evolve.

Neimeyer (2000) proposes five challenges of mourning (pp. 40–48), based on Therese Rando (1993) and William Worden's (1996) tasks of grief. The functions of sharing stories align with the challenges of mourning described by Neimeyer (2000):

1. Acknowledge the reality of the loss
2. Open yourself to the pain
3. Revise your assumptive world
4. Reconstruct your relationship to that which has been lost
5. Reinvent yourself

Using drama in grief support groups offers a safe medium that attends to these challenges.

1. *Acknowledge the reality of the loss.* Expressing stories through words or movement with others bearing witness can make the loss real.
2. *Open yourself to the pain,* Neimeyer (2000) states. "Without a willingness to embrace the pain long enough to harvest its lessons, we tend to proceed through the loss blindly, trying to orient to the demands of external reality without an internal compass" (p. 43). A grief support group can provide space for people to find and share lessons and explore and embrace feelings, including pain.
3. *Revise your assumptive world.* In sharing lessons learned with the group and telling and retelling the story, individuals are actively revising their assumptive world, which is the third challenge of mourning. Individuals in the group can embody the changes and share the ways life looks different before and after the loss.
4. *Reconstruct your relationship to that which has been lost.* The relationship with the deceased can be reconstructed by using drama in a grief support group. Neimeyer (2000) notes that death does not end relationships, it changes them. In the group, individuals can discuss the ways they still communicate with the deceased and share memories with one another. In the theater troupe, teenagers wrote letters to their deceased loved ones and read them out loud. They created skits reenacting rituals and traditions they carry out on birthdays, the anniversary of the death, or other special days, to help them feel more connected to their loved one.
5. *Reinvent yourself.* A grief support group that employs drama offers individuals the opportunity to reinvent themselves. Individuals can try on new roles and identities within the safety of the group. By virtue of being in the group, individuals take on a new identity as they acknowledge their loss, their connection to others in the group, and their will to keep living in light of their loss.

With any group, it is necessary to assess the developmental age of participants. For adolescents, the combination of drama and grief work seems to be a natural fit. According to Erikson (1959), the peer group is of great importance during adolescence, a time for individuals to try on different roles in search for identity. The group setting provides peer interaction. Drama offers a way for adolescents to explore new roles, the ways their identity has changed since the death, and how that plays out in their life.

☐ Courageous Kids Theater Troupe

One of the teenagers who participated in the theater troupe remarked:

I never really had such an effective way of expressing my thoughts and feelings toward death until I became involved in this. As soon as the group gets together, there's a sort of immediate connection that I'm sure comes from the common experience of having a loved one die. This connection is invaluable and becomes the foundation for a profound experience in which many aspects of death and grief are freely explored and eventually shared.

While a grief support group can be a nonthreatening environment to share and experiment with telling stories, it still takes time to build trust and for individuals to become comfortable in a group. And though the theater troupe is not a grief support group — the teenagers had already participated in a grief support group — it is essential to take the time to foster group cohesion and safety. Therefore the theater troupe started off the season, in September, with an overnight retreat.

The teens arrived on a Saturday morning and departed after breakfast on Sunday. In between cooking, watching a light-hearted movie, and spending time outdoors, they played games to get to know each other. Before diving into the sharing of feelings and personal stories, I led the teens through a series of low-risk trust building activities. I used a compilation of activities and games that I learned from Lola and gleaned from books and websites. I will share a few below, but I encourage you to do your own research and use the resource list provided for a more comprehensive perspective. Keep in mind that not every game will work, depending on group dynamics and the individuals in the group. The games are about process not product — they are a way to promote trust building and expression.

After warming up, I put on soft music and gave the teens big pieces of butcher paper to free write about incidents, memories, and feelings that stood out for them. I encouraged them to take their time. When everyone was through writing, they compared notes. The teens began to share their experiences and feelings with each other and learned what they had in common and the topics they wanted to explore together. For example, when one participant shared that her relationships with her family members had become strained since the death of her mother, another participant jumped in to reveal that his relationships had become more distant since the death, too. Another teen joined in the conversation and added that she had become closer to her family. From that discussion, the teens created a skit about family dynamics.

By the end of the retreat, loose skits, monologues, and vignettes were formed. We scheduled weekly two hour rehearsals, allowing for flexibility in consideration of the teenagers' busy lives. Rehearsals were a combination of checking in and spending time together chatting, playing games, and rehearsing and revising the material created during the retreat, as well as creating new material if the participants desired. As the troupe bonded, they wanted to spend time together that was not focused around rehearsing, so occasionally we would meet for pizza or other social activities.

The troupe met regularly for four months prior to performing in front of an audience. Shows were scheduled through the end of the school year. When the Fall came again, troupe members reconvened, along with potential new members, to talk about re-forming the theater troupe. Some "veterans" chose to be in the troupe again, while others wanted to be involved but no longer wanted to perform. They assumed leadership positions as cofacilitators. Veterans have talked about the fine line between telling their stories and overtelling their stories. They cautioned others to be careful not to share too frequently because then stories may lose their meaning.

It is important to note the demographics of the troupe. All of the participants lived in a college town, were white, and from various class and religious backgrounds. People from different backgrounds will have different responses to drama. The custom and art of story telling is embedded in some cultures while self-disclosure is taboo in others. Facilitators must be sensitive to the culture of the individuals in the group.

☐ Week 7 Curriculum

When followed sequentially, these activities will gradually encourage participants to be comfortable in the space and with each other. They have been selected because they are low risk and do not put individuals on the spot. Time and shared experience are essential to establish trust and connection in the group. Higher-risk activities may be added over a series of sessions. Be aware that grieving individuals have different comfort levels, and drama and theater may not be appropriate for certain groups. Be sensitive and provide encouragement. Be flexible and creative and provide adaptations of activities so that participants have alternate ways to be involved.

Before launching into the following activities, provide group members with a brief outline of what the group will entail. Emphasize confidentiality and remind them they have the choice to challenge themselves, but always have the option to pass by simply stating, "I pass."

A rough idea of how long each activity may take is indicated, but this is for the facilitator to determine based on the energy of the group. The origin of the activities is noted when known.

Activities

		Estimated Time Required:
1.	Check-in and ritual	5 to 10 minutes
2.	Activity of choice	60 to 90 minutes
3.	Closing check-in and ritual	10 to 15 minutes

Introductions/Name Toss (up to 15 minutes)

Materials Needed

Three to four beanbags or small stuffed animals that are easy to toss.

This simple activity encourages the learning of names and active participation. When used during the initial group of a series or in a single session, it works well because it is low risk. Some name games may be anxiety provoking because participants are put on the spot and may feel they have to be creative or smart in front of strangers. In this game, participants are not asked to show that they remember each other's names, although every name is spoken aloud many times. If this activity is used in the middle of a series of groups, once participants already know each other's names, they can be asked to speak the person's name they are throwing the beanbag to. Another variation for a group that has worked together before is for each participant to say a feeling or descriptive word about him- or herself while tossing the beanbag.

The facilitator should ask the participants to stand and join her or him in forming a circle. Toss a beanbag to someone in the circle and at the same time speak your own name. The participant will catch the beanbag, and then throw it to another participant while speaking his or her own name. Instruct the participants to throw the beanbag to those who have not yet received it. Ask participants to remember who threw them the beanbag and who they threw it to. Continue throwing and catching the beanbag and speaking names in the same order to establish a pattern. When a pattern is established, instruct everyone to speak each participant's name a few times through. This helps them learn the names faster because they are hearing them and saying them. Next, toss in a second beanbag, repeating the same pattern, with everyone speaking the names. Once the group is able to juggle both beanbags, add in a third beanbag.

Cover the Space (up to 15 minutes)
[adaptation from Augusto Boal]

This activity helps participants become comfortable in the room, in their bodies, and with each other. It creates a sense of connection between the group members and their surroundings and encourages them to start thinking creatively.

Establish a rectangular space in the room, large enough for participants to walk around freely without feeling crowded, but small enough that it is easy for participants to make eye contact with one another. Ask participants to walk around the space for a few minutes. They may look at each other, but may not speak or touch. Instruct them to make sure every area in the room is covered by someone at all times. Tell them to freeze and ask them to notice if there are areas in the room that are unoccupied. Ask them to move again, continuing to fill in the space. Gradually add in more instructions. You may ask them to move in different ways; for example, very slowly or close to the ground. Play with relationships, for example, by asking participants to move in pairs. Experiment with feelings and instruct them to move through the space as if they are late for a very important engagement, or as if they are going to meet someone they have not seen in a long time who they love very much.

Blind Circle (15 minutes)

This activity builds listening skills, trust, and awareness. It is also a great way to remind everyone the names of group members.

Ask participants to stand in a circle with their arms stretched wide so their fingertips are just barely touching the fingertips of the participants on both sides of them. Then have them drop their arms to their sides. Demonstrate this activity for them twice, once with your eyes open while you are describing the activity, and once with your eyes closed, to show that you are willing to take the risk you will be asking them to take.

Go into the center of the circle and wander around the space defined by the circle. When you approach a boundary of the circle, the participants in closest proximity to you must speak your name to redirect you, so you stay inside the circle. The second time you demonstrate, close your eyes. Offer everyone the opportunity to go into the center and encourage each participant to walk in one direction until they reach a boundary, change their pace, walking faster or slower, or change their movement, perhaps moving close to the ground or marching.

Either-Or *(15 minutes)*

The following is a very simple exercise that is often used early on in groups to help participants discover their commonalities. In this exercise, participants use their bodies to reveal their experiences or feelings. The facilitator speaks the following format:

Stand on this side of the room if _____; stand on that side of the room if_____. Or place yourself wherever you identify on the spectrum.

For example:

- You would love to play in the snow; you would prefer to play in the sand
- You want to read the book; you would rather watch the movie
- You would prefer dessert first; you could skip dessert
- You may consider statements related to grief,

For example:

- You often think about the person who died; you never think about the person who died
- You wonder if your feelings are normal; you believe your feelings are normal
- You feel guilt about some aspect of the death; you feel no guilt

As the group gets into the game, you may ask them to come up with their own statements to offer the group. This simple format may be revisited in later sessions as participants build trust and have more questions for each other.

There are many variations of this exercise. If participants are not physically able to move their bodies in this way, the facilitator may adjust the exercise and ask participants to raise their hand high in the air, keep it in their lap, or somewhere in between.

Tour of a Significant Place *(30 minutes)*
[adaption from Michael Rohd]

Materials Needed

Paper and pencils.

In this activity participants reflect on and share memories, which may encourage the surfacing and sharing of emotion. Ask participants to get into pairs, close their eyes, and imagine a physical place from their life (a room in a house or building, a place in nature ...) that they consider to be significant. It may be any place of significance, although you may suggest that it be one they associate with the person who died. Ask them to notice the colors, textures, and shapes in detail. Hand out the paper and pencils, then ask the participants to open their eyes and sketch the place they envisioned. Next, instruct them to take turns moving through their special place with their partner, as if they were both standing in it. The tour guide describes the physical space with as much detail as possible and can share stories and memories about the place if their partner asks a question that leads to a story. Be sure to mention they should describe the place as if they were actually there. Instruct them to switch roles after about 10 minutes. If the tour guide is stuck and feels they do not have more to share, ask them to share more details and encourage their partner to ask more questions. Before participants pair up for this exercise, you may choose to demonstrate by leading the group through a place that is significant to you.

Paths of Grief (20 minutes)
[Jaclyn Bovee, Courageous Kids Theater Troupe participant]

Materials (optional)

Paper and pencils.

In grief support groups I have cofacilitated, metaphor has been used in art-based activities. For example, group members may be asked to draw what their journey of grief looks like as a landscape. Group members may draw mountains to climb or waves to swim through.

This activity translates well into a physical exercise that one of the Courageous Kids Theater Troupe teen participants initiated. She asked everyone to move across the room as if they were moving through their path of grief. One participant moved as if he were climbing up a rock wall, trying to find that perfect ledge to rest on, but never finding it. Another teen pretended she was driving a car down a country road with the music blasting and the wind in her hair, when all of a sudden, she got stuck in a traffic jam for hours and just couldn't get out of it.

You may ask participants to draw their path of grief before exploring it physically. When you do ask them to act it out, have them all do so at the same time, so they will feel less self-conscious about others watching. This way, they will not feel the pressure to create a masterpiece. Offer them the opportunity to share their paths of grief after they have had time to practice. Participants may also want to try acting out one another's paths of grief. This may lead into a mirroring exercise in which one participant slowly moves through his or her path of grief and everyone else stands behind copying each movement.

Sharing/Closing (10 to 15 minutes)

Ask the participants to sit with you in a circle. Offer each group member the opportunity to share any thoughts they may have about their experience. You may ask them to share what they learned and what parts of the group were their favorite, least favorite, and most challenging. To end on a positive note, you may ask everyone to share something he or she is looking forward to.

☐ Children

When considering applying dramatic techniques in a children's group, the structure and content must be adjusted to be age appropriate. For example, sessions may need to take place in a shorter time interval and language should be simple. Children often express their emotions through play and through "metaphorical, non-verbal communication," and therefore expressive therapies including art, creative writing, and music help children work through their grief (Webb, 2003, p. 405). Dramatic activities are often playful, utilize metaphor, and can be verbal and nonverbal. Registered drama therapist Anne Curtis (1999) uses "improvisation, mime, puppetry, and role-playing in metaphorical situations" (p. 183) in her six-session curriculum *Circles of Life: A Creative Curriculum for Healing Traumatic Loss in Childhood*. She accounts for the level of cognitive development of the children by using simple language and caters to their energy level by leading exercises in which participants are physically active. Curtis asserts, "Physical movement breaks down mental barriers, allowing the freedom to respond emotionally" (p. 187). I have noticed this is true for teenagers and adults as well.

☐ Performance

Whether or not the group develops a performance is secondary to the shared experience and process within the group. The purpose of the group is process not product. However, a group may decide to create a performance based on the material generated during sessions. It must be the decision of the group members, not the facilitator. If some participants want to perform and others do not, everyone can still be involved if they choose to be. Nonperformers can provide valuable ideas, support, and feedback. A participant who is reluctant to perform may ask a performer to tell his or her story.

A performance can be an empowering experience for participants and for audiences. Audience members are affected because they see their own feelings reflected in the performance. The feelings of audience members are validated, and the performers are validated because audiences are visibly riveted, moved, and impressed by the sharing of the performers. Their feelings and experiences are heard and legitimized and they realize their stories are worth telling. Everyone grieves, whether it is for a death, relationship loss, job loss, or a geographical move.

☐ Last Words

The following poem was written and performed by a Courageous Kids Theater Troupe member, Justine Lee. She frequently changed the poem when she had new experiences that she wished her father could have been alive for. Another troupe member accompanied her on the guitar as she recited her poem.

You Missed Out

Justine Lee

You missed out on me entering the 6th grade
You missed out on my first boyfriend
You missed out on him and I breaking up
You missed out on me making new friends
You missed out on me failing math
You missed out on me passing math
You missed out on 190 of my soccer games
You missed out on Bern and I getting along
You missed out on five of my birthdays
You missed out on movie nights
You missed out on card games
You missed out on poker nights
You missed out on me actually keeping my room clean
You missed out on my first duck game
You missed out on graduation shopping
You missed out on my 8th grade graduation
You missed out on my first day of freshman year
You missed out on my first day of sophomore year
You missed out on my first day of junior year
You missed out on my first steady boyfriend
You missed out on me going to prom

You missed out on all the hugs I needed
You missed out on all the support I should have had
Daddy, you missed out on me growing up
But I missed out too
And the worst thing is
All the memories I used to have of you and I together
are gone
I don't remember your voice
I don't remember your smile
I don't remember your laugh
I don't remember your strong hands
I don't remember how it felt just to be with you
I don't remember you
When I look at a photo of you
I don't know who you are
Daddy you're a stranger to me
And that's something I wish I had missed out on

To facilitate means to make easier and there is no *one* right way to do this. In the context of a grief support group, the facilitator's role is to make it easier for individuals to share their feelings and stories about a significant death they have experienced. Grieving individuals are often not given permission to talk about their losses. Giving permission in itself is a form of facilitating.

Lauren B. Chandler is currently studying social work at Portland State University and is completing her field placement at The Dougy Center, The National Center for Grieving Children & Families. She is the former director of the Courageous Kids Theatre Troupe and works as a consultant to hospices and bereavement centers that want to create a theatre troupe program.

Resources

Boal, A. (1995). *The rainbow of desire.* New York: Routledge.

Boal, A. (2002). *Games for actors and non-actors* (2nd ed.). New York: Routledge.

Cossa, M. (2005). *Rebels with a cause: Working with adolescents using action techniques.* London: Jessica Kingsley.

Curtis, A. (2001). *Circles of life: A creative curriculum for healing traumatic loss in childhood.* Author.

Emunah, R. (1994). *Acting for real: Drama therapy, process, technique, and performance.* New York: Brunner/Mazel.

Kidder, B. (2001). *ImaginACTION: Activities that allow students to get up on their feet and moving* (2nd ed.). Fort Collins, CO: Cottonwood Press.

Rohd, M. (1998). *Theater for community, conflict and dialogue: The hope is vital training manual*. Portsmouth, NH: Heinemann.

CHAPTER **13**   Janet Shaw Rogers

Session 8

Grief and the Sacred Art of Ritual

"What is a rite?" asked the little prince. "Those also are actions too often neglected," said the fox. "They are what make one day different from other days, one hour from other hours."

— **Antoine de Saint-Exupéry,** *The Little Prince*

☐ Introduction

Most cultures around the world practice various forms of ritual associated with death, grief, and loss. Many aspects of these rituals have been carried forward from the past to the present day. Death and grief rituals have been part of our human journey for centuries — from the anointing of the body in Egypt to the ancient Aztec practices of burying grinding stones, corn, and chocolate along with the deceased. Preparing burial sites with food, precious stones, and metals, along with elaborate works of fine art was also part of the burial rituals of many ancient civilizations. These cultures wanted to ensure their deceased and revered loved ones were honored, well fed, and would have riches with which to enter the next phase of their journey following death. Entire towns, villages, and regions would enter into both public and personal rituals, which would serve to acknowledge death and enable a transition to take place within the community.

Today, in our modern societies, we also recognize the need to create and participate in ritual. A powerful and healing tool, ritual is still used to help us acknowledge major life transitions, especially in the areas of death, loss, and grief. The loss of structure, meaning, or control in one's life due to the death of a loved one, divorce, miscarriage, or a terminal diagnosis are all examples of transition or threshold experiences that lend themselves to being acknowledged and honored through ritual (Arrien, 1993).

It is because of the very traumatic nature of many of these transition times in our lives that ritual in particular offers a way to acknowledge the loss, as well as provide a structure if you will, which allows the reality of our own mortality to surface from our unconscious into our conscious mind. Through ritual we are able to bring our mortality and the concept of loss a little closer to home (Rando, 1984). As in the past, present day communities as well as individuals are also supported through ritual. Loved ones are able to come together in order to share feelings and stories about the loss and separation which has occurred in their lives (Rando, 1984).

Within our current Western cultural framework, there exist many diverse cultural groups. Each of these diverse groups practices traditions, rituals, and ceremonies that honor death and loss in ways that differ from one another. It is important to realize, even though the outer expression of many ethnic rituals may vary from culture to culture, that the essence of many of these practices remains the same regardless of their cultural origin. Honoring the passing of a loved one, caring for members of the community around a loss, supporting individuals through times of deep grief and loss, regardless of the circumstances of loss — these are the common values shared by a wide variety of cultures and ethnic groups the world over. The rituals of funerals, wakes, burials, cremations, grieving ceremonies, and mourning practices may look different in their outer form but the intention and essence from culture to culture remains similar.

☐ Grief and Loss Rituals from Various Traditions

In the Dagara tradition of West Africa, only the women of the village express their grief at the death of a loved one with loud, sharp, and piercing wails. These sounds serve to announce their grief to the rest of the village and act as a signal for the members of the village to prepare themselves for the grief ritual that takes place when someone has died. It is, however, only the women who can show their grief in this particular way. The men have other roles to play in the ritual of grief in the village (Some, 1993).

In the Jewish tradition, family members sit Shiva to express their grief at the loss of a loved one. The day of the burial is counted as the first day of Shiva and the mourning period extends for seven days. During this ritual time, Jewish family members focus entirely on their grief and loss by sharing stories of the deceased's life and their remembrances of their loved one. After sitting Shiva for seven days, the mourning period ends with a ritual. The lit candle is blown out in silence and the family members take a walk around the block to symbolically bring an end to the intense grieving period and mark their reentry back into the world of the living.

Throughout Mexico, and now in largely Hispanic areas in North America, there is an ancient Indo-Hispanic ritual that honors the ancestors and children. It is called the Day of the Dead — *Dia de los Muertos.*. It is a time when entire towns, neighborhoods, and communities gather to light candles, bear offerings to the ancestors, or *ofrendas* of *cempasuchil* flowers or orange marigolds to adorn the gravesites, along with *pan de muerto,* a special bread made in bakeries in October for the Day of the Dead festivities. The archetypal figure of death appears in the form of a tall, thin skeleton adorned often with a beautiful hat, dress, and gloves. One of her names is *La Caterina*. She, along with paper skeletons, are prominently displayed in shop windows, and carried in processions by community members as they journey to the cemetery and gravesites to place their offerings of light, food, drink, and flowers in celebration of the eternal cycle of life and death.

Another ritual that honors the ancestors takes place in parts of Japan during the Bon Festival in mid-August. It is believed that at this time, the spirit of the ancestors return. The Japanese create small boats or rafts upon which they place a lantern or a candle and let the raft float on the river. The name of this ritual is *Shoro Nagashi* — *shoro* means sacred spirits and *nagashi* means "to let it float with the current."

☐ What Is a Ritual?

Ritual is created through an action or set of actions that is first and foremost imbued with intention and awareness on the part of the practitioner(s). Rituals are designed to reframe "ordinary time" and create a "time-out-of-time" or, in other words, a timeless experience for the participants. They assist an individual as well as the collective in marking and honoring those threshold times of beginnings, endings, and transitions in our lives.

Well-known collective rituals such as birthdays, retirement parties, graduation ceremonies, and marriages are very familiar group rituals by which we honor, in a celebratory manner, many of life's threshold and poignant moments (Neimeyer, 2000) .

☐ How Ritual Can Help

It is during times of loss such as death, illness, and divorce that we most often need both physical and spiritual support to help us — both as individuals as well as a collective. We turn to ritual to help us face tragedy as well as to find expression for our grief and mourning. The enactment of ritual during these times can provide a crucial element of healing, by allowing us to express our deepest feelings about our loss. Our beliefs and feelings can be expressed through ritual when words might feel inadequate (Wolfelt, 1997). Therein lies the power of ritual, because ritual works on a symbolic level and with the unconscious, it assists us in bringing forward our unconscious feelings. Ritual, by its very nature, creates a structure in which these otherwise unconscious feelings might surface and become too overwhelming. The roller-coaster of feelings that can sweep over us like a tidal wave and swamp us with loss and grief now becomes manageable, in the safe and structured context of a ritual. In addition, collective rituals assist in supporting families, friends, and loved ones to communicate their feelings about the loss that has occurred.

The range of life situations involving loss and grief are varied. From the death of a loved one, to receiving news of a terminal diagnosis, or coming to terms with the loss of identity that can often accompany a debilitating trauma or disease process. These are but a few of the tragic human scenarios many of us face at some point in our lives. Even loss of employment, divorce, or miscarriage can often trigger feelings of grief and underscore the feelings of helplessness and separateness that may occur as a result of these traumatic situations.

With the news of a terminal diagnosis, for example, ritual also helps facilitate the deep acknowledgment of our own mortality along with a new reality or a new role for ourselves (Rando, 1984). This point is well illustrated by the many women today who are facing terminal cancer. In order to face their health challenge and acknowledge their mortality, many women choose to call together their sisterhood and ritualize the shaving of their hair, for example. The hair becomes, on the one hand, the symbol of loss and paradoxically the symbol of hope on the other hand, with its potential for regrowth. The regrowth of their hair, following chemotherapy or radiation, signifies a rebirth for the woman. Women attest to feeling empowered and changed by the rituals they have enacted prior to and following the diagnosis of a serious illness.

Ritual, then, allows us to move into greater connection with ourselves, our loved ones, and the Divine — that aspect of life related to mystery and the eternal. Through ritual we are moved out of our ordinary social interactions and into greater intimacy with ourselves, those participating in their ritual, and with Spirit. As Jean Shinoda Bolen writes in her book *Close to the Bone: Life Threatening Illness and the Search for Meaning*, "When an I-Thou element enters a ritual, divinity is present, linking the participants with each other and with the greater mystery. There is a shift away from the trivial into the eternal" (1996, p. 58).

Rituals become a way to honor and acknowledge the presence of grief, loss, and change that weave themselves into the very fabric of our human journey from birth to death.

☐ Modern Day Rituals of Loss and Grief

One of the most spontaneous collective rituals followed the death of Princess Diana in 1997 when people placed mounds of flowers, cards, and small offerings outside Buckingham Palace and Kensington Palace (where the princess had lived) in London to show their grief and affection for a woman who wanted to be known as "the queen of people's hearts."

Another spontaneous ritual involves the setting up of small roadside altars at the site of fatal traffic accidents. Friends and family of the deceased loved one adorn the roadside site with flowers and other symbolic memorabilia.

For parents who have lost a child, both personal and collective rituals have helped many couples cope with the immense grief that often accompanies such a devastating loss. The planting of commemorative trees, building birdhouses, constructing bicycle paths, creating pilgrimages to favorite spots of natural beauty are but a few of the true life rituals that have been enacted by parents and families as healing tools during the very anguished time of loss and bereavement.

☐ Kathleen and Alex's Goodbye Rituals

The following true-life story describes two rituals undertaken by a couple, Kathleen and Alex, who suddenly lost their 24-year-old daughter Amanda, as a result of an undiagnosed tumor.

A Collective Ritual

The first description is of a collective ritual the couple created for Amanda's friends. The other rituals are personal ones that Kathleen and Alex enacted in order to deal with their own grief and to heal.

A Goodbye Ritual for Amanda's Friends

When Kathleen and Alex received the news of their daughter's unexpected and tragic death, the couple journeyed to the city where Amanda had been living in order to begin the process of saying goodbye to their sweet young daughter.

Kathleen and Alex saw immediately that they were going to have to arrange and attend two different memorial services for their daughter within a week of each other, before they could come back home with her ashes. They had initially planned to have Amanda cremated in the city where she died. Then they would immediately fly to her childhood home bringing Amanda's ashes with them for a traditional family funeral for friends and family members.

It soon became apparent to Alex and Kathleen that their daughter had touched the lives of hundreds of young people in the city where she had been living. She had many close young friends the couple had never met because Amanda was going to school in a city far away from where her parents lived. Kathleen and Alex realized after meeting and talking to many of Amanda's friends just how much they were suffering. They knew that before leaving they would need to arrange a memorial ritual so Amanda's friends, most of them in their 20s, could attend.

The couple felt Amanda's young friends needed a way to make sense of the sudden death and loss they all so acutely felt. In addition, these young people needed a way to say goodbye to their friend Amanda and bring closure to their friendship, in a way that was significant and meaningful to them. So Kathleen and Alex made arrangements at the restaurant where Amanda had been working part time while she was going to school. Kathleen was able to find a beautiful, long piece of slate blue cloth, which was Amanda's favorite color, and together, she and Alex created an altar in the restaurant using the fabric along with precious objects that had been dear to Amanda.

The ritual took place in the restaurant during the morning hours before the regular business day began. On the altar Kathleen and Alex placed several symbolic objects. These had been Amanda's favorites: a toy black jeep, and huge black and white photos of the New York skyline. Amanda had always wanted to visit New York but never made it to the "Big Apple." Vases filled with blue gerbera daisies adorned the altar.

During the impromptu service of testimonials, several friends brought to the altar their personal offerings to show their love for Amanda. Those present spoke of the amazing connections they had with their friend. For Alex and Kathleen it was very healing for them to be able to hear just how much Amanda had touched the lives of others with her sweet, angelic, and loyal nature.

The stories and testimonials were gifts as well as offerings that brought healing to all present. Even though it meant extra work and added stress for Alex and Kathleen to orchestrate this ritual for Amanda's young friends, the couple felt that it was the right and most healing thing to do for themselves as well as for Amanda's community. To say goodbye in a place where these young people had shared good times together, and in a way where they could express their love for their friend Amanda, while amongst their peers, made the extra effort all worthwhile for Kathleen and Alex.

Kathleen and Alex's Personal Rituals for Amanda

Upon returning home with Amanda's ashes Kathleen and Alex knew they would create personal rituals for themselves in order to say goodbye to Amanda in their own way.

Amanda in New York

The very first ritual Kathleen entered into was to create a photo collage not just for herself but for all of Amanda's friends. Because Amanda had been "nuts about New York but never did make it there," Kathleen wanted to put her favorite photo of Amanda in a photo collage of the New York skyline, with Amanda in the foreground. In preparing this photo collage, Kathleen was able to go back and look through many of Amanda's photo albums. This allowed her time to be with many of her daughter's special moments. She was able to let go and grieve as she spent time reviewing Amanda's trips and important occasions that her daughter had celebrated with friends and family over the years.

Amanda's life came alive for her as she chose various photos from Amanda's albums to distribute to her daughter's friends. Once the collage was complete, which took some time given Kathleen's state of grief, she mailed over 100 copies of this precious keepsake to Amanda's friends. One level of letting go had begun.

The Tibetan Prayer Flags

An important ritual for Alex was taking Amanda's ashes to New York. He and Kathleen went to "the Big Apple," thus fulfilling a dream of Amanda's, one that she had not been able to complete while she was alive. Prior to leaving, the couple had been given Tibetan prayer flags by their neighbors. (Figure 13.1) A local monk had blessed them and told Alex and Kathleen that, "When you hang these your daughter's spirit will be set free and she will be at peace."

On the day they wanted to sprinkle her ashes from the Empire State building there was a torrential downpour so the couple then took her ashes with them onto a cruise ship. They had booked a get-away in the Caribbean following their trip to New York. Kathleen and Alex needed a break from their grief, their routine, and above all they needed rest.

After asking the captain to hang the gifted prayer flags, the couple was so surprised and awestruck as the sails were hoisted and the prayer flags were high above deck blowing in the ocean breeze, the crew began to play "Amazing Grace"! Every time thereafter, when-

FIGURE 13.1 Tibetan prayer flags. (Photo courtesy of Kathleen and Alex Kinasewich, Union Bay, British Columbia.)

ever the sails were hoisted, Alex and Kathleen felt they had been invited into this special ritual designed just for them. For an entire week, this daily ritual of hoisting the sails, the playing of "Amazing Grace," and seeing the prayer flags blowing in the wind gave them a sense of comfort and an experience of grace aboard ship.

The Memorial Float

As the first anniversary of Amanda's death was approaching, Kathleen knew that she wanted to do a personal ritual to commemorate her daughter's death. After searching the Internet for cross-cultural memorial rituals, she came across a Japanese ritual, mentioned previously in the introduction of this chapter, called *Shoro Nagashi*. After reading about the Japanese raft ritual, Kathleen decided, that she too, wanted to create a raft and set it afloat on the waters in front of her home. (Figure 13.2)

A year to the day of Amanda's death Kathleen enacted her version of this ancient-to-modern Japanese ritual. She realized it was time for both of their spirits to be set free — her own as well as Amanda's. She knew that

FIGURE 13.2   Amanda's memorial float. (Photo courtesy of Kathleen and Alex Kinasewich, Union Bay, British Columbia.)

by creating this ritual, although a bit different from the Japanese one, it would help her bring closure to her relationship with her daughter Amanda. She fashioned the small memorial raft out of a floatable material upon which she placed a glass globe with a candle. She gathered moss for the bedding on the raft. Then, she covered the raft with some of the ceremonial sweet grass which she grows on her property. Along the outer borders of the raft she attached pieces of bamboo to help it float and stay upright. She even tested out the raft in the bathtub to make sure it floated. All the while she was making the raft she was "balling her head off." As she says, "I had a tough time making the raft and yet I realized that this was all part of me being able to let go of Amanda and to let my feelings flow. I knew this ritual would really allow Amanda's spirit to be free. I asked the Creator to help me set her spirit free and to be an instrument in healing my grief."

Unlike the Japanese ritual, which does not include placing the ashes of the deceased on the raft, Kathleen wanted to include Amanda's ashes on her float. She placed a small amount of Amanda's ashes in a rainbow colored box, along with some of her favorite flowers, a lock of her hair, four sticks of incense symbolizing the four cardinal directions, along with a photo and a poem Amanda had written when she was a child. She canoed out onto the waters in front of her home at dusk and set the raft, with the lit candle, afloat in the current.

Once back on shore, Kathleen could see the raft from her veranda floating toward another beam of light coming offshore from a nearby island. The candle on Amanda's raft was already starting to dim. Kathleen said she instinctively knew that when the float met the other beam on the water Amanda's candle on the float would go out. (Figure 13.3)

> I just knew it was going to happen. The float met the beam of light from shore and the candle went out and so did the beam of light. Then there was a red flash! Then, there was no light at all. It was amazing! I had such a good feeling that Amanda's spirit was free. I felt that she was able to soar into a new energy and a new life was awaiting her.
>
> The red light for me was not only her passage into this new realm, but it was also a goodbye message to me that it was now OK to move on with my life.

With the completion of these rituals, Kathleen and Alex realized that the collective and personal rituals they had initiated and created had come to play a significant role in their own healing. The rituals reconnected them to the very qualities Amanda had demonstrated to her friends and everyone she had ever known — that of a generosity of spirit; always reaching out with love to people around her — friends, family, and even strangers.

FIGURE 13.3   Memorial float in the current. (Photo courtesy of Kathleen and Alex Kinasewich, Union Bay, British Columbia.)

In the recounting of these rituals there are some important points that warrant highlighting:

- When we give ourselves permission, we are all ritual makers
- In times of deep grief and loss there is a healing power in creating personal rituals

Kathleen and Alex's rituals illustrate the healing that can take place for couples and individuals facing tragic loss. The spontaneous, collective ritual the couple orchestrated with Amanda's friends, as well as Kathleen and Alex's personal rituals with the Tibetan prayer flags, the photo collage, and the memorial raft give us true-life examples of weaving the power of creativity into the healing power of personal ritual, which can arise even in the face of tragic loss.

It is important to include both secular and faith-based rituals for ourselves, family members, and other loved ones. "Public rituals can sometimes fail us precisely because they are designed to affirm communal values sometimes at the expense of individual needs" (Neimeyer, 2000). With this collective ritual, Kathleen and Alex were able to address the needs of Amanda's young friends to celebrate her life and their loss.

☐ **Week 8 Curriculum**

Activities

	Estimated Time Required
1. Opening ritual. Lighting candles and placing ritual objects on altar	5 to 10 minutes
2. Check-in	20 minutes
3. Enactment of ritual	1 hour
4. Closing ritual	10 to 15 minutes
5. Sharing time and taking down altar	30 minutes

Please note: The facilitator needs to be mindful of time and keeping each person's expressive offering to a reasonable time frame. The facilitator should check in with each participant a week prior, to know beforehand who is bringing what. Knowing the number of pieces to be shared, as well as who will drum, sing, act, move, or share an offering, will allow the facilitator to have the opportunity to plan for proper timing for all of the elements of the final session (from the check-in, the ritual itself, the sharing of food, to providing a closure time for the group).

Materials Needed

- Masking tape or sticky putty to hang collages on the wall
- A piece of beautiful fabric upon which the collages would be placed if not wall mounted
- Candles, matches, personal memorabilia, and altar makings

Notes for the Facilitator

- Have an extra supply of candles on hand — both votives and tapers are advisable for each session.
- Bring embellishments for the altar and the meeting room, such as water in a ceremonial vessel, flowers, natural objects such as stones, leaves, twigs, seashells, or feathers. These always add an element of the sacred to a space or altar.
- You will need to coordinate with the group if sharing food is to be part of the closing session. Plan accordingly for both space and time needs to accommodate the ritual, check-in, final closing, and sharing of food and goodbyes.

1. *Opening ritual:* You might choose to begin the last session of the course with the same opening ritual as in previous weeks to provide continuity but keep the check-in time much shorter to accommodate the ritual and closing.

2. *Check-in:* You might also choose to create a ritual with the check-in segment (see description of Council Process/"Talking Stick" ritual later in the chapter). Placing the sharing or check-in as the final segment of the closing ritual, will allow the participants to share their reactions about the various aspects of the final ritual such as the collage mandala or gallery, the walking meditation, or any other aspect of the course they may wish to reference for the closing ritual. Before any social time begins with the sharing of food or saying more informal goodbyes, it is suggested that the participants final sharing time take place within the time scheduled for the ritual. In this way, trivial conversation will be avoided and the ritual will allow for more heartfelt and intimate sharing by the participants.

3. *Closing:* It will be important to remember to bring closure to your ritual by taking down the altar and acknowledging to the group the end of the ritual portion of your time together. (See the description of closing in the Suggested Closing Ritual section below.)

Because this is the last session of the course, participants may have good-bye comments for the facilitator and for each other. Last goodbyes after a course such as this one should not be rushed.

☐ Suggested Closing Ritual

Bringing Your Offering

The ritual for this last session would involve (time permitting) each participant bringing to this last session at least one or two of their chosen art expressions from the modalities explored during the previous seven weeks. For example, participants could bring: a haiku poem or one of their written stories, or an entry from their journal, a song, a musical instrument (e.g. drums), a movement or drama piece, a sandtray story, or a photo. All participants who created a collage would be encouraged to bring their collage because all the collages are to be hung or laid out as a mandala.

Creating Sacred Space

The facilitator instructs the group to form a circle of chairs. As a group, each participant would help set up the community altar by bringing to the sacred altar space their candle, along with any memorabilia from the previous weeks, and any special offering for this last session.

If the collages are set out as a mandala or circle on the floor, the other personal ritual objects may be integrated with the collage pieces to form a large floor altar. Once the altar is in place each participant lights a candle. Then the group, along with the facilitator, will hang all of the collaged art pieces to create a collage gallery around the room. If wall space is not available, create a large mandala or circle with these collages on the floor in the center of the circle of chairs.

Adding a beautiful piece of material under the mandala will help create a sacred space for these artworks. The entire room then becomes the altar.

Entering into the Ritual

Next, the group enters into a walking meditation (see description later in the chapter) with each participant using their sacred witness to view the collages — whether hung on the meeting room walls or placed as a mandala on the floor. While the group is in walking meditation, have one or two participants drum with a steady, simple heartbeat rhythm.

This will allow the group to stay focused and the drumming will create a rhythm for the meditation walk. Reminding the participants to focus on their in-breath and their out-breath as they walk will slow down everyone's normal gait, which will enable them to allow a more focused and meditative way of walking. In this way, each participant's creative offering is viewed and honored from the detached place of the sacred witness and not from the critic's judgmental place. If the space is not conducive to all of the participants walking as a group, in a slow rhythmic way (taking one step forward with the right foot then both feet come together and pause, then leading with the left foot and repeating the pause, and so forth) then simply allow each participant to slowly walk throughout the room viewing each of the collage pieces in a silent, focused way. All the while the participants are walking, the drumming continues. If there are no drums or drummers playing, select a slow rhythmical piece of music for the group to move to in silent viewing. Remember to switch drummers so every participant is able to view the collage gallery. Once each participant has finished his or her walk each will return in silence to a chair in the circle.

The Artful Expressions

The drumming stops once everyone is in the circle, and the group comes together to witness each other with each one's chosen art form. Some participants may choose to read one of their Haiku poems or others may offer their expression by way of drumming or singing.

It might be that a couple of participants want to accompany one another. As an example, one person may want to read an inspiring passage from their journal or sing and the other person accompanies them with a simple drumbeat or a soft hum. In this way, all of the fertile soil that was cultivated in the previous seven weeks with each of the artful expressions can now be viewed and shared as a sacred offering. Sharing the offerings need not be a lengthy process.

There may be participants who choose, for one reason or another, not to present an art form to the group. As the facilitator, allow each participant to present what they feel comfortable with. There is no need to pressure participants. Some participants just might require some gentle encouragement.

Because this is the last session, extra time will be needed for the ritual as well as time to bring closure to the course. Allow time for any remaining dialogue from the participants that might need to be expressed before the group ends. Last good-byes after a course such as this one should not be rushed.

☐ Suggested Opening and Closing Rituals

1. Set up, as a group, a community altar in the meeting room
2. Have each participant choose a candle and place it on the altar
3. Place memorabilia on the altar and have participants light candles
4. Use the council process (see below) to have participants check in with the group
5. Select a piece of music and have the group listen to it in silence
6. Using a specific theme, each participant writes out and reads his or her prayer or letter
7. Have participants mimic drum rhythms to give expression to their emotions
8. Create a breath ritual: "Breathing in: "I calm my body" — Breathing out: "I release fear"
9. Have group members mimic several types of ritual movements and gestures to music — hands open and close at heart center, arms

raise to sky and extend to earth, bowing forward into circle (done to music)

10. With a drumbeat or music have group do a walking meditation
11. Ask participants to create and share a personal ritual within the course
12. End or begin with a gratitude practice: "I am grateful for _____."
13. Acknowledge the presence of the natural elements — fire, water, earth, and air, as well as the four directions north, south, east, and west

Note: Numbers 1–4 can become part of each session's opening ritual.

In the list of suggested rituals there has been an attempt to weave in many of the previous weeks' art forms and expressive modalities: music, movement, and creative writing. It is important to remember when each of these art modalities is incorporated and enacted as ritual so that an intention be set and verbalized to the group.

Create a beginning, middle, and end to each ritual. As the facilitator, being centered yourself and allowing the quality of vulnerability to be present within yourself but for the participants as well, will go a long way to ensuring that the element of the sacred and the quality of vulnerability are also present for the group.

Keeping the opening and closing rituals simple, such as choosing a candle and lighting it with a focused intention, is in and of itself a meaningful ritual. In this way, participants will be empowered to create their own rituals outside the course. Remember it is the intention behind the ritual that creates its power and healing.

As the facilitator you may wish to use the following list of questions to help you prepare your rituals for the course.

☐ Ritual Preparation: A Question Checklist

1. What is the purpose or intention of the ritual?
2. What elements would enhance or set the tone for the ritual — flowers, music, silence, movement?
3. How to begin and end the ritual?
4. How are the participants engaging in or enacting this ritual?

5. Is there feedback or sharing that needs to happen following the ritual in order for the experience to become integrated for the participants?

☐ The Council Process or Talking Stick Ritual

In many indigenous cultures the talking stick or council process is used to allow group members to share from their heart. Being fully present while speaking from the heart is the goal of the council process. Bringing one's whole self to what is being said is often done with the aid of a talking stick, stone, or bowl. This object allows speakers to focus both on their spoken words and their feelings.

When it is time to share, a participant will request the talking object, take a moment to center their thoughts, and then begin speaking. Keeping one's expression "lean" is being mindful of the other members of the group who may also wish to share. Once sharing is complete another member of the group then requests the talking object.

When the intent on the part of each of the group members is to be receptive and heart centered in speech, this sets the tone for a sacred group ritual. With the passing of the talking stick, stone, or bowl, the group is taken into a ritual of intimate sharing. Staying present to oneself while speaking and fully listening while others share, creates a quality of connectedness, and most importantly, trust, which then allows each person to feel safe within the group. At the end of the council sharing ritual, the talking stick, bowl, or stone is brought back to be placed on the altar.

☐ Walking Meditation

In many of the world's religions, such as Christian, Buddhist, and Judaic, the ritual of walking meditation is a very common practice. It allows the practitioner to enter into a very calm, focused state of mind. While in this contemplative state, one is able to access a greater quality of heartfulness as well as insight.

Buddhist monk Thich Nhat Hanh, in his group teachings here in the West, has created many group rituals involving walking meditation. He suggests starting with an in-breath taking a step forward with the right foot all the while silently repeating a phrase such as "I breathe in, I smile." The person pauses with both feet together. Then another step is taken with the opposite foot and the person says silently, "I breathe out, I release grief" — another pause, bringing both feet together before taking another step with the opposite foot.

With this deliberate and slow way of breathing, walking, and focusing the mind, one is able to extend the practice of mindfulness in all areas of one's life. It becomes especially helpful in times of grief and loss when the mind and emotions can become overwhelmed with grief. This practice offers a quiet place within.

□ Children and Teens

Children

Young children (7–10 years of age) usually have difficulty participating in ritual that is designed for adults. Their attention span is shorter, and their ability to conceptualize and reason differs from that of an adult. Children cannot be expected to participate in rituals the same way as do adults. They can, however, become engaged in ritual when it is designed for their age group and with their behavioral and emotional needs in mind. With a shorter time frame, and with an orientation toward play, children will respond and be affected in very positive ways.

Play rituals with puppets, stuffed toys, sandtray play, as well as drawing, coloring, making music, and sculpting with clay are several modalities that children will engage in naturally either by themselves or with other children. Because young children have little or no experience conceptualizing, the very concepts of loss or death and grief need to be explained and relayed to them in a different way from the way they are explained to adults.

In order to convey the meaning and reasons behind a tragedy that has occurred in a child's life and to have children share their feelings about this loss, designing ritual play is one way to have children share their feelings about death, illness, loss, and grief. These play sessions will help lessen their reactions of abandonment, fear, sorrow, and even guilt and anger which may surface for them. Ritual play will also help children say goodbye and commemorate a loved one's death or acknowledge a meaningful loss in their life.

With children the emotion of guilt can easily overburden them because of their magical thinking. For example, they sincerely believe they have the power to cause someone's death (Goldman, 2000). Children can be quick to feel they are the cause of any tragedy or loss that has occurred in their life. As the facilitator of a children's grief group, an important focus would be to normalize the experience of death and loss, as well as to identify the constellation of emotions for the children.

One of the roles of the facilitator is to act as the sacred witness to the ritual play the children create and to give the children honest answers to their questions using simple and direct language (Goldman, 2000). Another role is to be able to ask insightful questions. By asking questions of a child's puppet or stuffed toy animal instead of the child directly, the child has an opportunity to reflect on the question and try out different responses using their puppet or stuffed animal as their voice piece. In this way, feelings that may be buried or need a little encouragement to surface may be more easily accessed through the facilitator's questions. Puppets or stuffed animals are also a good way to have children talk to someone who has died.

Children's Ritual Play Session

Materials needed: hand puppets, stuffed animals, clay or Play-Doh, paints, brushes, and paper. Select a different play material each week for the children. One session might be puppets and the next week the children could play with clay.

Ritual

Children and facilitator can begin in a circle seated on chairs or on the floor. Have the children say their name and introduce their favorite animal to the group. Tell them why they are there and what you are planning for them in your time together.

Begin by asking one or two questions and allow the children to respond. The circle might need to dissolve into smaller groupings of children once restlessness begins. Remember to keep the time frame short to match their attention span.

Call everyone back to the circle and end each week with everyone holding hands and singing a song or playing a piece of music or dancing together in a circle. Coming back to the circle to end their time together is part of the ritual. The group could even create an altar together and each week the children could place their art "expressions" or other personal memorabilia, such as photos or favorite things they have created to honor their loss.

Teens

Teens and ritual go together. Teenagers relate well to symbolism and to the power inherent in symbol and metaphor. Ritual in a teen's life becomes a way to access the direct knowledge of a variety of emotional states. They learn about power and fear, for example, through rituals designed with their peers such as jumping over rivers and playing with fire and having sleepovers.

Teens have a high need for privacy. This trait can often keep them from experiencing or understanding personal loss and the host of emotions that can accompany tragedy and loss. Teenagers are emotionally very self-absorbed and usually seek advice only from their peers. They are awkward in exposing themselves to new learning situations. Adult experiences and insights are not readily listened to. It is sometimes difficult to have teens participate in a grief group for these very reasons. In addition, they are required to come into contact with other teens who may not be part of their social circle.

Teen Ritual

The previous listing of opening and closing rituals would all be suitable for a teen grief group. The description of the closing ritual would be very appropriate for this age group as well. As the facilitator you may want to invite the teens to design their own ritual once a level of bonding and safety among the members of the group has developed. Allowing them to feel a sense of ownership and creative input will assist in creating the bonding and safety. Allowing them to bring their own music goes a long way to winning a teen's trust.

Janet Shaw Rogers is cofounder of the concept design firm Rogers & Rosemary — a company dedicated to providing educational, emotional, and spiritual tools to guide people through times of personal change and transition. The Healing Box for Grief Loss and Endings has been designed to assist people in times of grief and loss. Janet is also a private consultant for women in business, providing leadership and vision for women entrepreneurs to realize their creative goals. She is also a yoga teacher of 25 years and leads programs for teen-aged girls.

Resources

Arrien, A. (1993). *The four fold way.* San Francisco: HarperCollins.

Bizou, B. (1999). *The joy of ritual.* New York: Golden Books.

Bolen, J. S. (1996). *Close to the bone.* New York: Scribner.

Goldman, L. (2000). *Life and loss* (2nd ed.). Philadelphia: Taylor & Frances.

Jeffreys, J. S. (2005). *Helping grieving people — When tears are not enough.* New York: Brunner-Routledge.

Neimeyer, R.A. (2000). *Lessons of loss: A guide to coping.* Keystone Heights, FL: Psychoeducational Resources.

Pucucci, M. (2005). *Ritual as resource.* Berkeley, CA: North Atlantic Books.

Rando, T. (1984). *Grief, dying and death: Clinical interventions for caregivers.* Champaign, IL: Research Press.

Saint-Exupèry, A. (1943). *The little prince.* Orlando, FL: Harcourt Brace Jovanovich.

Some, M.P. (1993). *Ritual.* Portland, OR: Swan/Raven.

Wolfelt, A. (1997). *The journey through grief: Reflections on healing.* Fort Collins, CO: Companion Press.

III

Section

Alternative Art Forms, Programs, and Stories of Art and Healing

14
CHAPTER

Deborah Koff-Chapin,
Carol McIntyre,
and Judith Koeleman

The Painters

What I recall clearly about the first true painting I ever did was the feeling that night that something real was happening.

—**Natalie Goldberg**, *Living Color*

☐ Touch Drawing in Grief Work: Drawing Out Your Soul
Deborah Koff-Chapin

I discovered Touch Drawing in revelatory play in 1974. A friend asked me to help clean up in the art school print shop. In the moment before wiping, I playfully moved my fingertips on a paper towel that had been placed over an inked glass plate. As I lifted the paper towel off the inked surface, I saw the traces of my touch imprinted on the underside of the towel. A rush of creative energy flooded my system. I realized that this simple, direct process had the potential to become a new and powerful form of creative expression. I felt called to share this dynamic process with the world.

FIGURES 14.1–14.3 Creative expression. (Photos courtesy of Deborah Koff-Chapin.)

As I have introduced Touch Drawing over the years, this calling has been affirmed time and time again. When offered basic instructions and a safe, supportive environment, people take to Touch Drawing like fish to water. Effortlessly, their hands dance upon the surface of the paper, translating their feelings into form and image. As I gaze across a roomful of people doing Touch Drawing, I feel like I am witnessing a sacred act: people gazing deeply into the inner mirror of their souls.

In a medium as immediate and direct as Touch Drawing, new channels of expression are opened, enabling feelings to flow forth uncensored. The act of *creating* with these feelings provides more than a purely cathartic release. It unleashes vibrant healing forces that guide the psyche toward coherence. Whatever darkness or pain may surface is fuel for the creative fire. Each successive drawing reveals another layer of awareness. With these imprints of the soul now on paper, nonverbal messages from the psyche are available for reflection by the conscious mind. Touch Drawing is a practice of creative, psychological, and spiritual integration.

These qualities make Touch Drawing a natural for grief work. I would like to share a few stories to give a sense of the power of this process. Tinky Timmons of Charlotte, NC shares her personal story as well as her experience doing Touch Drawing with others:

> When Deborah introduced me to Touch Drawing, I was going through an extremely difficult time in my life. My husband was leaving me for a younger woman, my best friend had passed away from cancer, and I was starting the process of healing from 17 years of child abuse. It was all I could do to breathe. My first experience of Touch Drawing was a huge turning point in my journey to healing from so much grief.

FIGURES 14.4–14.6 Images of a woman Touch Drawing. (Photos courtesy of Deborah Koff-Chapin.)

Grief is so overwhelming and is a hard emotion to explain even to one-self. The reasons for grieving are as diverse as each individual and the response to grief is multifaceted. Therefore, it is hard to find anything that works for all types of people. Touch Drawing seems to work for everyone — no matter what level of grief they may be in, what age they are, or what artistic abilities they may have. I have used Touch Drawing with cancer patients who have never even thought of drawing or painting, but just need to release something that is so devastating. When they are in the process of Touch Drawing, they are in a space of no pain, no grief, no suffering. They are watching their feelings appear out of the paper, and by gazing at the paper they seem to feel more at peace.

I have used Touch Drawing with abused children, and even though they don't know the depth of what they are doing, the process often brings tears they didn't know they had. That has been the case for myself as well. I have seen things coming out of my paper that amaze me and somehow show me how I am feeling even if I am not aware of the feeling at the time I am drawing. Often, I see a freedom and lightness there. I see an innocence of what my hands have done and realize that innocence came from a place deep within and it heals me in a way that no spoken word can.

I have cried while Touch Drawing, I have laughed while Touch Drawing, but most of all, I have healed while Touch Drawing. It is a powerful tool that one can use to heal from grief. It has facilitated my healing process and helped to bring me to a place of true inner peace!

Valerie McCarney is a Hospice volunteer and an Expressive Art Therapist in Saratoga Springs, NY. She had been using Touch Drawing with several of her other clients when she was asked to do a workshop for Hospice. She shares what happened:

> There were several people in the nursing home living with advanced ALS and multiple sclerosis. They had all lived there for a couple of years and had become very close. Then within six weeks, three of them died. This was very scary and sad for the remaining patients. The staff was worried because, although the patients were all upset, they were not expressing their grief. Instead, they were in a deep trauma state. (Figure 14.7)

FIGURE 14.7   Woman in a wheelchair touch driving. (Photo courtesy of Valerie McCarney.)

Because of my background, Hospice asked me if I would be willing to do an art session with them. Since many can barely move, I felt that Touch Drawing would work the best. We had volunteers helping, lifting their arms, and putting their hands on the papers. But once there, they could move their fingers around on the paper. I played different kinds of music and we talked about their feelings. Once the process began the energy in the room just shifted. Some of the people started to cry and express emotions that they had been holding in. To see people who were mostly paralyzed creating beautiful pieces of artwork was just wonderful. There was a man with advanced ALS and everything he drew looked like a spinal cord. I was told later he had been a chiropractor.

After we worked for about 45 minutes, I brought out a "word bowl" and the patients, with the help of the volunteers, chose words that expressed their feelings. We used glue sticks to put the words on their artwork. I took home the artwork and put it on foam board and brought it back to the nursing home for them to hang. They were all so proud. When the grief feelings came up again for them the social workers would take them down to the paintings to process, using the art and the words expressed as catalysts. It was truly healing for all of us involved. I find that for myself, having lost my mother last year and my father being in the dying process right now, Touch Drawing has been a way for me to be with all the feelings of grief and anticipatory grief. It is very healing and therapeutic.

Touch Drawing is serving Tinky and Valerie both in their work with others and in their own grief process. Without self-conscious effort, feelings of grief seem to naturally find their way to the surface to be reflected upon and transformed. Janyt Piercy shares how this occurred for a participant in a workshop she was facilitating:

One of my participants ended up doing some unexpected grief work. This woman was well into drawing and was doing faces. All of a sudden she came to me with a Touch Drawing she had just created. The woman was sobbing and showed me the drawing, explaining that the face was her dead mother's face. I held a space for her to talk and to cry as she needed to. This was a huge breakthrough for her. She was so moved by the experience that she went on to use Touch Drawing as a valuable tool in her grief process. She had felt her mother's presence manifest in the Touch Drawing session in the appearance of the face. (Figures 14.8 through 14.10)

FIGURES 14.8–14.10 Touch Drawings of womens' faces. (Photos courtesy of Deborah Koff-Chapin.)

Kathleen Horne (MA, REAT) describes a similar experience of drawing her mother's face, eight months after her death. She also did some reflective writing after the experience, demonstrating the power of verbal expression that has been catalyzed by the nonverbal experience of Touch Drawing:

> I could feel, as my Touch Drawing process deepened, the hovering around of grief. Suddenly, as I put my hands on the paper and began to draw, it was as though I was stroking her face as she lay in the hospital bed. The tears unleashed and I continued to draw — drawing after drawing, crying, and in awe as the series unfolded — taking me to a new place in my grieving process. My head was disengaged and my hands brought forth the wisdom. When I was done, I was done. Then this writing came:

> Grief appears, with an urgent intensity.
> Soft, and insistent.
> Grief of the mother. Grief of the daughter.
> Both aware that the loving angel of
> death is announcing its arrival.
> A space of timeless time, a space between worlds.
> I sit, you lie, in waiting.
> Touch: the only means of communication.
> The deep lines of life vanish from your
> countenance in preparation for leaving.
> Ultimate perfection.
> The cycle of return.
> The time draws near.

As you are saying goodbye to the Dance of Life
We gather around you, speaking in tears
and moans, laughter and silence.
The last Breath comes.
I let you go.
I have no choice.
I bow down before the eternal flame of Wisdom.
Your body is offered forth
Cradled, and at rest at last.
Love Holds.

Christina Wilson (MA, CEAT) uses Touch Drawing in the bereavement program she created for Hospice of the North Coast in Carlsbad, CA. Here she describes the format of her work with groups:

The session begins with the participants voluntarily disclosing to the group what they are struggling with in their grief (such as sorrow, anger, physical symptoms or illness, fear, anxiety). If a person wants to do this privately they can do so in their journal. Each participant lights a candle and sets an intention for their healing. The candle is moved to a safe table away from the drawing materials. The atmosphere in the room is quiet and subdued. I keep the lights low; bright enough to see everything, but not bright. I play very soft, meditative music such as the kind used for yoga. (Figure 14.11)

Then we begin Touch Drawing — at first with eyes closed, then open. Participants are encouraged to begin another drawing as soon as one is finished. We continue this for about 45 minutes or more. Then, we set aside our drawing materials, clean our hands, and begin to journal about our Touch Drawing experience. Usually there are one or two images that are deeply meaningful to the participants, so I ask each participant to choose a drawing and dialogue with it in their journal. Since we use the Creative Journal method (originated by Lucia Capacchione, Ph.D., ATR, REAT) the image speaks with the nondominant hand in the first person. The participant can then have a conversation with the image(s). Using Touch Drawing in this way has been very helpful for the bereaved in the groups. One participant who had lost her young daughter became more deeply in touch with her anger and rage through the Touch Drawing images that emerged. She then went on to integrate the images into other modalities of expressive arts.

To close the session, participants voluntarily share about their process and any new insights, feelings, observations they might have. They remarked that the experience of Touch Drawing is something that they feel takes them into a very centered place, very deep and calm. This is so helpful for the bereaved as they journey through the rollercoaster of grief. The candles are left burning until all participants have left, as a sign of their hope for healing, and to commemorate their loved ones who have died.

☐ Instructions for Touch Drawing

I offer the following instructions to support you in creating a meaningful and healing experience for the people you work with. I highly recommend that you do Touch Drawing on a personal level before sharing it in a public setting. The deeper your connection with the process, the more authentic your transmission of it will be. I also suggest you enrich the information presented here with the educational media created by The Center for Touch Drawing. I particularly recommend the *Touch Drawing Facilitator Workbook*, the audio CD *Touch Drawing: A Guided Experience*, and the video *Through the Veil*. These media were created to support you in having a deep experience of Touch Drawing. Find out more at http://www.touchdrawing.com.

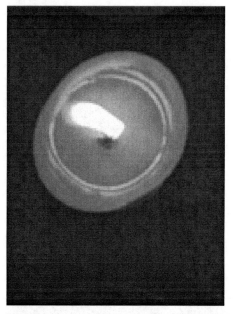

FIGURE 14.11   Candle. (Photo courtesy of Deborah Koff-Chapin.)

FIGURE 14.12   The drawing process. (Photos courtesy of Deborah Koff-Chapin.)

Technique

Touch Drawing is a simple yet profound process. All you do is roll oil paint onto a smooth surface and lay a sheet of paper on top of the paint. Wherever you touch the paper, an impression is made on the underside. A multitude of drawings can be created in one sitting. Each is a stepping-stone to the next, guiding you deeper into your self. It takes no special skill or artistic confidence to do Touch Drawing. All it takes is the willingness to be with yourself and allow whatever arises in the moment to flow through your fingertips. (Figure 14.12)

Materials

I cannot emphasize enough the importance of having the correct materials in the appropriate quantities. Touch Drawing can facilitate an experience of transparency between the art materials, the body, emotions, and spirit. But a glitch in choice or quantity of paint or paper can set participants up for a very frustrating experience. Try out the materials yourself before using them with a group.

- **Oil paint in a selection of colors.** A new product that is particularly practical is water mixable oil paint, which is easy to wash out. Acrylics dry too fast. A choice of colors is good, but not necessary. Let people select one or two colors that appeal to them to roll onto the board. Student Grade oil paints are not toxic. No toxic solvents are used in Touch Drawing.
- **Soft rubber roller.** The official term is a *printmaking brayer.* One per person is best, but one can be shared by two or three people if necessary.
- **A piece of plastic or any smooth, nonabsorbent surface for the drawing board.** Possibilities are Formica, dry erase board, Plexiglas, laminate, school lunch trays … experiment! One for each participant is important, so everyone can draw the whole time.

- **Enough lightweight paper to allow everyone to draw freely.** Think in terms of 25 to 30 sheets per person for a drawing session of an hour or so: less if it is shorter, more if it is longer. Wrapping tissue is the most economical and sensitive to the touch — and you can see the drawings emerge from your fingertips because it is translucent. But any other paper will work — newsprint, bond, vellum, sketch paper, etc. It is vital that everyone feels they can do as many drawings as they want. The freedom to express each moment in image without judgment is greatly supported by the fact that one is not limited in the number of drawings one can do. The movement from one sheet to another in a continuous flow is one of the keys to the power of Touch Drawing.

Preparing the Board

Put some thin dabs of paint on the drawing board. Roll the paint until you have an overall, smooth thin layer on the board. Place a sheet of paper on top of the paint. If you have put on too much paint, the paper will begin absorbing paint on contact. If this is the case, rub your hands all over the sheet to blot off the excess paint. Then put on a fresh sheet of paper. When you have the correct amount of paint on the board, it will take the pressure of your fingertips for the paint to adhere to the paper. You do not usually need to add new paint until you have done a few drawings. Just roll the board smooth between drawings. (Figures 14.13 through 14.15)

Privacy While Drawing

Each person should feel that they have the privacy to disappear into his or her own drawing journey. If someone is looking over one's shoulders, it is very inhibiting. Discourage social interaction between participants or any comments about the artwork during the drawing time. This will create a

FIGURE 14.13–14.15 Preparing the board. (Photos courtesy of Deborah Koff-Chapin.)

space in which participants can go much more deeply into the nonverbal realms.

Musical Support

When people are just getting started with Touch Drawing, it is helpful to have some musical background while they draw. It helps to keep them focused and moving. Once a group is more experienced with the process, it is wonderful to also draw in silence.

My audio CD, *Touch Drawing: A Guided Experience,* has gentle "heartbeat" drumming and chimes with occasional verbal suggestions similar to the ones I offer here. There is, of course, a wealth of incredible recorded music for you to explore. Anything goes, depending on the group you are working with. You may allow teens to bring in some of their favorites; if you are working with older adults, music from their era may help to set them at ease.

Offering Suggestions

There is a very fine line between supporting people in order to help them to enter the process and controlling their experience. When I offer suggestions, I try to keep them oriented to entry points rather than to content. This is not a guided visualization. It is a personal inner journey in which unique images arise from each individual. My focus is to direct people's attention inward, to support them to draw from their awareness in the moment. I always tell them that, while I may make occasional suggestions on approaches to drawing, they should not follow my suggestions if something else is moving through them in that moment. It is most important to follow their own inner impulses and move in their own timing.

Allow enough time for exploration of each suggestion before making another. Try to present them as gently and unobtrusively as possible. After a while, you can drop all verbal suggestions and allow participants to disappear into their process. Once they are engaged, they don't need any help knowing what to draw. As a matter of fact, they may never need any suggestions! Here are some possibilities:

Turning Inward

Take a few moments to center yourself before beginning to draw. Become aware of your body sensations, feelings, and thoughts. Accept whatever you are experiencing in the moment as your starting point. In the stillness before you begin drawing, turn to your source of spiritual sustenance and open to receive support. If you have a specific issue you would like to work with, bring it to mind and then let it go; offer it into the sacred space.

Beginning to Draw

Start by focusing on the physical experience of moving your hands on the page. Let go of the idea of "drawing a picture." Let your hands dance on the page, seeing how these incredible living tools can make marks in different ways. Try moving both hands together as well as using your dominant and nondominant hands individually. Explore the use of fingernails, fingertips, and palms of the hands. It is good to begin with your eyes closed, and explore both open and closed-eye drawing throughout the session.

When you have completed one gesture, pull the paper off the board. Barely glance at the image that has appeared on the page. Roll the paint on the board so it is smooth again. Place a fresh sheet of paper on the board. Allow yourself to enter a rhythmic process of moving your hands on the paper, pulling the paper off the board, rolling the paint smooth, putting on fresh paper, and touching your hands to the paper again.

As you complete each successive drawing, you can place them one on top of another in a pile. If you have used a thick layer of paint, your drawings may stick together. Put a clean sheet of paper on top of particularly wet drawings. (Figures 14.16 through 14.18)

Draw Whatever You Feel!

If at any time you feel stuck, draw what *that* feels like. Scratch up a sheet of paper if you want to. If you become afraid of what is emerging, give form to the fear. If you are finding the experience ecstatically joyful, let the feel-

FIGURES 14.16–14.18   Drawing learning. (Photos courtesy of Deborah Koff-Chapin.)

ing of joy flow out your fingertips and onto the page. Try not to let the idea of "making a picture" bring up your judging mind. If it does, just notice that your inner critic is talking, and don't let it run the show. Instead, try to draw the feelings the inner critic rings up, or draw a picture of the inner critic! Then go on the next drawing. Accept your feelings, *whatever* they may be, and translate them onto the paper. If you are doing this you are truly doing Touch Drawing.

When you *create with* your feelings, they will no longer block you. You will release them and move on to the next stage of your process. Be open to the unknown. When you have closed the drawing session, be sure to roll the leftover paint on your board smooth so that it is a good, flat surface for future Touch Drawing. (Figures 14.19 and 14.20)

Inner Face

If you would like to do so at this time, focus your attention on your face, how you experience it from the inside. Through the movement of your fingertips, you can project the sensations within your face out onto the page. Do this with your eyes closed at first, to more clearly focus on the sensations. It might feel as if you are projecting your face through your fingertips onto the page, or like you are taking off a mask. When you have completed one tracing of your inner face, bring your awareness to your face once again and do the same. Though you are engaged in the same process, the next face will be a unique expression of the moment. This simple form of drawing one face after another can continue deepening as you draw multiple faces. After a while it can feel as if one is looking into an inner mirror. The faces may even begin to feel as if they are living beings arising from another dimension onto the page.

A face can be created with the simplest of marks. You do not have to draw in a "realistic" style to create a powerful face. We are all capable of creating the archetypal image that we were first imprinted with as we

FIGURES 14.19–14.20   Inner face touch drawing. (Photos courtesy of Deborah Koff-Chapin.)

came into this world. All human cultures have represented the face in some way. The Inner Face is a core centering practice in Touch Drawing.

Inner Body Sensations

Allow your attention to move from your face to your body, either a part of the body or your whole body image. If you are feeling a physical pain, you can draw that sensation. You might translate body sensations into a recognizable human form or into abstract patterns and shapes.

Imaginal Body

Imagine that you are doing something that truly expresses how you feel in the moment. Really get in touch with how it feels to be in this position, or move in this way. Draw yourself from this awareness. Your "imaginal body" may take other than human form — animal, plant, element, landscape, abstraction. This approach can really open the door to your personal language of interior images.

Relationship or Situation

Bring to mind a relationship or situation in your life and just allow feelings and images to arise and be released onto the drawing board. Trust your intuition and try not to censor anything that comes to you as you draw.

Cloud Gazing

Spend a few moments just gazing at the page. Be open to "seeing" an image in the paper or the patterns of ink that bleed through. In this approach, you may have the feeling that the image is revealing itself to you. It is like seeing images in the clouds!

Ending the Drawing Portion of the Session

Be gentle as you bring people to closure. They have been in a very deep space. Give participants a few minutes warning by suggesting they begin to bring their drawing session to a close about five to seven minutes prior to closing time. About two minutes before closing, suggest that they bring their final drawing to completion.

At closing time, tell them to roll their boards smooth to clear them for the next time they will be used. Be sure participants don't try to wipe the paint off the board, as this may leave behind a strong textured surface. This act in itself can be done as a meditation to create completion of their process.

After the board is rolled out, have them place a clean sheet of paper on top of the paint and roll the brayer over the paper to both take up excess paint from the board and remove excess paint from the brayer. Be sure they take the paper off the board when done, or it may stick like glue and ruin the board for future use.

Viewing Drawings

To draw and to look can be enough. But reflecting verbally on the drawings, either through talking or writing can be very powerful. Witnessing one another's drawings after the session is enormously grounding. Although I would never force someone to share their drawings with anyone else, I always recommend that they do this. It is not uncommon for someone to feel like nothing much happened in their drawing experience. People who feel this way usually express great gratitude for the sharing time. Being witnessed helps them to step back and see more objectively what happened in their Touch Drawing session. It is good to have times when participants reflect upon their drawings in private as well. But until someone can appreciate their own visual language, the energetic attention of others is very supportive.

Physical Set-Up for Sharing

At the end of the session, participants should pick up their whole pile of drawings and flip it over. This places the first drawing on top. Seeing the drawings in the order in which they were created is much more powerful than viewing them randomly or from last to first. The organic process of transformation is much more apparent.

Witnessing the Images

I recommend intimate sharing in groups of two to three. When you first have people look through their drawings with partners, encourage them to take great care to be sensitive to one another. Many people have had negative experiences with others commenting on their "art." Remind them that Touch Drawing is first and foremost an internal process. The images are just the tracings of that process left behind, like footprints in the sand. You might suggest that each person who is about to share their drawings state their preference. Do they want to hear the comments of others or do they

FIGURES 14.21–14.23   Looking at each other's drawings. (Photos courtesy of Deborah Koff-Chapin.)

want to only share their own story as they go through their drawings? Or would they prefer to do the witnessing in silence? What you are trying to do is assist people to move out of the standard mode of looking at "art" to focus on insight rather than form. (Figures 14.21 through 14.23)

More important than interpreting the drawings is *deep seeing*. Giving deep, equal, and honoring attention to each individual's expression is the most empowering thing you can do. Truly "seeing" one another's images is seeing their souls. It is a rare gift to offer this level of attention to one another.

Writing to Reflect On Drawings

Writing is a natural adjunct to Touch Drawing. It can help an emerging awareness become more conscious. Even the simplest act of creating titles opens a new awareness. You can suggest that participants look through their drawings in the order in which they were created, and write a word or phrase on each one. It can be very enlightening to string the titles together on a separate sheet and see what the "whole" is saying.

FIGURE 14.24   Writing about Touch Drawing. (Photo courtesy of Deborah Koff-Chapin.)

You can also have participants look through their drawings and select one or two that particularly intrigue them. Suggest that they imagine that the drawing is a "being" and ask it to speak for itself in the first person. They may ask specific questions and explore a dialogue with the image. Their words may also take the form of poetry or a story. Another intriguing approach to writing is to use the nondominant hand. They might like to write out a question pertaining to the image with their dominant hand, and answer with their nondominant hand. This process can tap an aspect of the self that is rarely given voice. (Figure 14.24)

Shirley Silva is a certified thanatologist who used Touch Drawing to move through her own grief process. She shares some of her thoughts on how she used writing to deepen her relationship to her drawings:

> I carefully studied the meaning of every symbol or figure contained in the drawing, its relationship to other figures and to my grieving process. It was very important to me to contemplate these images in private and to document my appreciations and reflections in my spiritual diary. I reviewed my notes as time went by to determine improvements or to add new experiences with Touch Drawing. I would explore what the drawing revealed to me in terms of physical, emotional, mental, spiritual, or social needs concerning my loss and grief. Once the need was identified, I would write a plan of action to comfort or resolve that need and do it. I would then do another Touch Drawing session to see what my inner self was telling me about my metamorphosis. I now use Touch Drawing with my clients and they are amazed when they get in touch with their marvelous inner world by means of Touch Drawing. The healing and spiritual impact is transcendental if you work for it.

Using Movement and Sound

There are many other ways to tap the richness of Touch Drawings. You can suggest that each person select a drawing and position it on the wall or floor in such a way that they can move freely in response to it. Have them gaze at the image in stillness. Suggest that they begin to feel as if they are the image, and go into a position or movement that expresses it. They can make sounds or speak words that may come to them. Allow time for them to follow the expression through whatever transformations they are moved to make. (Figure 14.25)

FIGURE 14.25   Sharing images. (Photo courtesy of Deborah Koff-Chapin.)

Sharing Images with the Whole Group

After intimate sharing and personal processing, it can be wonderful to bring some of the images out for the whole group to see. The simplest approach is to have people select a single image or small series that they would like to hold up to be witnessed by the group. You could also have them lay the drawings out on the floor, if the room is large enough. It can be very moving for the group to hear the story behind the images being shared, or a writing that was inspired by the drawing. If the one who is being witnessed would like to hear the comments of others, they can then request perceptions and insights.

Closure of the Session

Some form of closure is important to help participants disengage from the collective energies and to support them to integrate the experience into their lives. It can be as simple as a moment of silence with those intentions. I also like to suggest that people get in touch with something from the session that they would like to nurture. I see this brief process as the opportunity to germinate the seeds that came to them through the experience. Giving thanks, either verbally or silently, helps to ground and close the collective field as well.

Clean-Up

Most people get only a little paint on their hands. Soap is fine for washing hands. Old toothbrushes or nail brushes will get out the last bits of paint.

Drawing boards take the paint more evenly once they have a dried layer of paint on them, so do not wash off the paint after workshops. They do need to be cared for properly, though. At the end of a session, check to be sure participants have rolled their boards smooth, blotted (not wiped) the excess paint, and removed the paper from the board.

Taking Drawings Home

Drawings can be rolled up and wrapped in a clean sheet of paper or a kitchen garbage bag to keep them safe in transit. Suggest that participants go through their drawings when they get home. It is helpful to number and date each series of drawings.

Recommend that people look at their images again when they have had a little distance from the drawing session. Just like with dreams, the drawings are appreciated more over time. It can be very touching to share the images with a close and trusted friend or family member. Suggest to your participants that they share their drawings in a focused and honoring setting, so that their viewing partner can appreciate the fullness of their experience.

Some More Stories

To close, I share a few more stories of healing grief through Touch Drawing. Margaret Wellens from Parkside, Australia, attended the five-day Touch Drawing Gathering in the summer of 2006. Inspired by the beauty of a bird's song, she had this experience of releasing long-held grief: (Figures 14.26 and 14.27)

FIGURES 14.26–14.27   Sharing stories. (Photos courtesy of Deborah Koff-Chapin.)

My first Touch Drawing experience was most significant for me because the process helped me to reconnect with a repressed grief that had been buried in my psyche for almost 60 years. When I was a child my younger sister, who was one of twins, died from pneumonia as a toddler. It was a quick death but a shock to us all. At that time, I thought everyone would cry over the loss of this joyful and innocent toddler. But to my surprise no one was allowed to cry or grieve, including my mother. I was upset. In fact, my sadness was actually choking my throat. I held back my tears like the others as we were told "don't cry." Years later, I found out it was a belief and custom for the older members of the family not to cry over the death of a baby. Since that time, I learned how to repress and push this feeling into my subconscious, which later manifested as symptoms of nasal congestion and hay fever.

One afternoon, when we were drawing outside in a tranquil and beautiful environment, I heard a bird sing a most spirited song. I was fascinated by its beauty and listened intensely to each sound and its echo. After a few moments of listening deeply to the bird song, a feeling of deep sadness came all over my being and my throat was sore. I had no idea what was happening nor where this feeling was coming from. I just felt sad and wanted to cry. At that moment, I just followed my feeling and drew what I felt, allowing the inner feelings and sensations to pour forth. As I was doing that, the past memories reawakened and images unfolded like a movie. The expressions of fear, anxiety, and hope on the faces of the loved ones when my sister died came back to me in a flash. I kept drawing, creating pictures to express and to release the sad feeling until I felt calmed and peaceful in my heart. The process of Touch Drawing helped me to reconnect with my deep feelings, releasing long held grief, and to break down the controlling pattern in my psyche. It is a medium for healing and transformation. It is also fun and I love it!

Carol Chappell from Norwich, Connecticut shares a story which communicates of the power of holding clear intentions and then letting go and allowing the deeper realities respond.

My first experience with Touch Drawing was a weekend workshop. My sister, Mary Ann, had died six months earlier, of ovarian cancer. I was her primary care person. She and I had just really connected as true sisters the year prior to her death. Part of my reason for wanting to experience Touch Drawing was the thought that it may help my very deep grief.

During one drawing session, at times, I would think of Mary Ann and ask for help from Spirit. When we were done, we paired up and

FIGURES 14.28–30   Images of butterfly drawing. (Photo courtesy of Deborah Koff-Chapin.)

looked at each other's drawings. That was significant, as my partner saw them through different eyes and that gave me a deeper understanding of the meaning. It was after that review that it suddenly hit me that the last three drawings of the session were of Mary Ann. The first (I thought I was drawing a person singing) was the face of grief — what I was experiencing; the second was Mary Ann's release to Spirit (there was a butterfly shape that seemed to be going upward to light); and the third was the face of a youth — happy and peaceful (which is how I always see Mary Ann when I connect with her now in my meditation). I felt in awe of the communication given to me by the Spirit within. (Figures 14.28 through 14.30)

What was so intriguing to me is that when I was doing these three drawings, I wasn't thinking of her consciously. The Spirit within me came through quietly with its own message in spite of my conscious thought processes.

Shemaya Blauer of Portland, Oregon (shemaya_toyou@yahoo.com) used Touch Drawing to help her deal with the collective grief of the Holocaust.

As a Jew one of my struggles has been how to experience and express the immense emotions that engulf me as I continue to learn about the Holocaust. In 1997 when I visited Auschwitz with my family similar fears arose as to whether I had the emotional vocabulary to walk through a concentration camp. Wandering through Auschwitz, I didn't know how to feel or how to make sense of it all. I wanted to be as open as possible to the experience yet didn't know how to do that without falling apart. A lot of the experience was really numbing, overwhelming. As we moved from one scene to another, my body fell into silence and I felt motionless.

In my hotel room a couple of hours later, Touch Drawing allowed me to move into those places where my body carried the silence and tap into that. In Touch Drawing, I was able to move back through the experience of walking through the gas chambers, past the ovens, on the grounds. I could allow my body to remember, to have that deep sense of knowing, and to create a form to hold it in. TD allowed me to move again, making those experiences mobile and alive. The pictures were not my best drawings. Though I'm attached to making something that looks good, I know that TD goes beyond that. It lets me go into my experience and have a handle to bring it to a different level. (Figures 14.31 through 14.34)

After drawing these images I remember feeling as though I had released some of the shroud of emotions that covered my being. Although nothing had changed and the unbelievable magnitude of the Holocaust had occurred, I felt that touch drawing had given me a larger perspective and a different way of bearing the weight of my emotions. As I return to these drawings almost 10 years later they still reflect the unbelievable horror of the Holocaust and provide a language beyond words to express my feelings.

FIGURE 14.31 Many Faces: I cannot look at them even now as they are starring at me. Who were these innocent souls, treasured mothers and fathers, sisters, and brothers? (Photo courtesy of Deborah Koff-Chapin.)

FIGURE 14.32 Innocence: 6 million innocent lives were lost, and the world lost its innocence too. (Photo courtesy of Deborah Koff-Chapin.)

FIGURE 14.33   Too Much to Bear: Enormous Pain. (Photo courtesy of Deborah Koff-Chapin.)

FIGURE 14.34   Symbols of Grief: How do I find meaning in my grief? Where do I put this huge burden that I carry? Symbols of Judaism appeared in my drawing: the tree of life and the menorah seem to hold space to honor those who perished. The train tracks are reminders of the gas chambers. (Photo courtesy of Deborah Koff-Chapin.)

I would like to close with the story of Marsha Roach Arbogast. She is an artist and writer. Here she shares how the natural integration of personal, cultural and spiritual healing that can happen through the creative process:

> I am a bicultural woman, Commanche/Cherokee and Caucasian. My grief around the child abuse and loss of culture I experienced had brought me to very dark places. I began to draw and paint to bring my psychic, somatic, and spiritual experiences to a visual state. The profound sense of touch I experienced in a Touch Drawing workshop deepened a tactile journey to one of alchemy, transformation, and transcendence.

FIGURE 14.35   Healing through drawing. (Photo courtesy of Carol McIntyre.)

My drawings revealed both my "Earth Daddy," my abuser, and my spiritual father in two separate pieces. The father that I found in a shamanic journey also appeared. I clearly saw that I had found safety and that I loved being Indian, that I had power and voice. I saw the beast of my own being and went down, down, down to the old places. I cried with the visions that appeared that day, and knew them to be the strange stirrings of my bumping heart.

In Touch Drawing, I entered a state of integration, healing and wholeness. I dialogued with my drawings, made copies of them, collaged the poetry onto the pieces. My senses told me that there is no way to lose if I lose myself in my art; for when I am lost that way, I am never more found or authentic. (Figure 14.35)

As a facilitator of creative process for grief work, you have taken on sacred work. I wish you the greatest blessings in all your endeavors! I hope to hear some of your experiences using Touch Drawing. Please sign the mailing list at http://www.touchdrawing.com and let us know you are facilitating. We will then be able to support your work through our e-newsletter, online special interest groups, and Touch Drawing Facilitator updates. (Figure 14.36)

Deborah Koff-Chapin is Founding Director of the Center for Touch Drawing. She is creator of *SoulCards 1 & 2*, and author of *Drawing Out Your Soul* and *The Touch Drawing Facilitator Workbook*. She has served on the board of directors of the International Expressive Art Therapy Association and is adjunct professor at California Institute of Integral Studies and Wisdom University.

FIGURE 14.36   Deborah Koff-Chapin with a touch drawing. (Photo courtesy of Deborah Koff-Chapin.)

☐ Painting the Dragon: A Group Painting Experience
Carol McIntyre

Finding one's passion through self-expression can be a daunting and exciting search. Creativity is a natural wellspring that moves through us just as does breathing the air around us. It's a journey that many long for and few are able to face on their own.

In this chapter I will explore how a group facilitates creative self-expression by describing some of our structure and process, also using some of the thoughts and feelings of our ongoing painting group that meets on Monday mornings. Acting as midwives, Barbara Schlumberger and I have facilitated a core group of painters with the group expanding and contracting over the last seven years. I have also run a group for my clients that maintains a core of about eight women. The group focuses on process rather than product. When process becomes the focus it allows for the individual to drop into the flow of one's being, which produces a sense of the ground moving out from underneath the painter. We will look at how this stirs and motivates the primitive energies from the depths of one's being to be expressed through the creative flow.

As we gather for our sessions, we first meet in the talking room to set the circle and the intention for the day. We will talk about how open or how closed one feels in her creative process that day and perhaps will volunteer something from her outer life as well. One of the intentions that we all hold as a group is to maintain safety for this exploration which comes in various forms. The most important one we have is not to comment on each other's paintings; a good comment can stop a person's process just as a negative one might.

Actually, one voice that does begin to chat almost immediately as one begins to paint is the judge or the critic. This will begin to drown out the intuition if we don't keep the class mostly in silence and free from the normal exchanges that people seem to make about their creative work. In order to allow the maximum amount of freedom, we do not show or share our stories about our paintings at the end of class. At times the women may need to paint something sexual, aggressive, or just something that is taboo for them. To allow difficult issues or emotions to happen the conditioning and voice of the judge has to be disregarded; we can't believe or even really listen to it.

As the intuition begins to take over the brush moves in a spontaneous way. This usually takes a while before one can relax into one's body sufficiently to begin to move from that place, the place of the dream maker. This is an awakened dream state that allows one to tap into the deepest flow of one's being; a deep meditative state.

We are not talking about just splashing paint on paper, although at times that may be necessary as well, but allowing a curious inventive exploration of the symbolic realms that comes in a caring and direct way with the brush. As this happens there may be material from the past that begins to manifest in the present moment. It brings with it the emotions that the individual will look to the group for support. Here are some thoughts and feeling from our group that they have shared with each other.

Gail says, "Together we create a rich soup of feelings and experiences which words cannot fully express, but by painting together there is a visceral feeling of the richness of what we share. We each unconsciously provide the flavors and textures that make the soup such a nutritious support for one another." Esther follows with a similar thought, "Life is a solitary exercise and in a group it can be held in this soup of exploration."

Some speak of the intense aloneness that they experience as they dive into the unknown and feel attracted to being in the group so as to be in that groundless state. Heather states, "For me, the act of creation has always been a way for me to dialogue with the Great Mystery and my own soul. For the most part it's a private process. When I allow myself to expand this ritual into a group setting it takes on a whole new meaning — of ritual and connection. The ritual of painting in a group opens and expands my awareness to others and our interconnectedness. Our combined intention creates both a powerful gateway into the mystery and a stronger container to hold each other as we face the Unknown." (Figure 14.37)

Jolene says, "The group provides a safety net, community, creative energy, emotional and creative support, the ability to be witnessed. It's a scary journey into the unknown. Generally my travels are not smooth and graceful but the group gives me courage by way of silence and observation. Although we paint in silence the energies that are created in the room are quite remarkable, energy that I can 'hitch' a ride on. The energy

FIGURE 14.37 Woman painting. (Photo courtesy of Carol McIntyre.)

FIGURE 14.38 Community of painting. (Photo courtesy of Carol McIntyre.)

of others helps me keep my brush moving. The group brings me out of isolation and gives me a sense of belonging."

As Caroline reflects on what makes the group work for her she states, "The group can provide a congenial and supportive atmosphere in which to face dragons; to explore the corners of our psyche; and to express the truths contained in our deepest beings. It provides a holding environment and is a reminder we are not alone. The spontaneous laughter and tears are a measure of the heart of us all." (Figure 14.38)

Most talk about the witnessing, not being judged, the silence and the empathy that the group provides. At each session we meet in the talking room before we paint in order to set the circle and again after we paint for a closing of the circle. It allows each person to check in with what their concerns and hopes are for the day and to set their intention. The check-in is usually not too much about material from their outside life more from their inner experience in the moment and their process about painting. Once in a while there will be a need by an individual to reveal more, but the main focus is on the here and now. This allows for the group "to anchor me, kind of like being in a river together, all connected by the current," according to Kate. Kathleen speaks about "being drawn into an energetic instinctual level that allows for the empathy to flow."

Throughout the thoughts and feelings and written words of the group there was a consistent mention of the group holding and allowing the courage to be there in the individual. The group has the capacity to do just the opposite as well, but in this structure and with the intention to hold and support, it allows the painter to take these basic destructive energies and also the light forces to the piece of paper.

In the center of the room is a table with over two dozen different colors of paint. On the wall we use large sheets of paper, from there we move back and forth between the table and the painting. We supply palettes for mixing more colors as well. We use a professional quality of nontoxic Prang tempera paints. In actuality you don't even need the paints; a pen and paper is enough. But it is the colors that help people to free some childlike part of themselves, the part that loves color and the feelings that come from them. (Figure 14.39 and 14.40)

FIGURES 14.39–14.40   Paints in the classroom. (Photos courtesy of Carol McIntyre.)

The facilitators act as midwives, holding the intention set by the group and the individual. They help deliver those stated goals of deep self-expression. In order to reach those levels of self-expression there needs to be a high level of surrender and letting go, which is experienced by many ego deaths along the way: a breaking apart of early conditioning and rules that they have made for themselves. Usually through inquiry and play there can be a freeing of these early conditionings. One begins to see it doesn't really matter what is being painted and yet at the same time it does matter and it is done with great care. With the judge ever ready

FIGURE 14.41 Paintings on display. (Photo courtesy of Carol McIntyre.)

FIGURE 14.42 Paintings on display. (Photo courtesy of Carol McIntyre.)

to participate in this endeavor the struggle is on and courage is needed. This is where the group provides this great holding of compassion and courage.

To look around the room and view another person standing or sitting on a stool painting, facing the same little deaths and births, automatically conveys a strength beyond words, a courage, a sense of feeling being communicated throughout the room. The feelings aren't always easy ones, especially in the beginning, just like meditation. There is a tendency for the bottom of the river to be stirred up and brought to the top. There might be a lot of tears or anger, and many times fear and even terror. These are not easy feelings to face on one's own. Generally when people are at home painting they are called in many directions, answering the phone, other's needs, things to be done in their environment, distractions in general. It takes great discipline to stay with that level of feeling and creative flow if one is on their own. By the structure of the group this discipline is provided automatically. (Figures 14.41 and 14.42)

There will be great distraction even with the group and the support of the facilitators to keep it concentrated in the room. Many find being hungry calls them, being tired, needing to call someone, or handle some impending disaster at home. It will take the holding of the group, the facilitator, the ongoing movement of the group in the background to begin to call them back, to help release them from the grips of the outer world.

The group will act as the anchor, the many arms of the container, many times the most important reason to return to paint. Maybe it is that early primate in each of us that calls us back to be in community, to be held in silence, to be held in feelings and emotion, to be held by words, to be held by intention. It allows the courage to face the expansiveness, to be in the Mystery and to feel all that it feels to get there. Barbara, who coleads some of the groups with me, says, "The freedom to soar to unknown places while staying connected to myself and others seems to be the magic synergy that enhances the entire process. Just as bees need the entire colony to make honey, humans seem to need one another to access the deeper realms of their nature." (Figure 14.43)

Carol Huntsinger McIntyre, marriage and family therapist, has been in private practice for over 20 years. She has worked for Home Hospice both as a volunteer and on paid staff and for the University of California, San Francisco Medical School Residency program at Sutter Hospital. For 8 years she has facilitated a personal and professional support group for doctors as they go through their 3-year program. Carol has completed the teacher training program at the Painting Experience in San Francisco and taught painting groups in Saint Helena and Santa Rosa. She continues to offer classes with Barbara Schlumberger at The Painting Place, Mon-

FIGURE 14.43   Bearded man with halo. (Photo courtesy of Carol McIntyre.)

day morning painting classes, and a program, for professionals, "Painting From the Inside — A Meditative Approach," as well as workshops offered on a seasonal basis.

☐ Painting through the Pain
Judith Koeleman

Born in 1957 I lived the life of an international army brat before settling in British Columbia. Campbell River on Vancouver Island is where I have called "home" since 1980. I never get tired of the natural surroundings, and the inspiration to my practice in the arts has benefited by this ambiance.

My world came to a staggering impasse after my 17-year-old daughter died in a skiing accident on Mount Washington in March 2002. My self-confidence shattered and I felt an enormous amount of anxiety in the months after her death. My work in the service sector was too stressful and I made a conscious decision to find quiet work, for a time.

Six months passed and I asked myself what was my purpose in life, where was this path taking me? My son needed me. My husband and step-father of the children needed me, and I needed them. I read many books about grieving, which helped me to understand that everyone grieves in their own way and their own time. I cried a lot. It felt good to release the pent up feelings. In my mind's eye I felt that if I cried enough, surely I would get a grip on this grief. I prayed for guidance and an inner calmness began to emerge, helping me through this period. I can only explain this feeling as faith. There was also comfort knowing that my daughter had a deep faith, which assisted in releasing my inner grief as well.

There were several days when anger and self-pity prevailed, on these days I would make sure to take long walks and let physical exercise be my release. The need to nurture my soul and redefine my place in life became a priority so I worked on the inner mending by expressing these deep feelings through art. Choosing the right color of acrylic paint became an essential part of how to express my emotions. The boldness or subtleness articulated my inner feelings without words or the need to supply an explanation to others. Next, the mark making became the focus, soft long strokes, short abrupt dabs, to squiggles or slashes, spatters and drips. Adding water to the paper and then holding the paper up vertically, created interesting drips. Another method was by adding water from a sprayer and tipping the paper back and forth so the medium created interesting mixes with the shifting. The more I experimented the more confident I got. I would let the first works dry and then go back and put another layer on top adding to the story of emotions, which signifies the complexity of feelings.

Primarily I paint intuitively; combining flat, vivid fields with heavily textured subjects in the abstract. Art making is a bold adventure that has allowed me to take risks and to engage in deep learning as I move through the stages of loss. Painting and expression has both provoked and demystified grieving for me. Through this process I have gained greater clarity about the world around me, who I am, and where I'm headed in a way that embraces all the elements of my life.

As I took greater risks, the more I opened myself to art the more I found myself taking steps toward the journey of healing. My smile returned and the laughter soon followed.

Getting to Know One Another by Color and Mark Making

Supplies Needed

- Multiuse white paper
- A box of colored penciled (prism)
- Colored felts
- Sharpener and scissors, glue stick

FIGURE 14.44 "Judith." (Photo courtesy of Judith Koeleman.)

Ask each group member to write down his or her first name on the white paper. Let them know they can use all the supplies on the table for this task. Encourage that they add a design, decoration, or symbol, which conveys a personality trait that they would like to share (Figure 14.38)

Judith: For me I like a certain amount of order and routine but my creative and expressive energy seems to bubble and burst forward.

Color with Feelings and Emotions

Materials Needed

- Paper cut in 4 x 3 inch squares
- Pencil crayons, colored felts or acrylic craft paint and small paintbrushes
- Premake eight or nine examples: facilitators can title each square.

The group is asked next to match a color that expresses the feeling or emotions that the facilitator has suggested; the group can add new ideas. Combining colors to make a new color should be encouraged. Everyone's square is then collectively gathered to show the difference in color preference. (Figure 14.45)

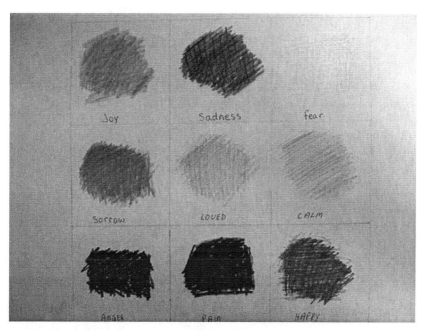

FIGURE 14.45   Color and emotions. (Photo courtesy of Judith Koeleman.)

Color and Mark making

Materials Needed

- Watercolor paper, heavier weight or small canvas
- Acrylic paints: red, yellow, and blue, purple, green with black and white
- Water in plastic container, cover for table and rags
- Paper plates or plastic lids for paint palettes
- Several 1-inch brushes, larger ones encourage less detail
- Palette knives and/or spatulas, straws, and blow dryer

You may substitute colored pencil crayons and felts or use black indian ink for contrast splatter, you can tilt your paper to give drips over background. Indian ink stains so use cover for table an old plastic tablecloth works well. Or use acrylic paint with water for a runny consistency.

The group starts by selecting two or three acrylic paint colors with the use of black and white that best describes the feeling and emotion they have in mind. We are now focusing on combining color and mark making. The group should be encouraged to stand so their arms and hands give sweeping motions. Give everyone personal space; the floor can also be used. Splattering of paint and the smearing with hands gives freedom to express. Encourage the abstract and the making of different marks. Dots, slashes, swishes, and slices. Blow the paint around with a straw or blow dryer. Dab with a rag, scrap off, add white to lighten, add black to darken (a little goes a long way). The mixing of colors will create new colors all on their own. Set a time limit of 5 to 10 minutes; this will inspire spontaneity. Stop and access if the marks are conveying their emotions. If not, start again with new paper or scrap off paint before it dries and start again (dry with blow drier before next layer). Try a different color choice. Use thin slices between thick strokes. Use a dark color beside a light color. Add white to the colors in the background. Add text or drawings when dry. Add felts. Glue on a post card, picture, or past drawings.

Paper usually comes in 22" × 34" so you can halve a sheet or use large sketchbook paper that can be ripped out for individual use. Some books come with perforations for this purpose.

The painting titled "Stage 2" represents emotional release. Collectively the nine panels then signify the last stage, acceptance. (Figures 14.46 and 14.47)

Judith Koeleman was a successful business woman for 27 years before she returned to college majoring in the arts. She graduated from North Island College with honors. She works in sculpture, print making and painting. She lives near Campbell River on Vancouver Island and has numerous works in public and private collections.

stage 2   nine panels   16x20 inches   mixed media   2004

FIGURE 14.46   Stage 2: Physical Pain. (Photo courtesy of Judith Koeleman and Brian Kyle.)

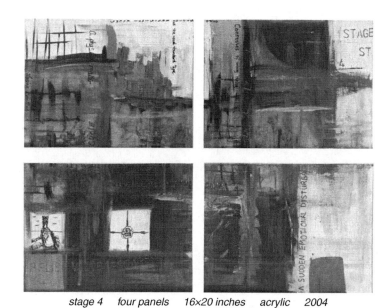

stage 4   four panels   16×20 inches   acrylic   2004

FIGURE 14.47   Stage 4: Physical Pain. (Photo courtesy of Judith Koeleman and Brian Kyle.)

15

Sara Baker and
Sara Spaulding-Phillips

The Writers

Whoever finds love beneath hurt and grief disappears into emptiness with a thousand new disguises.

—Rumi

☐ Woven Dialog Workshops
Sara Baker

Listening is like holy silence.
Listening is like the rain.

— Rachel Naomi Remen

When we become ill, or someone close to us dies, we are thrown into a chaotic world where our "normal" lives disappear. We can feel a loss of control over our bodies and our circumstances, overwhelmed by our new role as patient or bereaved. Suddenly, instead of being the actors in our lives, we are tendered passive, or *in-valid*. Fear, despair, and guilt can often threaten to overtake us. Sometimes we don't know who we are anymore. Yet through writing, we are able to connect with our authentic self and give it voice. Our writing becomes the place we can awaken our feelings, and the workshop becomes the safe haven where we can share those feelings.

What Happens in a Woven Dialog Workshop?

In a Woven Dialog Workshop, a small group of people gather to write and share their writings. Poetry, images, fairy tales, and the work of others is used to seed the imagination, but the primary texts are those created by participants themselves. By learning active listening and by writing observations about what has been read, members are able to respond to the writer in a way that reflects back what has been written. This allows the writer to "see again" his or her writing. A group dynamic is created that allows for trust and support and containment of feelings. Many participants have commented on the relief they have felt after writing a particular piece; others have said, "I didn't know I felt that way."

Participants can expect:

- to learn methods of unlocking the healing powers of the unconscious
- to develop self-compassion as you discover your unique voice
- to find a supportive atmosphere that allows for a safe exploration of feelings

The Tools for the Writing Workshop:
Listening and Observing

I would like to invite you into several sessions of the Woven Dialog Workshop, which I run at the Loran Smith Center for Cancer Support in Athens, Georgia. These particular workshops took place in the winter of 2005, and while I have changed the names of the participants, the rest is all a true account from my notes on these sessions.

What I would like for you to notice is that while there is a well-defined process, which consists of the reading of patients' texts and written observations on these, followed by discussion, the process allows for openness to the promptings of the participants. Unlike a writing class in a classroom, there is no curriculum to master. Rather, literature is used to "seed" the imagination, but the focus of the group is on the work produced by the participants themselves. The skills practiced include active listening and learning to make observation. The goals are to become more proficient listeners to their own and others' voices. Every group is unique, and every person brings his or her own ineffable mystery to the table. We have found that keeping to "close readings" of texts, with written observations, slows down responses and bypasses easy psychologizing. It allows for both revelation and privacy. As you will see, the process allows for the respectful witnessing of each other's wounds and struggles, and for real therapeutic moments.

Notes on Session 2, Week 1, January 18, 2005
Literature: Second Helping, by Doug Dorph

Around our table this January afternoon, we have Jane Ann, a breast cancer survivor of 67, Barbara, a woman in her early 60s who is dealing with a metastasized abdominal cancer, Sally, a nurse in her late 40s who is dealing with grief about her mother's death and her father's imminent death, Carol, a lawyer in her 40s, a single mom, who is in treatment for breast cancer and who has recently lost her sister to cancer, and Debbie, in her 70s, who is a year and a half out of treatment.

We began, as always, with Barbara leading us in centering breath. We introduced ourselves, our illnesses, griefs, and writing experiences. The older members were wonderful in explaining what we do, especially Barbara, who says that she has learned how to listen, and Carol, who emphasizes that the participants are safe here. I could see that Carol was nervous and on edge, full of emotions. She said that her sister died of breast cancer just before she herself was diagnosed. She said that she thought she had been handling it fine but then fell apart. Debbie said that her cancer diagnosis was several years ago and she had sailed through, but suspected that she had feelings she wasn't dealing with. She is very contained, quiet, and interior.

I had former members tell their alter ego names and the new members then told theirs and explained them: Carol, the attorney said she was Hope, an earth mother who loved gardening, cooking, kids (although Carol doesn't know how hopeful Hope is). Debbie told us that she had always disliked the name Debbie — her mother said she had been named after one of her father's old girlfriends. He must have been insensitive, Debbie commented wryly. She said she was Marguerite, who was flamboyant and sophisticated. Marguerite was a caregiver, Debbie said. "I have always been a caregiver," she said, "maybe too much."

I handed out the poem "Second Helping." We read it silently and then out loud. Jane Ann said she didn't really get it until it had been read out loud. I gave them instructions on writing observations and feeling responses. They wrote theirs and then we began to read the writings; old hands going first. Everyone had good points to make — Barbara that she liked the writer, Jane Ann said that the poem was about mindfulness. Sally said she could see him at the Thanksgiving table, carefully sampling all the tastes. Carol said she was angry that everyone thought that traumas like heart attacks and cancers were supposed to make you such a better person. We recognized her feelings, talking about how that attitude could serve to avoid real feelings, and could be an easy "out," then we went back to the specific poem — observing that it was not a manifesto, but simply one man's singular experience. We talked about the difference between our responses to a poem and what was actually in the poem. Debbie noticed the repetition of the word now, and how effective it was.

We talked about the different kinds of poetry — most of them were shocked to learn that poetry doesn't always have to rhyme. I was concerned that they become close readers, and that they differentiate between what is on the page and their responses to it. We talked about the "abiding image," about following the image that holds energy for you, even if you don't know where it will lead. Debbie wanted to turn that into "theme," into abstract ideas, but I held to the idea and potency of image. We talked about images in dreams. We talked about the donnee and leaving the donnee, about how a poem contains feelings, allowing a safe place to explore them. I pointed out the simple authentic language of the poem, the use of concrete words, the lack of sentimentality or adornment. Barbara said, "Wow, I'm learning a lot."

Group Process. The group melded very well — I was gratified that the former members were so skilled in their welcoming of the new members. I could see that Carol was dealing with an overflow of raw emotions — she had a hard time sitting still. Debbie is very soft-spoken, and yet everyone gave her time and listened; they made room for these new people.

Notes on Session 2, Week 2, January 25, 2005
Literature: Silk Cord, Morning Poem

We began by checking in about our week. Debbie said she had a good week — few details. Barbara said she had a very good week — no cancer markers. She was very happy. Carol said it was no okay week; again, she seemed on the verge of tears. Then we checked in with our alter egos. Marguerite said she was fine, Charmayne said she was so excited she was dancing on the ceiling, but then her father's voice cautioned her to not be so happy. Hope said she was able to do something for her son that she had wanted to do and felt happy about that. Helen (my alter ego) said she had a good week painting, but when she learned her daughter-in-law was in a workshop with a famous painter, she was blinded by jealousy and discouragement. I wanted to model that it isn't always essential to have "model" emotions, and our alter egos really don't have to!

After our meditation, everyone read their poems. Debbie's was a haiku-like poem:

> When cancer came to call
> Everything in my life changed.
> It became richer.

Barbara responded to this by noting its economy, and saying, very adroitly, that she was like a cat hanging on the curtains, she was curious about the details. Carol noted that the language "came to call" was treating the cancer like a visitor, so that it achieved some normalcy. She also noted that when she heard "everything changed" she expected some negatives, but the poem surprised by being positive. I was also struck by "came to call" — as if it were a "gentleman caller," but cancer is no gentleman.

Barbara wrote an amazing poem about being stuck. Carol noticed that while it was about being stuck, "the lines seemed to stumble over each other." She noted the c and f sounds, which were crackling like the ice she described. Debbie noted the heart of it, or the essence: she said that it was a poem about being blocked, like the glacier in the poem. I noted the extended metaphor of being frozen, the similes: like ice crackling in a glass, like a glacier, like a kid with his tongue frozen to a pole. There were also wonderful images: "icicles dripping a myriad of words." And word choices such as "icy tumult." I noted the paradox of writing a dynamic poem about being stuck.

Frosty Feelings

> Since the assignment to write a poem,
> My mind has been frozen in fear.
> The literary ice queen has me in her frosty grip.
> My very own emotions crackle around me
> like melting ice cubes in hot water.
> A myriad of mixed words drip from
> the icicles forming in my head.

In all this chilly turmoil
My heart beats with the anticipation of creating.
But the flow of words between the
heart and head is blocked
Solid as a glacier.........unmoving.
I feel stuck like an unwitting kid
Frozen to a frosty metal pole,
Powerless to move or to speak.
So I wait expectantly for movement,
The freedom of the thaw.
Wondering in quiet frustration
what glowing expressions
may be locked up in this freezer of my mind.

Carol wrote a lyrical piece around the images of finches at her feeder, turning from gold to brown and wondering if she would ever turn gold again. Debbie noticed the poem was open ended, because it ended with a question. Someone noted the image of fluttering combat at the feeder also indicating the fighting for life (Will there be a place at the feeder for me?). Someone else noticed that it began and ended with the same image, but the colors were reversed.

Finches

Since the finches turned from gold
To brown,
There is less peace for me
In their coming and going —
My gut a reflection
Of their fluttering combat
For a place at the feeder.
Will the light return for me too,
When the finches go back from brown
To gold?

Group Process. For a smaller group, I felt it worked very well. It gave Debbie a chance to have more air time than she might otherwise have had, and allowed us to go deeply into everyone's work. Carol is a quick study, very intellectual, and has a strong personality. I felt she was becoming more comfortable with her ability. Barbara is a good foil — the therapist in her draws out Debbie and her strong personality balances Carol's.

I hope the reader will see in this small glimpse into the workshop the richness of imagination and perception these participants exhibited. I think one of the most therapeutic aspects of this process is that through exercising the imagination and creating texts, the participants gain a sense of their own agency. This agency is often lost in the context of treatment and social forces. By creating an imaginal space which is engaging — first through the creation of alter egos, then through the exploration of, and writing of fairytales and poetry — participants are invited to play, rather than to "fix" an illness or grief. Participants can then experience what Bellruth Naperstek calls the "joyous self love that comes from accomplishment."

Second, because the focus is on the writings, rather than on the participants' "issues," emotions can be expressed and witnessed, without reducing the person to a pathology. For example, in the poem about the finches, fear and hope are expressed by someone who could not easily speak directly about these things. "Poetry," says Robert Frost, "provides the one permissible way of saying one thing and meaning another. People say, 'why don't you say what you mean?' We never do that, do we, being all of us too much poets. We like to talk in parables and hints and indirections... ."

Finally, although these are notes from the first two workshops early in the sessions, I hope readers will note the generosity and attention given by the participants to each other's work. This attention enlarges into empathy and understanding over time, and this provides for a "weaving" of community. Work written in the workshops becomes part of the communal pot, the communal context. We learn from and about each other.

Sara Baker, has facilitated expressive writing workshops at the Loran Smith Center for Cancer Support in Athens, Georgia for the past three years. She presented her work on the Woven Dialog Writing Workshop at the International Meeting of the Society for the Arts in Healthcare in April 2006. She has published fiction, plays, and essays in numerous venues, and has been an Artist-in-Residence for the State of Georgia. She taught for many years at the University of Georgia and Georgia Institute of Technology.

☐ Fierce Writing
Sara Spaulding-Phillips

Long ago, an elephant walking across my chest in the middle of the night began a creative journey that continues to this day. My heart attack and the open-heart surgery that followed engendered in me a gratefulness to have had this powerful experience, come through it with ease, and be given a second chance. My enduring spiritual faith, meditation practice, and understanding of the natural cycles of life in relation to seasonal changes helped me during this critical period of recovery. I experienced a radical transformation in regard to life, death, and the mysteries enveloping them. My physical crisis was in fact a spiritual initiation into the deep mysteries inherent in life and death.

Once recovered, I wanted to share these insights with others. I was eager to spread the word, almost evangelical in my fervor to bring others to see how death could be a joyful and wonder-filled experience. While I recognized that how we live, whom we serve, and how passionately we live our lives is most important, I could now see how, if not faced, accepted, and honored, grief, death, and loss could be crippling. Taking care of all the unfinished business of the past frees us up to live life more fully and passionately.

And so my writing seminar "Preparing for Our Death" was born. The class was a container for a group of people to honor their losses and move on with their lives. Ten people signed up, and that first class was a powerhouse. Most of the participants had no idea of the depth of their grief and its unrecognized yet profound effect on their lives. They hadn't really paused to consider it.

Because of my newly won camaraderie with death, I found that my own resulting delight and laughter freed up an easiness within the group as well. And with this liberation, the dark side soon came flowing out. Tears, laughter, anger, and joy were released with a lot of learning along the way. Through our writing we came to terms with grief's crippling effect on our souls. Night after night, by reading aloud our writing, we poured balm on our battered souls.

There were those who had never fully grieved the loss of their mothers, fathers, husbands, wives, lovers. Mothers who had lost babies or couldn't have children mourned those losses as well. People even lamented lost opportunities.

One 50-year-old man sought the group for physical as well as emotional and spiritual reasons. Because of severe fibromyalgia, he had been obliged to give up his previous way of life, retrain himself, and carry on. Two cancer patients in different stages of the disease dealt with the devastation wrecked on their bodies. There was a man whose beloved therapist had died within the past two years. One woman, born on October 31 and therefore comfortable with the dark side, nevertheless needed healing from the loss at a young age of her first husband in a tractor accident. Another woman's mother was inexorably slipping away into Alzheimer's grasp. She needed to record the hysterical yet poignant incidents in her mother's life so she could write herself into greater acceptance and understanding.

The classes continued into the fall and winter — appropriate seasons, as folks were literally facing the darkness. And then the well ran dry. I couldn't get a class going. My tight-knit community of brave souls had already faced mortality. No one wanted to dwell in the "cottage of darkness" anymore. What to do?

The answer was obvious: after facing death, we now wanted to live our lives boldly and with intention. Living on the edge, living with passionate commitment, living life to the fullest: living fiercely is all of that. And so the class "Fierce Living" was born. New, essential questions challenged us: Who am I in this world? What is my reason for being here? What is my spiritual or soul work now? At its heart "Fierce Living" was about coming to terms with what really matters.

The classes took off. While I first taught on my own, I was later joined by another Sara who loved the work as much as I did and was as comfortable with the dark side as I. Seven years of teaching "Fierce Living" profoundly changed my life. I retired from 30 years as a psychotherapist and began an altogether different practice, a creative, life-coaching practice. My commitment to living fiercely and with passion drew me along an ever-expanding path of spiritual service and creative art. I began to paint again, channeling my near-death experience into what I call sacred art.

To this day I paint and write while practicing spiritual mentoring and a personal form of shamanism, work that feeds me and, I believe, inspires others as well. While death may have drawn me briefly into that "cottage of darkness" long ago, only by recognizing and accepting it was I able to emerge alive, aware and able to live with true ferocity.

Sara Spaulding-Phillips, is a psychotherapist, writer, teacher, and mentor for writers living in Santa Rosa, CA. "Preparing for Your Death" and "Fierce Living" syllabi with 10 weeks of lesson plans are available upon request. (www.saraspauldingphillips.com)

Debra Mier, Laura Thomae, and
Carole M. McNamee

Programs in Art

It is a fact that even the best ideas and visions and programs do not in
themselves have a lasting impact on man unless he is given a chance
to act, to participate, and to share ideas and aims with others.

—**Erich Fromm**, *On Being Human*

☐ A Multimodality Camp for Grieving Families
Debra Mier

Willow House is a child and family bereavement program located just
north of Chicago, which has addressed the needs of hundreds of families
in the area. Our mission is to help children who have experienced the
death of a parent or sibling, and our family-focused approach allows us
to support their parents in their own grief processes while they learn how
to parent a grieving child. As the Program Director for this organization,
I have had the unique opportunity to get to know families during one of
the most difficult times of their lives — the death of a mom, dad, brother,
or sister. We meet monthly with these families, in their area, using a
group support model. Children meet monthly with others their own age,
and their caregivers meet with others who share a similar loss (i.e., newly
widowed or bereaved parents).

Due to the wide range of ages and types of loss represented in our pop-
ulation, it is often challenging to develop supportive programming that
meets the needs of such a diverse group. I find myself constantly drawing on my background as a registered drama therapist to develop innovative programming that invites families to share their grief experiences in

newly relevant ways. It is always amazing (and humbling) to observe the diversity of ways in which children and adults process their grief, and to acknowledge that, as a result, no one modality will fully address the needs of the entire group. Some individuals are more comfortable processing verbally, some nonverbally through art or music or movement. Our monthly support groups employ a range of techniques for self-expression, but in any given month, it is challenging to meet everyone's needs. One of the reasons I look forward to our annual Family Camp is that it enables me and my colleagues to provide a myriad of activities over the course of an entire weekend. We work to structure the experience mindful of the unique demands of the individual families attending camp — and a weekend-long experience enables us to provide opportunities for self-expression that address the multiple needs of all participants. Over the years, we have learned that the key to providing a rich camp experience for everyone is to start with a rich theme that provides opportunities for ritual, movement, art making, and music and sharing.

Years ago I had the wonderful opportunity to live and work in Japan. During that time, I was exposed to seasonal traditions and rituals that beautifully honored nature, life, and death. In particular, the annual *O Bon* festival spoke to me. Also called the "Festival of Lights," *O Bon* is an annual three-day event, celebrated nationally, through which people in Japan honor their ancestors. It is believed to be a time when those who have died are welcomed home for a visit. Lanterns are hung in doorways to guide the ancestors and welcome them home. Families travel to their hometowns to be together and prepare special foods that were favorites of those who have died to celebrate their return. During those three days, entire communities join in folk dances (known as *bon* dances) as part of the festivities. The festival concludes in a ritual called *toro-nagashi* in which floating lanterns are lit and released as a farewell to the ancestors and as a means to ferry them on their way.

As I was developing a theme for last year's family camp, I thought about the *O Bon* festival. The name of my organization, Willow House, comes from the combining of cultures. In Western culture the willow tree symbolizes death, grief, and mourning while in the Eastern tradition, it symbolizes beauty, grace, endurance, and strength. It occurred to me that the *O Bon* festival I experienced first-hand in Japan would provide the perfect theme for camp — by exploring how another culture approaches this unique yet collective journey, Willow House families would be opened to new possibilities for hope and healing. My colleagues and I recruited volunteers and researched the festival. We spent months planning, adapting, and preparing, and were excited when a record number of families signed up for camp. While it would be impossible to recount the full breadth of the camp experiences, I would like to share some selected moments that may be particularly relevant to those interested in expressive arts therapies.

Kamidana

During *O Bon*, various food items and photos of loved ones are placed on what is called the kamidana or "god shelf." This small houselike structure became the centerpiece of our memory table and children were invited to assist in the decoration of it throughout the evening. As families arrived, they each placed a framed photo of the loved one who had died on the *kamidana*. In front of the photo, they placed a small portion of their loved one's favorite food. M&Ms, flan, apple pie, popsicles, "gushers", Nutter-butters and a hard-to-find orange soda were included among the items. Families then shared their food items with one another.

This opening ritual was a great way to begin camp, since it evoked powerful memories of family meals. It was also the perfect avenue for additional sharing, with other families and also between members of the same family. As caregivers and volunteers mingled and enjoyed this unique potluck, the children spent hours decorating the kamidana and writing notes to their loved ones who had died. A note left by one of the children simply stated, "I never knew you liked watermelon." Several of the volunteers were struck by this statement, which points to the impor-tance of continually sharing memories of the person who died, reminding us that the task of getting to know someone is never really complete.

Hachimaki and Fans

The *O Bon* festival also offers unique costuming opportunities, which was important for me as a drama therapist because this would assist the chil-dren in taking on the role of a festival participant. Costuming enables us to establish aesthetic distance, thereby affording the opportunity to explore new and possibly threatening things safely by taking on the per-spective of a character. The intent was that by wearing a costume piece or having a unique prop, children would have the necessary distance to explore their grief in a unique way. I have found over the years that this can be achieved very simply, without elaborate costumes. On Saturday, we had group time for both children and adults, and used that time with the children to allow them to make their own costume pieces.

In Japan, *hachimaki* are simple headbands worn to signify a person's determination to take on the task at hand. They are worn during festi-vals and any time there is a difficult task to achieve, such as studying for an exam. We wore our *hachimaki* to acknowledge the hard work of grieving and our determination to approach it together. Children were provided with a list of adjectives translated into *kanji* (Japanese characters). They were then asked to identify a *kanji* symbol that described them and another that described the person who died. They drew those symbols on their *hachimaki*, and with the help of volunteers, tied the band around their head to costume themselves for the remainder of the camp weekend.

Fans in Japan are not just devices to move air to cool us down but are also used by warriors, performers, and laypeople as a means of communication. Symbolically, they represent the road of life, beginning at the base and fanning out into the various roads into the future. Group participants reflected on the direction and twist and turns their lives had undergone since the death of their loved one. They then decorated their fans, using some of the same *kanji* symbols they drew on their *hachimaki*.

Bon Dance

At the end of their group time, fully costumed, the children each developed personal gestures that captured the essence of the *kanji* they had chosen to describe themselves or the person who died — strong, silly, brave, and shy. The children practiced these gestures as a group, exploring the power of embodying these traits. The self-described "shy" child had an opportunity to embody strength and power and to move through space feeling strong and powerful. At the same time, children who described themselves as "powerful" were able to embody shyness and sadness. The process allowed for a rich exchange of feelings and responses to grief. They were now prepared for the *bon* dance.

On Saturday afternoon, all the children came together to learn a 500-year-old dance traditionally performed by entire communities. These folk dances are not complicated in nature, and are designed to be repetitive so that every member of the community can take part, regardless of skill level or physical ability. Knowing that the activity might not appeal to all age groups, a number of percussion instruments were available to provide opportunities for even the most resistant of teens to participate. This also allowed us to mirror the Japanese tradition, since *bon* dance is typically performed in a circle, around drummers. We adapted the dance by having the children insert their personalized gesture at a defined moment in the music. The children later performed the dance for their caregivers at the closing of camp.

Toro-nagashi

Saturday evening, we made lanterns in honor of the person who died. This family-based art activity involved the decoration and personalization of rice paper panels that were attached to a small, simple three-dimensional wooden frame. Families brought photos of their loved ones, and children and adults worked together to create memorial collages. Many families chose to use the *kanji* adjectives that described their loved one to add to the collage. When completed, these lanterns were beautiful objects of art. One by one, the families shared the meaning behind their work, and one by one the lanterns were lit and carried out by volunteers to form a path that led to the campfire.

Traditionally the *toro-nagashi* lanterns are released on the water and are therefore not kept. Our lanterns were designed to be retrieved so that families could take them home as a remembrance of the weekend. It became apparent during the art making that families were concerned that their lanterns would be damaged by the lake water. We spontaneously adapted this ritual to ensure that families could retain their beautiful art as a keepsake. Instead of guiding their ancestors back to where they came from, these lanterns guided families forward on their path. (Figures 16.1 through 16.3)

FIGURE 16.1   Lantern on the water. (Photo courtesy of Debra Mier.)

FIGURE 16.2 Lantern path. (Photo courtesy of Debra Mier.)

FIGURE 16.3 Lantern path. (Photo courtesy of Debra Mier.)

During the closing camp ceremony, families had an opportunity to talk about their camp experience. Many remarked that the beauty and simplicity of this different cultural approach moved them and offered new rituals they would adapt and make their own to honor their loved ones. Volunteers and staff acknowledged that the Japanese *O Bon* festival provided the perfect framework to allow participants of varying ages, backgrounds, experiences, and belief systems to explore their unique grief journeys through ritual, art, movement, dance, costuming, and music. I was honored, too, to have the opportunity to weave this cultural ritual I had learned about so many years ago into the lives of the families I work with today.

Program Information

Willow House is a social service organization dedicated to helping children, teens, families, and communities who are coping with death and dying. Services include support groups, educational resources and referrals, community outreach, and special programs and workshops. These programs are community-based so that they are easily accessible and foster peer support and interaction among the bereaved within the comfort and familiarity of their own communities.

Debra Mier is a licensed clinical social worker and registered drama therapist with a background in social work and bereavement. She has worked for three Chicago-area child and family bereavement programs, and is presently the Program Director at Willow House. In addition, she serves on the board of the National Association of Drama Therapy. Before entering the field of bereavement, she worked with a variety of special populations as an expressive arts therapist.

☐ Arts in Hospice, Illness, and Grief
Laura Thomae

The medicine of art is that it releases and contains the psyche's therapeutic force.

— **Shaun McNiff**

Give sorrow words: the grief that does not speak, whispers in the o'er frought heart and bids it break.

— **William Shakespeare**

Keystone's Therapeutic Arts (in Wyndmoor, Pennsylvania) program is founded on the basis that the creative arts therapies provide powerful vehicles for facilitating insight, meaning making and healing in those who are facing death or coping with the loss of a loved one. Engaging in art experiences provides an aesthetic container for expressing and exploring emotional and spiritual aspects of the grief process.

The therapeutic arts have proven to be a valuable and positive force in helping patients and their families enhance coping skills and give voice to the complex emotions that are part of the grief process. Music and arts experiences also can help patients and their loved ones create personal and communal rituals for grieving, remembering, and letting go. The arts provide us with tangible symbols and metaphors for expressing that which cannot be expressed easily in conversation (talk therapy).

One of the greatest benefits of utilizing music and art experiences in palliative care hospice and bereavement is that each encounter with the creative process is unique; it is immediate, adaptable, fluid expression that in supportive settings can be explored within the safety of the aesthetic container. Thus art experiences allow for release and expression of the many complex and often conflicting emotions. The immediacy of creating is especially suited to the nature of the grief process. Grieving persons cycle through many different feelings and emotions, music and art experiences meet the individual where they are providing a supportive aesthetic structure through which to explore whatever arises.

Art Communicates before It Is Understood.

— **author unknown**

Many of the patients and family members I work with are unsure of how they should be feeling, acting, what they should be doing. Everything they have previously known has now changed, there are no "operating rules" in this new territory. Many are responding to family, cultural, and other external pressures of what the "good patient" or the dutiful bereaved should do. The arts offer a place for conflicting emotions to be "out there," while at the same time, the arts offer metaphors and symbols that convey the meaning beyond words.

It is very important when using arts in therapy to be aware of the power of these tools and take responsibility for using them only when you are trained and have done your own personal work to be able to support the patient/client with what can be opened up within the art experience. Of all the arts I believe that music is the most visceral and therefore the most potent vehicle for change. However, the wrong music and the wrong intervention can do more harm than good. The activity of cocreating and improvising with patients and their family members can be very raw and emotional and not every musician is trained and able to handle what may come up when working with someone who is going through an intense grief process. Harold Arlen said that:

> Words make you think a thought, music makes you feel a feeling, a song makes you feel a thought.

Music therapy utilizes music as the primary mode for facilitating the creative process of moving toward wholeness in the physical, emotional, mental, and spiritual self. Keystone's music therapist works with bereaved individuals to promote expression and healing of emotional and spiritual grief. Group music experiences include: projective music listening, songwriting, lyric substitution, music assisted relaxation, music playing, and improvisation.

Keystone Hospice Grief Group Examples

Children's Bereavement Workshop

This workshop is for children aged 6 to 12 who have recently experienced the loss of a loved one. Through a combination of arts experiences, movement activities, and discussion children will have the opportunity to express their grief and experience with supportive methods of coping with loss. Each child is asked to bring a photo of their loved one to place in a memory frame they will create in the workshop.

Children are very open and resilient; they often cycle quickly through many different feelings and emotions. For example, a song I played called "If You Miss Me From Singing Down Here," brought up strong feelings and tears for many of the children in the group. I kept singing and the music supported their expressions of pain and loss. When the storm had passed the children easily transitioned to a discussion of placing favorite memories of their loved one in a memory frame around a favorite photo. The music provided a supported release for the pain of their loss. Creating the memory frame provided the structure and focus for the expression of joyful memories.

Coping with the Holidays

This is a daylong workshop for adults. This workshop focuses on strategies for coping with the demands of the holiday season while grieving the loss of a loved one. Art experiences are offered to reduce stress, express feelings, socialize grief, honor the grief journey, and create healing rituals for the bereaved.

Many participants report they find support, strength, and gain new insights through creative expression. For example, I introduced a music and movement experience to address participants' issues of feeling "detached," "having no energy for the holidays," and "dreading family and social interactions." This movement experience involves everyone standing in a circle and going around the room, with everyone first creating a movement or gesture to symbolize a feeling about their loss, and then adding a sound to go with it. The participants choose a partner whose expressions touched the individual, and together they explore those sounds and gestures by mirroring them back to each other. The last direction for this movement experience is to respond to one's partner's gesture with a new one that starts where the other person finished (if the partner started with her hands in the air then the other person starts his or her response in the same place). This was very moving for everyone. The group members were struck by how they felt transformed by giving their expression to someone and having it mirrored back to them, and they were astonished by how their gestures were responded to. By creating and responding to different sounds and movements they gained insight into their own process and also were able to see other possibilities and means of coping for themselves. Movement experiences can be very grounding, increase awareness, and mitigate the detachment that can lead to depression in the grief process.

Honoring our Legacy of Caring: Staff Memory Shares

These workshops are held regularly to support healthy acknowledgment of grief and loss experienced by the hospice staff. In these groups staff members find common ground in creating healing works of art. Sometimes we open by singing favorite songs of beloved patients or holding a meditation after reading the names of the patients who have passed. Hymn singing is especially powerful for this group as we have a number of staff who are very religious and find solace in their faith. We have written collective poems and songs to remember those who have gone and honor our work with them.

Creating together creates a strong community and offers support to hospice staff who inevitably experience loss on a regular basis. It is important for us to grieve our patients and to allow for the expression of these feelings with our coworkers. This supports and models healthy grieving in the workplace.

Examples of Arts Experiences

Mandala Quilt

The mandala quilt is utilized in staff memory shares and bereavement groups.

Materials

8½×11 papers with light pencil circles drawn in the center (I use a Styrofoam dinner plate or Frisbee), several boxes of pastels. Oil pastels are less messy than chalk pastels.

Directions

Each caregiver in the group creates a mandala that expresses his or her memories or feelings about a patient or the caregiver's role in caring for that patient. The mandalas are then arranged together to create a quilt, each square represents those who have passed. Participants are invited to share something about either their process in making their mandala square or the patient they are remembering; for example, what words describe your mandala, what does it say about the patient or the care you

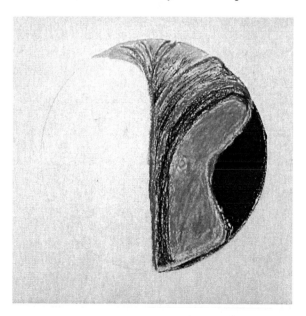

FIGURE 16.4   Mandala drawing by a survivor of breast cancer. (Photo courtesy of Carole M. McNamee.)

give? Do the colors you chose represent a feeling of energy; what characteristics of that patient do they remind you of. What word/feeling is the first to come to mind when you look at the mandala? Let other group members also respond to the drawing if OK with participant. (Figures 16.4 and 16.5)

Also have participants response to the effect of the quilt: what qualities describe the quilt; what words or feelings come to mind; what does it say about the care you give; your strengths; talents as a caregiver; your experience of patients and families?

Caring Hands Remember

Materials

Paper (minimum size, 8½ × 11); multicolored pastels (several boxes so that everyone has a choice of many colors)

Directions

Our hands are powerful tools for healing. Ask for examples of how participants use their hands for healing in their work. Then invite everyone

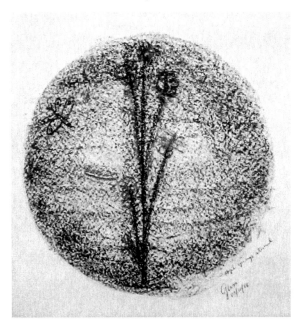

FIGURE 16.5   Mandalas created during first group meeting by woman diagnosed with colon cancer. (Photo courtesy of Carole M. McNamee.)

to pick two colors from the pastels: one that represents what each person gives in his or her work, one that represents what the person receives.

In some Eastern traditions it is believed that we give energy with our right hand and receive it with our left. With the color that represents what the caregiver gives from her work, she should trace her right hand (or dominant hand) on the paper, then write a word or two that expresses what she gives; repeat the process for the receiving (nondominant) hand, writing words that reflect what she receives from her work.

Note: I often play soft music in the background, instrumental classical, meditative, or new age, to set the mood and create a holding space for the experience. The participants are then invited to share what they experienced in the process. We close with a group honoring of what it means to give and receive in our work and how both are necessary.

Music-Guided Relaxation

Relaxing instrumental music is played while the therapist guides the participants through a relaxation and visualization exercise to center and focus. This starts by encouraging participants to visualize themselves "leaving cares and worries at the door."

General Format for Bereavement Workshops

1. Welcome and introduction (song or poem by facilitator to set tone of group)
2. General group rules: listening, respecting confidentiality
3. Personal introductions (hopes, fears, expectations for today)
4. Art experience (e.g., mandala, collage, poem) utilizing key issues stated by participants in the introductions. Art experiences can focus on remembering the deceased or creating an affirming piece of art to use as a touchstone when things are difficult. Group processing of experience.
5. Lunch
6. Music experience (songwriting, song choice, and reflective listening and discussion, group drumming or guided imagery). Group processing of experience.
7. Workshop closure

Reflective Questions:

1. Is there one thing you would like to carry with you from this group?
2. Did you learn anything new about yourself. (e.g., strengths, resources, coping skills)
3. Song, poem, movement, or meditation led by facilitator

Laura Thomae, is coordinator of the Therapeutic Arts Program at Keystone Hospice, Wyndmoor, PA. She is also a board certified music therapist, consultant, professional singer, and recording musician. She has presented on music therapy at a number of national and local conferences and workshops including Performing the World '03, an international conference on performative psychology; The American Society of Aging/National Coalition on Aging (ASA/NCOA) 05; The Society for Arts in Healthcare and National Hospice and Palliative Care Conference '06.

☐ An Expressive Arts Group for Cancer Patients: Finding the Creative Fire
Carole M. McNamee

Introduction

Cancer is the second leading cause of death in the United States, responsible for 22.7% of the deaths in 2003 (American Cancer Society, 2006). Cancer patients are challenged by psychosocial issues including coming to terms with mortality, lack of control over their own lives, and a sense of self that is subsumed by their identity as a cancer patient (Kaye, 1991; Wheeler, 1998; Zemen, 1998). Support groups are now commonplace to help patients and their families cope with illness and the challenges posed by the treatments themselves. These groups are typically provided in hospital settings, involve education about the illness and the effects of treatment, and the sharing of experiences. Experiential groups and art therapy groups in particular provide unique opportunities for cancer patients to give and receive support, to express themselves nonverbally, and to reestablish their identity as individuals (Ariail 1996; Ferszt, Massotti, Williams & Miller, 2000; Luzzatto & Gabriel 2000; Malchiodi, 1999; McLeod, 1996; McNiff, 1998, 2004; Nainis et al., 2006; Öster et al., 2006; Serlin, Classen, Frances, & Angell, 2000; Targ & Levine 2002). In major cancer centers, and particularly in settings that treat children and adolescents, expressive arts groups are a more common means of support. More recently, Collie, Bottorff, Long, & Conati (2006) described the use of distance art therapy groups to provide opportunities for women with breast cancer living in remote areas.

This section describes an outpatient expressive arts group for adults diagnosed with cancer, offered in a nonhospital setting in a rural area in Southwest Virginia. Descriptions of the group structure and the creative arts activities, as well as examples of participant artwork and associated narratives, are highlighted. Participant comments on the process of art making are poignant expressions of their experience.

In spring 2006, seven cancer patients participated in "Finding the Creative Fire," a program exploring the effects of creative arts experiences on levels of distress in cancer patients. This program was offered by The Arts in Healthcare Project, an outreach effort of The Family Therapy Center of Virginia Tech. The participants met as a group for two hours each week for eight weeks and engaged in a variety of expressive arts experiences, including mandala drawings, collage, mask making, painting, soapstone carving, and collaborative art. Patient responses to the creative arts and the group experiences were overwhelmingly positive and can be summarized by one participant's comment at the end of the eight weeks — "It [the creative arts group] should be an integrated part of cancer therapy."

At the close of the project, participants provided feedback on their experiences, which indicated that they felt an increased ability to express themselves, an increased understanding and acceptance of their response to their illness, a feeling of not being alone, and a recognition of art as healing. All seven participants expressed a desire to share their work and associated narratives in an exhibit. The participants felt a desire to educate the public about the experience of being a cancer patient.

Project Participants

Workshop participants were recruited through letters and flyers sent to local physicians, counseling practices, and religious organizations. Most of the participants reported hearing about the workshop from multiple sources, including individual physicians and clergy.

Eight participants were interviewed and attended the first meeting. They were all female and ranged in age from 20 to 69. All had been diagnosed with cancer within the previous 18 months and their diagnoses included five with breast cancer (one metastasized), one with stage 4 ovarian cancer, one with metastasized colon cancer, and one with Hodgkin's lymphoma.

Of the eight initial participants, one decided not to continue participation following the first session, stating that she preferred to pursue her interest in crafts rather than engage in the workshop's creative activities. The remaining seven participants all completed the workshop.

Format of the Sessions

The workshop met for approximately two hours each week using the following format. The first 30 to 45 minutes were devoted to verbal responses to selected questions. Initial questions asked about early experiences with art and learned attitudes about being creative. Later on participants were asked to respond to group process. After the first few sessions, it became clear that participants wanted more time to talk and share, so we opened the studio earlier, and invited participants to come early to talk and get caught up before the workshop began.

Following the question/response period, participants were encouraged to leave their "internal critics" in a basket provided in the waiting room. If their internal critics were insistent upon watching, they were asked to give their critics a task to perform, such as making only supportive comments. Having taken care of their inner critics, participants then engaged in the creative arts activity chosen for that day. Participants were encouraged to remain silent as they worked to facilitate focus on their own process. Activities in the first few sessions included collage, mandalas, and scribble drawings, all viewed as less threatening to those who might feel artistically challenged. Upon completing their projects, participants were encouraged to journal in response to their creations. In the final approximately 30 minutes (we often ran over), participants would display their work and share their responses to it with the group. Occasionally, participants would receive feedback from the group and some education took place about how to deliver that feedback.

The Creative Arts Experiences

Mandalas

During the first workshop session, participants were introduced to the mandala and provided with oil pastels and a sheet of 14″ × 17″ paper with a lightly drawn 11-inch diameter circle. Participants were asked to simply draw with an awareness of the circle. Responses to this exercise varied with only one participant expressing discomfort with the process. Upon completion of the mandala, participants were asked to give their mandalas a title and to then either journal or create a mind map* using the title as a focus.

Several mandalas from that first meeting are shown in Figures 16.4, 16.5, and 16.6. As products of the first meeting they reflect a range of responses and the diversity of the group. In the mandala shown in Figure 16.4, the artist shared that it brought up feelings that she thought she had been done with and indicated that the artwork was giving her something to think about. Her later reflections upon this effort included

I started with the pink to yellow spring of life and hope. A gray women has her head bowed before a darkness yet has a sunshine heart. With the left half, I had absolutely nothing to add. This was one of the first times I began experiencing art as process.

The mandalas shown in Figures 16.5 and 16.6 were created by a woman diagnosed with colon cancer. I often suggest the use of both white and black backgrounds when creating mandalas. It can also be helpful to suggest the use of the nondominant hand. Use of the nondominant hand is especially helpful when participants have trouble letting go of expectations for the "product" or final result. This participant came to the workshop with a background as a scientist with no prior experience with the arts. She appeared to surprise herself with her responses to the creative arts activities.

Below are her reflections on the mandala shown in Figure 16.5:

The idea of mandalas was totally new to me. At once I thought that this was going to be a fun thing to do. I chose bright colors initially because I was in a happy mood. Then for some reason I shaded it with a little darker color — I was trying to reflect my current situation of a HOPE for things to get better with my colon cancer but also accept the fact that right then my cancer situation was a little "iffy" and thus, the little darkening colors.

About her second mandala shown in Figure 16.6, she commented:

Again, I was in a sort of optimistic mode but quite unsure of the future about my colon cancer. I knew there was a lot of energy within me but presently confined and limited by my disease and my treatment.

The mandalas shown in Figures 16.7 and Figure 16.8 are those of a woman who had been diagnosed with stage 4 ovarian cancer approximately four months prior to the workshop. She was extremely upset with the events that preceded her diagnosis when she felt her symptoms were

---

*The term *mind maps* refers to the process of focusing on the mandala title and recording word associations in four- to five-word chains. Once a chain appears to have come to completion, a new chain begins by refocusing on the title. The mind map process terminates when focusing on the title yields no new chains.

FIGURE 16.6 Second mandela created by a woman diagnosed with ovarian cancer. (Photo courtesy of Carole M. McNamee.)

not taken seriously. Her anger with her circumstances and her physician was profound. The mandala in Figure 16.7 was created at the initial intake appointment before the group's first meeting. At that time, I encouraged the participant to create a second healing mandala when she was ready. At the first group meeting, the participant acknowledged that she had not yet created a healing mandala and chose to do so at that meeting. That mandala is shown in Figure 16.8.

Participant reflections on the first mandala were as intense as the images that appeared as she drew.

> Oh my God. ... the urgent panic, the rage at the dying of the light. Sliced open, ripped apart. Full of Cancer and death. ... no way to express the violation (that was now necessary) because of the doctor's betrayal and sin. ... Awful to remember. The shock. I am glad I have a record of it. For so many go through this. I wish now I had had more time to elaborate on it to express to others how hard the journey is.

Several weeks later, her mandala, shown in Figure 16.8 reflects a calmer state of mind. She reflected on this mandala:

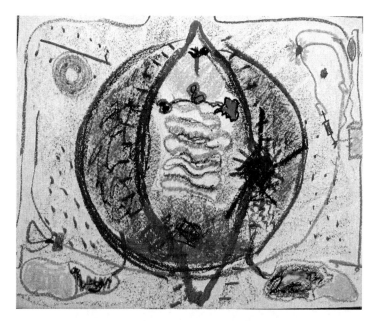

FIGURE 16.7   Mandalas from a pre-workshop meeting with the facilitator and in the first workshop session. (Photo courtesy of Carole M. McNamee.)

FIGURE 16.8   Made by a woman diagnosed with ovarian cancer. (Photo courtesy of Carole M. McNamee.)

I needed to make one [a mandala] for myself. I could only rely on myself. I had to direct my own healing, participate in it fully. "No bastard seedling left," "was attacked," and "there must be some left," describe my anger and desperation. I had to focus on "healing and restoring" and I am convinced this visual process was paramount in my getting hold of it. It is beautiful. I want to hang it on my wall with my journaling and the mind map. I love the image of "we lay upon each other." I think of how my dog nestles up to me when I feel bad — and how my husband's healing, loving hand pats on my shoulder, my side, in bed, when I moaned in pain.

Collage

In the second session, participants were directed to look through selected collage materials, cutting out images that evoked significant positive or negative responses. Provided materials included magazines with art, sculpture, wildlife, cultural, landscape, family, and current events themes. The images were then assembled in one or more collages and participants were asked to reflect upon their chosen collections of images. This was a particularly comfortable exercise for all participants and the discussion of chosen images was open and honest.

FIGURE 16.9 Collage with images reflecting the artist's experience of breast cancer. (Photo courtesy of Carole M. McNamee.)

The oldest member of the group and one who was more challenged by the art activities, created the collage shown in Figure 16.9. The images provide an obvious view of her struggle with breast cancer.

Her comments reflect her relief at being able to work with collage materials. "I was pleased to work on the collage because it didn't require drawing. I found pictures which conveyed an idea of what it is like to experience breast cancer."

Scribble Drawing

In the third meeting, participants were directed to create a scribble, using one continuous movement on an 18" × 24" sheet of paper. To encourage looseness in their scribbles, we practiced using large sweeping arm movements in the air before putting pen to paper. Thirty seconds is typically enough time to create a usable scribble. Next the participants were directed to focus on their scribbles visually, noticing any images that emerged from the scribble. This process was repeated with the scribble placed in all four directions. Participants then chose which images and direction they wanted to develop and to outline and fill in their images.

Figure 16.10 shows a scribble drawing created by the youngest member of the group.

Reflecting upon the experience of her scribble drawing, this young woman commented:

FIGURE 16.10   Scribble drawing by youngest participant in the group. (Photo courtesy of Carole M. McNamee.)

When I drew this picture, I remember feeling like I was the girl in red. Frail, tangled-up, dreaming of comfort and warmth. I wish I were the girl in blue, resting comfortably on a big couch instead of trying to find balance on the orange ball.

I see that the girl has her eyes closed. I didn't want to be conscious of the changes and everything that was happening to me. I wanted to get away and forget everything.

Healing Stone

In week 4, the participants first drew names to identify partners. Participants were then invited to create a "healing" stone to give to their partner. Dendritic soapstone of varying sizes and shapes was provided and participants each selected a piece to carve. Because soapstone is soft, sandpaper of varying grades was sufficient for the carving process. Masks were also provided to prevent inhalation of dust. At the close of the session, healing stones were exchanged along with words of support and encouragement.

Full-Body Painting/Collage

In week 6, participants created full body painting/collages. They began by creating or tracing an outline of their bodies on 2′ x 6′ sheets of paper. Tempera paints and collage materials were provided and participants were

FIGURE 16.11   Full body painting/collage using tempera paints by a woman with a recurrence of breast cancer. (2′ x 6′). (Photo courtesy of Carole M. McNamee.)

FIGURE 16.12   Collaborative mural created by six members of the study using tempera paints. (Photo courtesy of Carole M. McNamee.)

free to use any combination to embellish their self-images. Figure 16.11 shows one participant's painting/collage.

The quote below provides a reflection on the internal process of this participant as she created her "super hero."

> … started with a happy face, felt pretty good that day … but the paint kept dripping and I realized while my head was OK my body kept wanting to cry. [I] added the crown and feathers to show jauntiness and humor to balance the sad — made her a "super saint" as if she is "Cancer Wonder Woman" or some super hero."

Collaborative Mural

In week 7 of the workshop, six of the seven participants were present and engaged in the collaborative mural shown in Figure 16.12. Participants each found positions along the wall and began to paint. Every 5 to 10 minutes (as directed), participants shifted their position to the right (circularly) so that each participant contributed to each section of the mural. Upon returning to their original position, participants were given the opportunity to provide any final touches. For most of the participants, this project appeared to be the highlight of their experience. Below are a few participant comments associated with the experience of creating and viewing this mural:

> I love the power of the group to accept and receive each others offering, to recognize what each was saying and to add without undoing — the process of listening actively. It captures the survival and power of love among us — what we can do together!
> It's the group's child — no one can understand it or know its meanings like us.
>   … a wonderful project especially later in the group as we had gotten to know and trust each other. Finding ways to make our own make on others' art and then being OK with what others had done

FIGURE 16.13   Clay mask created in week 5 by the youngest participant in the group. (Photo courtesy of Carole M. McNamee.)

to my own beginning marks was fascinating. … one of my favorite projects, it feels good to look at.

I love the mural … I am amazed that in the "middle" of all the images and ideas and activity, I discerned some spirituality…

Clay Mask

The clay mask activity began in the fifth meeting when wet clay was rolled and shaped into individual masks. In two cases, the participants chose to place the clay over their own faces to mold it. In others, the masks were shaped over a ball made of plastic bags. Tools and extra clay were provided to help decorate the masks. The masks were then fired and returned to their creators for painting/embellishing in the eighth session. Figure 16.13 shows the clay mask created by the youngest participant in the study. Below are the comments of the creator of this clay mask:

Once I started sculpting the clay mask the first thing that came into my mind was something that I'd seen months before; a ritual in an African tribe where mothers hold their children down while the father cuts patterns and designs in the child's face. When interviewed the parents explain the importance of knowing that life is full of pain. One cannot live until one has felt pain. ... I see the pain and suffering I have felt, but I also see fierce eyes with determination.

☐ Summary

In spring 2006, The Arts in Healthcare Project sponsored a research project, "Finding the Creative Fire," which explored the effects of creative arts experiences on levels of distress in cancer patients. Seven participants met for approximately two hours each week for eight weeks and participated in a variety of creative arts experiences, including mandala drawings, collage, mask making, painting soapstone carving, and collaborative art. Participant responses indicate that participation in creative arts activities had several benefits including the feeling of not being alone, increased awareness of other's experience, increased understanding of their illness, increased acceptance of their illness, and the opportunity to express feelings.

I always was in better spirits when I left class. It was a bonding of cancer survivors. It was fun. They [the leaders] made all of us feel artistic.

I have a better emotional vocabulary to describe my feelings about the return of my cancer and the process of my explaining my situation to others. I wasn't surprised by the feelings that came out in the art but was able to explore more deeply and fully through the art process.

I am more accepting of the fact of my illness — before I was looking at it as something that I had shoved under a rug — I did not want to confront that fact that it is there. Now I know that it is there and I can deal with it also on the conscious level, not just on a medical scientific level. I am more at ease talking about it and more accepting that I am indeed going through the effects of cancer [treatment] and not rejecting the reality.

It [the group] was something that was different from my realm of experiences (being a science person) and it was a release of some tension as well as [experiencing] a creativity that I did not know existed within me.

... knowing that no matter how bad a situation is, there is always hope.

At the close of the project, all seven participants expressed a desire to share their work and associated narratives. Sharing their work is just one more step in a healing process.

While medicine is in charge of the crucial treatment of these patients, it is clear that the creative arts activities described in this chapter provided opportunities for an improved quality of life and healing for the soul.

Carol M. McNamee, Director, the Arts in Healthcare Project at the Family Therapy Center of Virginia Tech, Blacksburg, VA. Carol uses the creative process to facilitate individual and family wellness. She earned her PhD in marriage and Family Therapy from Virginia Tech, and an MS and PhD in computer science. She has published many publications on creativity and holds workshops on wellness and creativity throughout the United States. She is an affiliate research professor at the Family Therapy Center at Virginia Tech.

Resources

American Cancer Society. (2006). http://www.cancer.org/docroot/PRO/content/PRO_1_1_Cancer_Statistics_2006_presentation.asp?, accessed September 16, 2006.

Collie, K., Bottorff, J., Long, B., & Conati, C. (2006). Distance art groups for women with breast cancer: guidelines and recommendations. *Support Care Cancer,* 14(8), 849–858.

Ferszt, G., Massotti, E., Williams, J., & Miller, J. (2000). The impact of an art program on an inpatient oncology unit. *Illness, Crisis, and Loss, 8*(2), 189–199.

Kaye, R. (1991). *Spinning straw into gold: Your emotional recovery from breast cancer.* New York: Simon & Schuster.

Luzzato, P., & Gabriel, B. (2000). The creative journey: A model for short-term group art therapy with post-treatment cancer patients. *Art Therapy: Journal of the American Art Therapy Association, 17*(4), 265–269.

Malchiodi, C. (1999). *Medical art therapy with adults.* London: Jessica Kingsley.

McNiff, S. (2004). *Art heals: How creativity cures the soul.* Boston: Shambhala.

McNiff, S. (1992). *Art as medicine: Creating a therapy of the imagination.* Boston: Shambhala.

Nainis, N., Paice, J., Ratner, J., Wirth, J., Lai, J., & Shott, S. (2006). Relieving symptoms in cancer: Innovative use of art therapy. *Journal of Pain and Symptom Management, 31*(2), 162–169.

Öster, I., Svensk, A., Magnusson, E., Thyme, K., Sjödin, M., & Åström, S. (2006). Art therapy improves coping resources: a randomized, controlled study among women with breast cancer. *Palliative and Supportive Care, 4,* 57–64.

Serlin, I., Classen, C., Frances, B., & Angell, K. (2000). Symposium: Support groups for women with breast cancer: Traditional and alternative expressive approaches. *The Arts in Psychotherapy, 27*(2), 123–138.

Targ, E., & Levine, E. (2002). The efficacy of mind-body-spirit group for women with breast cancer: A randomized controlled trial. *General Hospital Psychiatry, 24,* 238–248.

Wheeler, W. (1998). *Path through the fire.* Northford, CT:

Zemen, L. (1998). *Whose breasts are these, anyway? Making the most of breast cancer survival: A workbook.* Onancock, VA:

Sandra Baughman
and Laura Kiser

Programs for Teens and Children

Happy hearts and happy faces,
Happy play in grassy places—
That was how, in ancient ages,
Children grew to kings and sages.

—**Robert Louis Stevenson**, *Good and Bad Children*

☐ Teens and Creative Arts
Sandra Baughman

Grief support programs that include interventions such as creative writing, music, and the visual arts are helpful in assisting adolescents in their attempt to achieve an emotional balance on their journey through grief. Adolescence is a particularly difficult time of life to experience loss. Teenagers are faced with the monumental task of integrating their need for nurturing while breaking away in search of independence. The inclusion of the arts in a group support setting for adolescents creates a safe expressive place to share feelings and concerns that would otherwise go unaddressed. Creative arts-based programming offers grieving teens an avenue of expression that other forms of intervention do not. The physical act of involvement in the arts often allows adolescents to release unspoken pain, thereby creating a foundation for healing.

My experience with the use of art in grief support is primarily with children and adolescents. An effective program is one that uses various aspects of the arts to help identify high-risk individuals as well as building a safe environment to explore and cope with feelings of loss. Identifying high-risk teenagers can be achieved by having the group members create coping dictionaries. The initial act of creating the cover, manipulating the materials, and the informal discussion that ensues during the activity is extremely effective as a prelude to the sharing of thoughts on coping that will ultimately become part of the project. A young man who continually exhibited anger and inappropriate behavior, rarely participating in the group discussion and sharing, reached a crossroads during this activity. Group members were encouraged to embellish the cover of their coping dictionary with images of their feelings. As the group assembled images for their books, the young man blurted out "Sometimes I just want to kill myself." His immersion in creating the dictionary cover allowed him to open up and reveal a serious issue that staff could then address.

Another powerful arts-based activity for adolescents involves the use of music and words. We were fortunate enough to have access to a creative writing professor from a local university who enthusiastically volunteered his time to our program. He graciously donated his band as well as his expertise in poetry and worked with our students to help them to use words to free-associate their feelings. An advantage to bringing in someone with experience teaching creative writing is their willingness to share their own emotional journey. Group members will often relate to them in a way they may not be able to relate to other adults in the program. At the next session the band acted as a background to a sort of "open-mike" night for the group members to share their creative poetry. As always, the option to pass was available. Many of the teenagers participated and a few who were uncomfortable getting up with the band asked someone else to read their work. When the entire group hears feelings expressed by others, it is often a relief to know that they are not alone in their grief. The sharing of words and music provided a basis on which healing dialogue could take place. Music brings adolescents together in a very positive way.

A wonderful way to reach adolescents at their level and provide a creative way to memorialize someone is to put oneself in their shoes. The graffiti project offers a sense of permanence, which is important to this part of the grief process. Group members chose a name or word with a special meaning. Once that was done, students prepared their own board to resemble a portion of a brick wall, mixing paint and sand to create a brick effect. Once dry, the special word or name was carefully drawn out and then painted, paying special attention to the typical graffiti style. Adolescents embrace this type of project as they connect to it on many levels.

A creative arts-based grief support program can reach adolescents at their own level. The use of arts-based activities as the core of the program, as opposed to merely being a part of the program, attempts to connect grieving adolescents to their emotional self. Each project offers a path for individuals to find a way out of despair, depression, anger, and fear.

Immersion in the arts through carefully selected mentors, materials, and themes can reveal a sliver of light at the end of a very long tunnel.

Sandra S. Baughman is a graduate student pursuing a master's of science degree in hospice (bereavement programming) at Madonna University, Livonia, Michigan. She is an Arts for the Spirit Coordinator in the Oakwood Healthcare System and owner and instructor at The Creative Cottage Fine Art Studio in Northville, Michigan.

☐ The Grief of Children: Creating a Family Mark
Laura Kiser

When children experience the death of someone close to them, communication of the feelings associated with this loss can be difficult to articulate and express. Verbal communication is often too overwhelming and children may not feel they are part of a supportive environment that would allow for such difficult disclosure. My role as an art therapist and licensed clinical professional counselor in a palliative care and hospice center and in pediatric hospitals has allowed me to work with children, adolescents, and families who have experienced loss on many levels. This section will focus on the use of art therapy as an effective intervention when working at a bereavement camp for children who had experienced the death of a family member. Through the creation of memory boxes children were able to preserve the memory of the individual who had died. As these boxes were later assembled into a camp totem pole, children had a symbol of the support they had received from other children and validation that they were not alone in the grief process.

The Loss and Grief of Children

Some of the losses that children experience can be easily recognized while others are harder to decipher by those providing support. Death of a family member or friend, abuse, divorce, destructive or uncontrollable acts of nature or man, and a violent neighborhood or home environment are easily identifiable losses that children experience (O'Toole, 1998). Other losses that affect children in a less obvious way include extended hospitalizations, changes in family pattern or structure, academic difficulties, personal or family health changes, adoptive or foster home changes, and friends or family moving (O'Toole, 1998). Children's reactions and adaptation to these losses are greatly affected by their understanding of the loss, the information they receive, their support network, and their ability and permission to grieve.

Grief is the natural and normal response to the distress we experience when something in our life changes due to a loss of some nature. Children grieve the deaths of family members and individuals that are close to them. Grief is not something that surfaces when someone is mature enough; it affects everyone at all ages. According to Wolfelt, "Grief does not focus on one's ability to understand, but instead on ones ability to feel" (1998, p. 20). Grief is how we adapt to the loss we experience and transform our lost physical relationship to a symbolic and abstract relationship (O'Toole, 1998). Grief manifests into feelings, mental responses, and physical reactions. Children can feel anger, sadness, emptiness, fear, anxiety, shock, and disbelief, as well as betrayal, guilt, shame, blame, and relief.

Due to children's incomplete emotional and cognitive development, the signs and symptoms of childhood grief are less obvious and of shorter duration (Heegaard, Jones Clark, & Zambelli, 1989). This does not mean that children experience grief in a less intense manner. There are many debates over a child's ability to understand death and at what age this occurs. Many believe that children prior to the age 3 or 4 are unable to achieve complete mourning and that by adolescence most children can mourn (Heegaard et al., 1989). Despite all of the controversy regarding complete mourning, children react to loss at all ages and experience grief according to their cognitive and emotional level at that time. Children experience grief at each new developmental stage, needing to process their loss repeatedly in order to understand and grow.

Throughout the grieving process, there are many factors that children need to reconcile. Children need to accept the reality of the death and attempt to establish meaning from the loss. They must find new ways to include the deceased person in their lives through the maintenance of memories and the creation of memorials. Children need to adjust to the changes; especially to an environment in which their loved one is missing. These tasks can be accomplished successfully with a supportive network of family, caregivers, and friends. Bereaved children need to feel secure and understood in their grieving process. They need to feel heard when discussing their uncertainties and may need to seek out understanding and supportive adults other than their family members if these adults are also grieving (Heegaard et al., 1989). How a parent responds to the death affects the child's reactions and understanding of the loss. Grief counseling and bereavement groups can provide the supportive space for children and families to express themselves.

Group Work with Bereaved Children

Since many bereaved children are at risk for psychological or emotional difficulties, preventative intervention strategies are often necessary (Heegaard et al., 1989). Due to the complexity of children's grief, support that is goal oriented and provides structure and education can be a beneficial component to the grief work.

Group therapy is a crucial element to the therapeutic process because it validates a child's grief by assuring them that they are not alone, that grief is natural and normal, and that it is beneficial to express grief in appropriate ways. Group therapy can provide a social sanction for expression and promote adaptive mourning responses (Heegaard et al., 1989). Our society has youth trained to believe that death is a forbidden subject. By participating in a bereavement group, children can be a part open communication with others regarding the death and their feelings surrounding the loss.

Art Therapy with Bereaved Children

Children have always used art to communicate, especially when they are trying to depict conflicts or complex thoughts or feelings that are too difficult to articulate in words. The act of creating a concrete representation of a feeling allows a child to become an active participant in their grief process, combining their image and their verbal processing of the image to acknowledge feelings and promote change. Art therapy enables bereaved children to surpass the intellectual and emotional limitations associated with understanding and conveying feelings about death (Heegaard et al., 1989). This is especially important in the grief process as children attempt to preserve their relationship with the individual who has died, focusing now on an abstract and symbolic relationship instead of a physical one. Hrenko cites Cook and Dworkin's study (1992), stating, "Artistic creations can serve as concrete reminders of more abstract ideas, values, or emotions. These creative works often seem to encapsulate the essence of what the bereaved shared with the deceased" (Hrenko, 2005, p. 85).

Therapeutic Effects of a Camp Environment

Michalski cites Beyers (1970), Kelk (1994), Levitt (1994), Schwartz (1960), Shasby, Heychert, and Gansheder (1984), stating that as camp programs offer participants invaluable opportunities to grow and develop, the advantages extend to participants return to nature, increased self-worth, improved and supportive relationships with both peers and adults, and greater ability to take on responsibility (Michalski, 2003, p. 54). For children that may feel isolated or dissimilar to their peers due to situations such as the death of a sibling or parent, the camp environment can offer an experience that provides connections, enhanced relationships, and the crucial validation that these children need.

While working at a palliative care and hospice center, I had the opportunity to provide art therapy services to pediatric hospice patients, children experiencing anticipatory grief as a family member was dying, and children in the bereavement program. I assisted in the creation of their first bereavement camp that would provide a therapeutic program for children who had experienced death. This camp was a weeklong day camp that provided bereavement services to children in the community. Transportation services were provided to and from the camp, allowing children who lived in communities where resources were insufficient despite the large number of children needing services to participate in this experience. Children were between the ages of 6 and 13, and all had experienced the loss of a family member. The activities and interventions were led by some of the counselors from the hosting hospice organization, counselors from a local bereavement organization that had partnered with the hospice, and volunteers who had been trained by the hospice's children's bereavement counselor. The camp provided activities that promoted connection through the sharing of feelings associated with the loss, team building, education on grief responses, creative interventions, and physical activities such as swimming, hiking, and experience on a ropes course. This balance allowed children the space to invest in new activities and develop new relationships through creativity and growth.

I was asked to provide an art experience that would be a part of each day's schedule during the week. I wanted to provide an intervention that, within this safe and therapeutic environment, would lead to creativity, exploration, and connection through the process of art making and verbal processing. I chose to introduce to the children the idea of constructing a group totem pole assembled from sections individually created by each camper. The totem pole theme felt appropriate as an intervention because of its connectedness to family, storytelling, tradition, and memory keeping.

The word *totem* means family mark. It is a common misconception that totem poles were tools in religious practices, representing a god or gods and worshipped by those who created them. The figures and carvings on a totem pole often represented ancestors and became symbols of their identity and records of their history (Wright, n.d.). These structures became a family's mark, a record of who they were and a concrete representation of that generation and previous generations. It is this documentation of history and memory keeping that appealed to me as an intervention that promoted the goals of this bereavement camp.

The children and their family members were invited to an opening event the day before camp started to allow campers an opportunity to interact with the other participants while being surrounded by their family members. This also gave the parents and caregivers a chance to connect with each other, meeting other adults who were experiencing similar losses and perhaps sharing related struggles. At the end of this family event I introduced the totem pole project to the campers and their families. I educated them on the meaning of totem poles and clarified that the symbols, often portrayals of animals and people, represented the story of the carver and the tribe. The campers were informed that they were each going to create one part of the totem pole; their family mark. Children were given handouts that offered descriptions from many cultures around the world of the symbolism of certain animals. Some examples were:

> Fish-knowledge
> Antelope-grace, beauty
> Bear-nurturing, protective
> Butterfly-metamorphosis
> Bee-rebirth, soul
> Birds-freedom, sight
> Dog-guidance, protection
> Dragon-strength, wisdom
> Leopard-courage, speed
> Frog-hidden beauty
> Decker & Komando, n.d.

I encouraged the children to take the handout home and discuss with their families what animal or animals they thought represented their family unit. It was stressed to the families to include their entire family, even the family member or members who had died. This handout was a design used to generate conversation between the children and their parents and stimulate their imaginations as they thought about the person who had died in a different way.

As the children arrived on the first day of camp, there was apprehension as well as excitement. Although most of the children had met the day before, it was still daunting to be a part of a group that was unfamiliar. The facilitators and counselors provided a team building physical activity that began the process of connecting and sharing. With some of their energy spent, I gathered the children together to begin the art activity. It was obvious that the children had put much thought into deciding what animals could represent their families as the dialogues began about which animal or animals they had chosen. Creativity was encouraged as children wanted to combine multiple animals into one new species. Some children's decisions were based on characteristics identified as being connected to certain animals, while other's decisions were based on animals that the child liked or connected them to the family member who had died. If a child was struggling with ideas, a counselor would sit with that child and have a conversation with them about their family; asking them to highlight certain characteristics and personalities of the members. A few of the children needed guidance through this process because recollection was difficult and emotional. As the children shared stories and memories about their family in this accepting environment, they seemed relieved and were able to identify what animals they wanted to represent their family unit.

Excitement grew as the materials were handed out to begin the creation of these three-dimensional animal sculptures. When everyone had received a 12 × 12″ box with a fold down top flap, the curiosity of the campers was roused and questions began about how a box could be turned into an animal. I stressed that the box was a very important element to our animals because not only was it was going to be the base of our animal design, it was also going to become a memory box, a container to safely hold feelings and memories of the family member who had died.

Cathy Malchiodi (1992) states that, "Art has often been made in memory of someone who is lost or departed. In some cases, all art expression may serve as an act of remembrance" (p. 117). Boxes have been used often in art therapy as containers that represent security, structure, and safety; vessels that can hold the important and the sacred. It was in these boxes that the children could use paint, markers, and collage to create a significant space for memories of those that had died. Children were encouraged throughout the week to bring photos, drawings, and other items of special significance and emotional connection that could be placed inside the memory box.

These first few sessions would be designated for the development and construction of the animals. The box would be the base of the animal and the campers could use newspaper and duct tape as sculptural materials to create wings, heads, tails, arms, legs, and other parts of the animals that emerged from the box. The top and bottom of the boxes were to be kept flat so these containers could be opened and used as a memory box and so the animals could be stacked on top of each other when constructing the totem poles on the last day of camp. The facilitators and counselors were able to assist the children with any construction and help problem solve as children transformed these boxes into animals waiting to emerge from these containers.

The many roles of the facilitators during this activity were crucial to the children feeling successful and safe in their process of constructing their animals, creating their memory boxes, and building the totem poles. Molding the newspaper into something the child thinks represents the animal and manipulating duct tape to secure these structures on the box can be difficult and frustrating. It was important that the facilitators helped the children when they were frustrated, but that they kept their expectations or opinions to themselves. Assisting the child empowers them in the process but taking over can inhibit their creativity and imagination. As the facilitators worked with the children they often mirrored the actions of the child, allowing for a dialogue to begin about the process and creating a space for the child to share what their choices represented as they created their animals. Through this constant encouragement and reflection, the facilitators became essential partners through this process and journey.

As the children worked for two days on the construction of the animals, it was remarkable to witness the intention that was emerging from these boxes. "I'm making mine into a bear and a dog because my dad loved dogs and he was strong and powerful like a bear. He helped me when I was scared because he wasn't scared of anything. My box has the head of a bear but a dog tail and legs. I'm going to paint it brown and yellow because those are the colors of our dog." Stories and memories like these were shared often with the facilitators and other campers during the process. The third and fourth days were set aside for painting and adding embellishments to these creations. Acrylic paint was used and yarn, raffia, glitter, sequins, and other assemblage materials were provided. One camper whose box was transformed into a butterfly stated, "I am going to paint the wings of my butterfly purple and pink because those were my mommy's favorite colors. I need lots of glitter for the wings because my butterfly has to be pretty."

The final day of construction was set aside for the completion of the memory boxes. Children used fabrics, beautiful papers, and paint to adorn the inside. Pictures had been brought to camp throughout the week and were glued inside of these boxes. Small items that reminded the child of their family member were also placed inside these containers. The children had worked with the facilitators throughout the week on writing down memories about their family member. These stories and memories were a large component in the children's grief process as they shared their reminiscences and articulated their feelings. These stories were also placed inside of the memory boxes.

On the last day the children gathered at the camp before going to a nearby park where there would be a picnic for campers and their families to celebrate the camp experience. The children came together with their animal sculptures to share with the others how the process of creating these family mark's had been. The children articulated the meaning behind their choices for animals to represent their family units and their choices of what was placed inside the memory boxes. The nervousness that had been felt on the first day was clearly gone as the children felt cohesiveness with the group and were comfortable sharing difficult feelings with these other children who had similar experiences. The final component to this process was going to be the construction of the totem poles at the picnic site at a nearby park. Children were each given a beautiful stone that would help to mark the sacred space at the park where the assembly could begin. As we formed a line to begin our walk over to the park, some of the children volunteered to beat special drums along the way. The image of these children walking down the street and holding these animal sculptures while the sound of the beating drum resonated was powerful. The group was remarkably quiet, seeming to understand the power of this ritual and its connection to their families. When the group arrived at the park, the children walked around searching for an appropriate spot. Criteria for appropriateness, as clarified by the campers, included level ground, proximity to the lake, proximity to the picnic site, and sufficient sunlight that would illuminate the totems. Everyone placed his or her stone on the ground creating a large circle that would surround the totem pole site. The group then decided that three totem poles should be built so that the structures were sound, not vulnerable to the elements of nature. I chose to put the construction of the totem poles into the hands of the children, having them decide where each family mark would be placed. The process went effortlessly as the campers made their decisions based on animal types and aesthetics. They were insistent on not having two of the same animals in a row or similar colors in close proximity. The result was an incredibly unified collection of animals and family marks that stood tall and created a prevailing presence. The last piece to this ritual allowed the campers to acknowledge the difficult and emotional grief work they had all done individually and together. Each child was given a small container of bubbles and asked to think of a wish for all of the other campers. Simultaneously, each camper blew their bubbles, sending their wishes out into the world. This physical representation of the support and wishes each camper shared was an affirmation to the power of their group. A Polaroid picture was taken of each child next to the totem poles before the totem poles were dismantled.

Conclusion

Art therapy was a successful addition to the curriculum for a bereavement camp for children who had experienced the death of a family member. Art making provided a powerful outlet for the expression of feelings associated with grief. The goals of the art experience were to create a connection between campers who often feel isolated in their grief, promote effective and appropriate ways of communicating grief, encourage the development of a symbolic relationship with the deceased family member, foster creativity, and create a safe and secure environment where these children felt supported. These children left with the "tools" needed to be active participants in their grief work and the confirmation that they can find positive support systems through this process.

Laura Kiser, is a registered art therapist and licensed clinical professional counselor who has extensive experience working with child, adolescents, and families in pediatric hospitals and palliative care and hospice settings. She has guest lectured at universities and to communities on the use of art therapy in hospital settings, end-of-life issues, and grief work. She currently is providing art therapy and counseling services to children and families at The Children's Hospital at Montefiore in the Bronx

Resources

Cummings, R., Michalski, J.H., Mishna, F., & Worthington, C. (2003). A multi-method impact evaluation of a therapeutic summer camp program. *Child and Adolescent Social Work Journal, 20*(1), 53–76.

Decker, J., & Komando, V., (Date not provided). Animal symbolism — Many cultures. Retrieved September 7, 2006 from http://www.princetonol.com/ groups/iad/ lessons/middle/animals2.htm.

Heegaard, M., Johns Clark, E., & Zambelli, G.C. (1989). Art therapy for bereaved children. In H. Wadeson, J. Durkin, & D. Perach (Eds.), *Advances in art therapy.* (pp. 60–80). New York: Wiley.

Hrenko, K.D. (2005). Remembering Camp Dreamcatcher: Art therapy with children whose lives have been touched by HIV/AIDS. *Art Therapy: Journal of the American Art Therapy Association, 22* (1), 39–43.

Malchiodi, C.A. (1992). Art and loss. *Art Therapy: Journal of the American Art Therapy Association, 9*, 114–118.

Piccirillo, E. (1999). Hide and seek, the art of living with HIV/AIDS. In C. Malchiodi (Ed.), *Medical art therapy with children.* (.pp. 113–132). London: Jessica Kingsley.

Wolfelt, A. (1998). *Helping children cope with grief.* Bristol, PA: Accelerated Development, Inc. (Original work published 1983)

Wright, Dr. R.K. (n.d.). Totem poles: Heraldic columns of the Northwest Coast. Retrieved September 20, 2006 from http://content.lib.washington.edu/ aipnw/wright.html

J. Earl Rogers
and Janet Feldman

Alternative Art Forms

The human Essence is the part of us that is innate and real, and can participate in the real world.

—**A.H. Almass,** *Diamond Heart, Book Four, Indestructible Innocence*

☐ ActALIVE: Addressing HIV/AIDS-Related Grief and Healing Through Art
Janet Feldman

The HIV/AIDS pandemic has, since the early to mid-1980s, left more than 40 million people infected worldwide, more than 20 million dead, and many more millions who are affected by it in one way or another, from widows left to support their families to orphans who have no family left at all. In this context, grief is ever-present, and healing seems a challenge almost beyond measure. The good news is that the human spirit, ever undaunted, is alive and well and living in the artistry and creativity which has been applied to address HIV/AIDS, not only in terms of prevention and education, but also with regard to grief and healing, struggle and transcendence.

The international arts coalition, ActALIVE (http://www.actalive. org), is composed of 300 members in 30 countries, both individuals and

FIGURE 18.1 Mural from brightly colored handprints. (Photo courtesy of Janet Feldman.)

organizations, who use the arts for educational and healing purposes.* One of the most compelling motivators for creative solutions to addressing the myriad of challenges HIV/AIDS presents is that grief and loss are endured so regularly, especially among the very young and those of the "first" generation, whose adult children have died from HIV/AIDS-related complications, leaving behind their parents and descendents.

Visual Arts: Education, Expression, and Empowerment

A number of empowering, educational, and enjoyable activities have been developed to enhance coping skills, encourage a sense of hope for the future, and improve the chances of healing. One of them, called "The Hands Project," has been developed at the Lifehome Center in Phuket, Thailand (http://www.lifehomeproject.org). Groups of women and youth are brought together to make a mural, on paper or cloth, from their brightly colored handprints, which they press onto the material, signing their names underneath the imprints (Figure 18.1). These murals have

---

*ActAlive has participants who belong to organizations mentioned in this chapter, SOLID, Playback Theater, Memory Book Project, Memory Box Project, Body Maps, NACWOLA, Save the Children, that, to date, are not themselves members of ActAlive. These organizations are included here because of their long-standing work related to art, health, grief, and healing, and because ActAlive has members either affiliated with these entities, or who carry out HIV/AIDS-related prevention activities based on artforms developed by them, such as "memory work."

been created as far afield as Kenya, where the technique was brought to a home for children orphaned by HIV/AIDS.

This activity is simple and fun, but also profound in its ability to help people to feel visible, to encourage a sense of well-being and community, to allow for expression of emotion when words and other forms of active engagement are not possible, or do not in themselves convey what is in people's hearts and minds. Another activity, which has proven to be both uplifting and educational, is the making of "peace tiles," so-called because this project began as a creative gift for children affected by war in Northern Uganda. Conceived by artist and educator, Lars Hasselblad Torres, the process involves making collages on small wood tiles (8 inches square) — using a wide variety of materials, from found objects to newspaper clippings, to personal mementos of significance — and gluing the design so as to fix it to the tile. The results of this work are displayed in murals of 30 tiles each.

The International Peace Tiles Project (http://www.peacetiles.net) began as a single exercise, meant to provide uplift to youth struggling to cope with the loss of families and of childhood itself, and has since branched out to encompass other themes and subjects, such as HIV/AIDS, sustainable development, and urban visions (for healthier cities in the future). For World AIDS Day, December 1, 2005, ActALIVE members (Lars is one) and others in 12 countries organized tile-making workshops that involved 1000 or more youth in the production of hundreds of tiles. These were developed into murals, which were shown in eight countries that included Nigeria, Senegal, Kenya, The Gambia, South Africa, the United States, India, and Switzerland. Three international murals — composed of mixed tiles from different countries — were shown: one in South Africa, one in Switzerland (at the headquarters of the Global Fund for AIDS, TB, and Malaria), and one in India. An Indian mural was shown at the Marquette Children's Museum in Marquette, Michigan, and youth there interviewed their Indian peers about this art project, as well as the challenges HIV/AIDS presents to their families, communities, and country. (Figure 18.2)

In India, nonprofit Gram Bharati Samiti (http://www.gbsjp.org) in Jaipur involved 40 schools and assorted organizations in their World AIDS Day project, and hosted a conference on that day at which the murals were exhibited and awareness about HIV/AIDS was raised. Murals in India and a number of the participating countries were then donated to schools, children's homes, Hospices, or the youth wing of hospitals.

The beauty of this project is that it can be done on both an intimate and a massive scale: an individual can make one tile, small groups can gather to make tiles on specific themes, and coalitions of people and organizations can come together — as they did in India and around the world — to create art that is accessible both locally and globally, to the individual and

FIGURE 18.2   Peace Tile made for World AIDS Day 2005, by the Global Aware-ness Club, Gulf Islands Secondary School, SaltSpring Island, British Columbia, Canada, for their sister school, Pitseng High School, Lesotho, Africa. (Picture by John Martin-McNab, for SOLID. With permission.)

to the collective. Regardless of the size or numbers involved, educational messages can be conveyed, health enhanced, and a sense of hope and well-being increased. An added bonus is that the resulting product can be donated to help youth who are coping with illness, loss, and grief.

An HIV/AIDS lesson component is often included as part of the work-shop program, an important adjunct to the creative activity. Research and anecdotal evidence suggests that HIV/AIDS education is often more effec-tive when paired with "entertainment" in some artistic form, and the tes-timonies received from those who have hosted workshops and created murals speaks eloquently to this point.

Theater and Music: Poetry in the Note of Life

Theater arts have proven to be equally powerful and compelling in terms of addressing the educational, psychological, emotional, and spiritual dimensions of the HIV/AIDS pandemic. Many members of ActALIVE use theater for educational purposes ("edutainment"), ranging from a peer counselor in Nigeria (Richie Adewusi of YouthAid Projects) who has written a family drama — now being serialized for television audiences there — to an accountant and part-time playwright in Kenya (Stan Tuvako, a volunteer for KAIPPG International, and cofounder of the ANFORD youth group) who has created a multimedia performance piece for youth, called "Poetry in the Note of Life." This play contains poetry, spoken words, music, dance, and song — in many sections composed by youth themselves — and is performed for and by youth.

One nonprofit administrator in Kenya (Ron Odhiambo of the St. Egidio Community) has written a play about the Peace Tiles — both the concept and mission, as well as how to make them — and taken it on the road, performing not only in Kenya but also Uganda and Tanzania. This play has also been filmed in Kenya — by Kenyan and American youth who took part in a joint storytelling project called JUMP (Juveniles Using Media Power), during the summer of 2006 — and plans are being made to distribute it more widely as an educational resource.

JUMP (http://www.jumptochangetheworld.org) uses film, photography, and audio (podcasting) to help youth create stories about their lives, with the goal of instilling a sense of pride and confidence, building bridges of understanding between youth of various countries and cultures, and changing the world for the better, one youth interchange at a time. All of the Kenyan youth who took part in 2006 have been in some way affected by HIV/AIDS — including loss of parents and other family members — so the project for them, and for the American youth as well, proved cathartic as well as educational and creative. JUMP, conceived by educator Robin Worley (Hawaii), will continue to address similar subjects in the future, providing an outlet for grief and loss, and an uplifting way to express and convey to others the challenges so many youth face today.

In a compelling book on this subject, called "Playing for Life: Performance in Africa in the Age of AIDS", author and communications professor Louise Bourgault (Northern Michigan University) discusses theater, song, poetry, and dance as avenues for expression, education, and empowerment around the pandemic. "One Life to Live," a South African play combining drama and dance, tells the story of a domestic servant who struggles to become a professional singer. HIV/AIDS prevention messages, as well as the gender inequality faced by women (itself a risk factor for HIV infection), are subjects conveyed to audiences via visual and auditory entertainment.

This method is especially effective for those with limited literacy (who cannot read written texts), or who know and use a local language only.

The South African song, "Come On," contains the exhortation to provide care and support for people living with HIV/AIDS: "Brothers and Sisters ... come on, come on, let's take initiatives, let's all be involved, let's care for these people with HIV/AIDS, let's keep them strong and looked after." Music is one of the most frequently used and popular methods to convey HIV/AIDS information. Often, new lyrics are added to older and easily recognized tunes, thus linking something traditional and familiar with the unfamiliar concepts and issues being addressed. "If You Don't Know AIDS By Now" ("… you will never, never know …") uses the chorus of a well-known American song to convey its prevention message ("… don't get too excited, and do unplanned things, because one mistake you make, can ruin your life forever.")

One project working at both the local/personal and global levels is One World Beat (http://www.oneworldbeat.org), which yearly organizes concerts, drumming, and other activities worldwide. Between the years 2002 and 2006, thousands of people in 45 countries have taken part in events ranging from an informal living-room get-together in Switzerland to a stadium in South Africa during Festival 2006, where 4000 participants gathered for an hour of drumming, linked to others in 16 countries who were doing the same thing, at the very same hour.

One World Beat has had a consistent focus on making a difference through music, which it seeks to do by encouraging activism and caring on the part of individuals and groups, by linking people in such a way that they feel a sense of global unity, sharing, and purpose. HIV/AIDS and health concerns — for people and for the planet — are a primary focus for this organization, as are peace and healing. Everyone is welcome to take part, whether a professional musician or a music lover who drums out a tune on a tabletop.

This kind of broad appeal and involvement of both professionals and amateurs alike can also be found in the work of Playback Theater, an international organization with chapters worldwide. The Playback method takes as its raw material the true stories of people's lives, converting them into drama which is accessible, highly charged, and deeply moving. Themes include HIV/AIDS and healing, and coping with grief and loss. One recent project, in New Orleans, works to help people address the enormous sense of helplessness, fear, anger, and sadness felt in the devastating wake of Hurricane Katrina, which destroyed large parts of the city in August 2005. http://www.playbacknet.org/iptn/index.htm http://www.playbackschool.org/Katrina_March_Trip2.htm

Writing for Your Life

The written word has proven equally compelling as a medium for expression of longing, grief, struggle, hope, insight, compassion, rage, and joy, in addition to its ability to motivate action and bring about change. Author, journalist, and yoga expert Michael McColly has for many years been writing about HIV/AIDS and health, subjects brought closer to home by his own HIV-positive status. Michael's new book, *The After-Death Room: Journey into Spiritual Activism* (2006), is a memoir which examines HIV/AIDS from numerous perspectives — including the individual and the global, the physical and spiritual, the intellectual and emotional — and through a cross- cultural lens, following the author as he travels the world, meeting a wide range of activists, from Zulu healers in South Africa to Buddhist monks in Thailand, sex workers in India to mullahs in Senegal, African-American ministers to artists in Vietnam. http://mccolly.ecorp.net

Writing becomes part of what the author does to address the effects of HIV/AIDS in his own life, in addition to whatever his work can do to help others both survive and thrive, despite or even because of this disease. The personal links to the political, and reportage blends with autobiography in such a way that insight, understanding, and a feeling of connectedness emerge, which can aid personal and planetary growth and healing. Yoga is an integral part of this work as well: Michael teaches simple Yoga exercises wherever he goes, believing this to be as effective and necessary as writing or any other form of activism to address HIV/AIDS.

In the epilogue to the book, he makes a compelling case for the role and power of individuals to help themselves, others, and the world, no matter who we are, where we are, what our circumstances or health condition. For those struggling with illness, loss, and grief, as well as those trying to provide comfort and give needed support, his insights are especially pertinent and valuable:

> We tend to believe that the solutions to complex social problems require great leaders, technological feats, enormous sums of money, and reams of think-tank experts. But the causes of injustice and suffering are never- ending. They demand another kind of intelligence, one that does not always follow reason, the correct political ideology, or religious doctrine. In fact, suffering confounds us precisely because we believe we have the will to eliminate it. Every religious tradition reminds us that our only choice is to embrace and learn from suffering. Almost everywhere I went around the world, activists asked me to stay and help them. Their pleas revealed to me a simple truth about political and social change: it begins and is sustained by individuals taking action.

Community Actions and Personal Expressions

In Canada, a large-scale event called "Time to Deliver: Community Action

FIGURE 18.3 "Time to Deliver" flags installation, composed of 8000 flags representing the numbers who die each day from HIV/AIDS, exhibited to date in eight Canadian communities and at the Toronto 2006 International AIDS Conference. (Picture by John Martin-McNab, for SOLID. With permission.)

on AIDS" is a public engagement that brings the urgency of HIV/AIDS home in a potent, visual way: a field of 8000 flags, arranged in the shape of a red HIV/AIDS ribbon surrounded by white crosses, confronts visitors with the dramatic and tragic scale of the pandemic. There is one flag for every person who currently dies from HIV/AIDS-related causes, each and every day. This moving tribute is a powerful way to connect communities in the fight against HIV/AIDS and to mobilize support for initiatives that address health issues and poverty. (Figure 18.3)

Currently installed in eight communities across Canada, "Time to Deliver" is proving to be a moving focal point to bring awareness and spur action on issues surrounding the disease. Through this public-art piece, the nonprofit SOLID (Salt Spring Organization for Life Improvement and Development) is calling on community groups worldwide to make their own "Day of AIDS" installations. Organizations with a focus on global issues, health, poverty, and gender equality are invited to participate in the campaign to mobilize communities, awaken the public, and step up action on the part of governments, groups, and individuals. (http://www.solid-saltspring.com) (Figure 18.4)

Over 8,000 Deaths Every Day
Promises Made
TIME TO DELIVER

Community Action on AIDS.
Victoria / Whitehorse / Kelowna / Calgary / Regina / Kenora / Toronto / Montreal / St. John's
VIDEA / ICAD / SOLID

In Partnership with

FIGURE 18.4   Connecting communities in the fight against HIV/AIDS. (Photo courtesy of Janet Feldman.)

This type of action makes a potent and unforgettable statement about the issues and urgencies brought on by HIV/AIDS, which has conse-quences at the individual and interpersonal levels, and at the commu-nity, national, and global levels. The exhibit encourages viewers to get informed and involved, to take action, donate, and volunteer. It provides an opportunity for community-based organizations to become involved in an international public education campaign through public art, linking these grassroots organizations together into a network of like-minded and determined groups who can share skills and resources, community-to-community, across the planet.

One additional aspect of this project contains an important element related to grief, support, and healing: in the spirit of engaging people to act meaningfully, the flag project takes on another life when the flags are taken down. Artists, teachers, grandparents, or anyone handy with a needle and thread is invited to transform flags into squares for quilts, which will be assembled by SOLID and sent to Lesotho to act as warm blankets for orphans who live in the mountains.

On a smaller scale in terms of size, but hopefully equally effective, is a   project in the works — organized by ActALIVE and Arts for Global Development (http://www.art4development.net) — which will ask people to decorate postcards, using HIV/AIDS as a theme. These will be displayed both in physical settings and online. The goal is similar to that of the Peace Tiles: to encourage expression and hopefully aid in education, healing, connection, and communication around the effects of the pandemic.

Puppets Perform, People Are Persuaded!

Puppets are playing a vital role in HIV/AIDS education and prevention, and on related human-development challenges and issues: domestic abuse, prison life, cultural diversity, political and social freedoms. Gary Friedman Productions (http://www.africanpuppet.com) makes use of puppets to address all of these subjects, working in diverse communities around the world, from Australia to South Africa to Fiji in the South Pacific.

Writing eloquently (on his website) about his artistic medium of choice, Friedman says:

> Puppetry has a unique ability to bring people together to examine community social issues. Our productions combine both music and humor, two proven ingredients for crossing cultural and language barriers and reaching people internationally. The puppet is a visual metaphor, representing "real life," but is also one step removed from the real world. It can inform and educate at the same time. Puppetry holds up a mirror to society and gives people a chance to look objectively at themselves. It especially enables people to laugh at themselves, and is less threatening than the human performer. Puppetry can be used to challenge social and political barriers, as well as stereotypes, because it represents a "neutral" (observer). Puppets do not necessarily have to belong to any particular culture or language group or social class, so they can be adapted to the target audience. They can also say more than the 'live' actor, especially (effective) when tackling taboo issues like sex, dying, and racism. It can deliver the strongest possible message in a light-hearted manner, without offending or frightening the audience.

While Friedman does puppetry for a living, many who use puppets do so on a more informal basis. In rural Western Kenya, giant puppets in vthe shape of a person stroll through the streets on World AIDS Day and other occasions, dispensing educational materials as they move through crowds excited by their imposing visual presence. Puppetry is becoming an important component of many community health programs, from India to Japan to the United Kingdom.

Memories and Maps: Books, Boxes, and Bodies

In Uganda, the National Community of Women Living with AIDS (NAC-WOLA) and the international development nonprofit, Save the Children, have developed the "Memory Project" as a way of helping children and families cope with the effects of HIV/AIDS, including the loss of parents, the resulting stress and grief, and the need to move beyond sorrow to focus on survival as well as healing.

The making of a Memory Book can improve family communication about the difficult issues of HIV status, death and dying, and estate planning. These books also serve as a precious reminder of family history and traditions, and are sometimes the only possession parents can leave for their children. Many people express gratitude for this kind of project, which can increase a sense of empowerment, hope, and purpose, because one is doing something constructive and meaningful. A participant writes: "I am very optimistic now; I have been taught and I teach others, I enjoy talking about good nutrition and having a positive attitude." Another says: "I am not worried about the future. The Memory Book and training have helped me explain to my children that I am positive and that one day I will die, so I have been able to prepare them. But I also explain that everyone dies one day, and I am just the same."

A training program has spread the project throughout Uganda, and partnerships have helped to extend its use to other African countries, including Kenya, Zimbabwe, Ethiopia, Tanzania, and South Africa.

In South Africa, writer and therapist Jonathan Morgan has established the Memory Box Project, which first debuted at the July 2000 International AIDS conference in Durban. Made from recycled cardboard boxes, Memory Boxes are similar to Memory Books, telling stories which range from loss and despair to hope and healing. Morgan has most recently developed the "Ten Millions Memory Project," which aims to reach 10 million African children with memory-work activities by 2010.

And in conjunction with a group of HIV-positive women, Morgan and others have developed a project called "Body Maps," in which human figures are drawn on life-size panels of butcher paper. Each one is unique, expressing a gamut of emotions and varying in style and complexity, though all reflect each woman's thoughts and feelings, fears and aspirations, and views about the virus residing within her. The process is described in this way: Body maps are made by tracing two bodies, of the artist and a partner. The artist then goes about filling in the traced body with images, words, patterns, designs, and scars. A type of art therapy, the maps are used in conjunction with group therapy, photography, and writing in order to help each woman deal with her HIV-positive status.

For more on these techniques and this general approach to grief and healing, there are a number of resources, including a pdf on how to make a Memory Book:

http://www.healthlink.org.uk/projects/hiv/imp_stories.html
http://www.scfuk.org.uk/scuk_cache/scuk/cache/cmsattach/1838_
     Memory_Books.pdf
http://www.mrc.ac.za/aids/june2004/millions.htm
http://www.philadelphiawriters.com/articles/10_2004/bodymaps.
     htm (g)

The Art(s) of Acting ALIVE

This section has attempted to give a brief overview of the variety of artistic responses, media, and tools which are being used to address the many dimensions, issues, challenges, and effects of HIV/AIDS. The essential and invaluable role of art, artists, and of the creative spirit which resides in every individual is daily being tried, tested, utilized, and called upon to take up the vital and urgent work of prevention, education, support, comfort, growth, and inspiration, with ever-increasing regularity, effectiveness, and success. From personal wellness to social healing, art helps us to truly "feel" and also "act" more alive, which in turn increases our willingness to continue living — despite life's struggles and inevitable sorrows — and links us at the same time to something more transcendent. It is this "larger view," and the spiritual dimension which is tapped and nurtured by rising to meet our daily challenges in fresh and creative ways, that places human suffering within a more "workable" frame of reference, allowing us to move beyond grief, loss, and pain into spaces of joy, hope, compassion, and activism.

On the eve of an International HIV/AIDS Conference in Toronto, convened every two years in a different location around the world, I was asked … as an artist and community activist — to answer this question: "How can we bring about an end to AIDS, as world citizens fighting the pandemic, making it our individual and combined mission over the next two years?" I include my response in closing, with the hope that together we can "act" to keep the world "alive," and each of us within it!

I approach this question as an activist, artist, and founder/director of two HIV/AIDS and development nonprofits.

As an individual, I think it is important to educate oneself, to keep updated   on HIV/AIDS-related issues and challenges, both locally and globally. This is one form of activism, and there are many others: writing letters to news media and politicians, talking with friends (and complete strangers!) about what we learn, engaging in creative projects, linking with others in collective activities on a range of issues, from lack of treatment access to more funding for programs. Working with people affected by or living with HIV/AIDS, volunteering with a local nonprofit (or starting one!), reaching out to support efforts halfway around the world, becoming a member of a discussion group, marching in demonstrations.

As collective entities — whether that be organizations, networks, coalitions, dynamic duos, or in whatever form — we can also do so much to address and reverse this pandemic. ActALIVE is a good example: the coalition is composed of 300-plus members in 35 countries, all of whom are activists in their own right. As an organization, we have engaged in endeavors such as the coproduction of an edutainment music CD in Sierra Leone, cocreation of an *African Youth HIV/AIDS Best Practices Handbook* — with 95 creative projects from 25 countries — and in an arts project called "Peace Tiles," which involved 1000-plus youth from 12 countries in tile-making workshops and mural displays on HIV/AIDS themes, for World AIDS Day 2005.

As artists, activists, and world citizens, we have a powerful role to play in bringing about an end to HIV/AIDS. Art — and creativity in all forms — is already saving lives, instilling hope, and offering new solutions to a disease which has sometimes been seen as unstoppable. The acronym, ActALIVE — which stands for "Arts for Creative Transformation: Activism, Lifeline, Inspiration, Vision, Education" — reflects the multifaceted role that arts, and the creative spirit within each of us, can play in stopping this pandemic for good. The slogan of one prevention and education campaign says it all: "Make Art, Stop AIDS!"

Janet Feldman is founder/director of two HIV/AIDS-related nonprofits: one is the international branch of a Kenyan HIV/AIDS and development organization, KAIPPG (http://www.kaippg.org), and the other an international arts coalition called ActALIVE (http://www.actalive.org), whose members use the arts and media to address HIV/AIDS and development. She is an editor of the arts and development e-journal *art'ishake*; cofounder and adult ally of the Global Youth Coalition on HIV/AIDS; board member of JUMP; news director for One World Beat; cocreator of development projects which focus on ICTs/ODL, nutrition and food security, empowerment of women and youth, health and education, and poverty-alleviation.

Resources

Bourgault, L. (2003). *Playing for life: Performance in Africa in the age of AIDS*. Durham, NC: Carolina Academic Press, , pages 169-170.
McColly, M. (2006). *The after-death room: Journey into spiritual activism*. Cambridge, MA: Soft Skull Press.

☐ Mask Making
J. Earl Rogers

> Masks have the power to transform the consciousness of both the wearer and the viewer.
>
> **— L. Raine**

A fun and engaging artform is the making of masks. Teen and children are especially attracted to masks making and it is an excellent alternative to other artforms. It can be done in two hours or be a day-long process. While teens and children enjoy the process, I have worked mostly with adults and find it equally rewarding and inviting. Websites that can provide more information on mask making are listed at the end of this section.

Mask making has been a part of human culture since the earliest of times (Strong, 2001). There is usually a strong element of ritual involved with the creation and functions of the mask and the emotions of the maker/wearer are often to be seen expressed in the mask. The most famous masks are those deriving from the old Greek plays, tragedy, and comedy. The smiling face of comedy and the sad face of tragedy are comment visuals used at many plays and theaters today.

Historical evidence of masks has been found in many different societies and civilizations with depiction of masks as early as 20,000 BCE. The mask brings forth the sense of a particular myth and the spirit of the unknown and has been involved in many sacred practices. The mask is another way to tell the story of human history and shape the story of individuals. It tells the story of magic, sadness, fear, rage, spirit, and allows the wearer to become the story and move out of the personal. Think of wearing a mask at a costume party and what freedom it offered in your interactions. Masks are a useful means to tell the story of loss and express grief. In many traditional societies masks are more than just art objects, but functioning objects that carry much power. They can be used for healing, initiation, and worship. Masks seems to carry similar characteristics throughout the world in most societies (Sivin, 1986).

Masks can be used by the bereaved in a metaphorical sense to convey different aspects of the deceased or the emotions of the grieving. They tell the story of the person we lost and characteristics not easily spoken of. The masks can also carry strong emotions which are difficult to express in normal conversation.

There are many methods to make masks easily. For small children the mask can be made on a blown-up balloon using paper-maché. Paper plates, paper cut-outs, or paper bags all can be used to form the basis for the mask. Then paint, collage, or drawing can be applied to the mask by each individual (Sivin, 1986, p 23).

Plaster of Paris masks are easy to make and fun for groups (see the website http://www.montefowler.com/mold1html).

There are two easy ways to use the materials listed below. First, the mask maker places a paper towel over his or her face and a partner covers the face with plaster of Paris strips. Leave room for the person to breathe or use straws to breathe through. The eyes can be covered, leaving the eyes closed, or openings left for the eyes and then trimmed or decorated later. If the eyes are closed and covered, cut out eye holes with an X-Acto knife after the mask has dried. The second is to cover the face with petroleum jelly (keeping all hair out of the way) and apply the plaster of Paris strips.

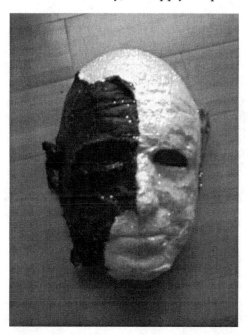

FIGURE 18.5 Plaster of Paris masks made by Janet and Tio (1997). (Photo courtesy of Earl Rogers.)

FIGURE 18.6 Plaster of Paris masks made by Janet and Tio (1997). (Photo courtesy of Earl Rogers.)

FIGURE 18.7 Plaster of Paris masks made by Janet and Tio (1997). (Photo courtesy of Earl Rogers.)

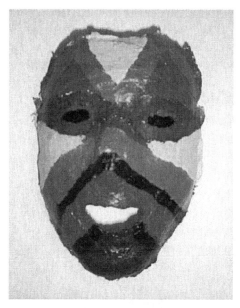

FIGURE 18.8 Plaster of Paris masks made in workshops by Tio and Janet (1998–2000). (Photo courtesy of Earl Rogers.)

FIGURE 18.9 Plaster of Paris masks made in workshops by Tio and Janet (1998–2000). (Photo courtesy of Earl Rogers.)

This can be done by the partner, or with adults and older teens, small mirrors can be set up and each person can apply the strips to their own face. Allow the plaster to dry and then wiggle the face muscles and the mask will pop off. Then using paints and materials the mask can be decorated.

Materials Needed

- plaster of Paris strips (available at craft stores)
- paper towels or petroleum jelly
- old towels for clean up
- X-Acto knife
- acrylic paints and objects for decorating
- small paint brushes
- hot glue gun for attaching decorative objects

Apply damp paper towels over the person's face and then plaster of Paris strips, or cover the face with the petroleum jelly, being sure to cover all areas where the plaster of Paris might be applied. Pull the hair of the person out of the way or use strips of cloth to hold the hair back. If the eyes are being covered by the plaster of Paris make sure to give extra coats of jelly to the eyes and eyebrows. Keep the eyes closed until the mask has been removed. Dip the strips into a bowl of warm water and apply to the partner's face. About three coats of the strips will be needed to make a sturdy mask and to allow the mask to be smooth. Do not get the petroleum jelly to get into the eyes as it can sting. Once the masks are dry the painting and decorating can begin. An opening for the nostrils or mouth can be left so the person can breath, or straws can be used in the mouth or nose. The painting and decorating can often be the longest part of the process and it may take more than just two hours for the completion of the mask.

Alternative methods could include buying premade paper or plastic masks and then decorating as with the self-made masks. Papier maché can be used in place of plaster of Paris. The process is a bit longer. The website at http://www.kinderart.com/multic/machemask.shtml gives an excellent description of how to use the material, and offers a course for mask making for children.

Resources

Bridgewater, A., & Bridgewater, G. (1996). *Carving masks: Tribal, ethnic and folk projects.* New York: Sterling.

Maskmaking. Retrieved September 4, 2006, from http://www.sunnyday.org/art_ lesson_plans/mask_making_history.htm

Paper Mache Masks. (1997–2006). *Kinderart.* Retrieved September 5, 2006, from http://www.kinderart.com/multic/machemask.shtml

Portelli, P. (1997–2006). Face cast. *Savoir Faire Productions.* Retrieved September 5, 2006, from http://wwwsavoirfaire.ca/archive/2_recipe_12.3.html

Raine, L. (2000). Making sacred masks. Retrieved September 5, 2006 from http://www.spiralgoddess.com/masks.html

Sivin, C. (1986). *Maskmaking.* Worcester, MA: Davis.

Strong. S. (2001–2002). Soul unmasked. *Harbinger Project.* Retrieved September 4, 2006 from http://www.harbingerproject.com/issue38/unmasked.htm

Thomas D. Moore, Sandra M. Walsh,
Lisa Wayman, and Penny Allport

Stories of Art, Grief, and Healing

Letting our stories out is a way we begin to understand our struggles and reconcile them.

—**Charles Garfield**, *Sometimes My Heart Goes Numb*

☐ A Son's Good-bye
Thomas D. Moore and Sandra M. Walsh

At one time, after my father had his stroke, and was still at home with mother taking care of him, the thing my father loved more than anything else, was for me to play the violin for him. But we got to a point when he was at home, where the emotional intensity that was present in him by my playing was too much for him. Often his eyes would well up with tears — it was too much for him. He would say, "T.D., you are going to have to stop playing — I can't take it anymore."

That last night in the nursing home, I had asked him earlier in the afternoon, "Would you like for me to come over and play for you a little bit after dinner because I have to leave in the morning?" By then, time had passed — it was almost two years later and I hadn't played for him in about two years. He said, "Yes." Thinking back now, I guess the playing gave him pleasure instead of causing him stress.

That night ... well, I came and I brought a music stand because I decided I would read a lot of pieces for him. I had a recital I was supposed to do so I planned to play my recital pieces. Then after that, I read from a volume of unaccompanied Bach. I was trying to find music that I thought he would like, and since the Bach doesn't have a piano accompaniment, it was appropriate. I played for about 2 hours — just Dad and me in his room. It was nighttime, dark. Knowing it would be dark, I had brought a stand light. I didn't ask anyone for permission — I started playing very quietly and a nurse came in almost immediately — I asked if it was OK and if it was too loud and she said it sounded beautiful and not to worry about it. I guess it was dusk — around 6:00 p.m.

Several times while I was playing, the door opened and I was aware of the fact that at some time it was left wide open and I just kept playing. Then finally, I thought — it was approaching 8:00 p.m. — you know nursing home residents go to bed early — I thought I should stop. A nurse stepped into the room and she said, "Would you please come out here — with your violin. Then I realized, they had turned the lights off in the hallway — there were a lot of people in the hallway, there must have been 40 or 50 people in the hallway, all in wheelchairs basically, mostly wheelchairs. The nurse told me, "You have no idea how much this has meant to these people, you have really given a lot to these people." She explained, "No one applauded because it wasn't a concert for them, it was a spiritual experience." She said something to that effect, I remember. So when I stepped out into the hallway I was overcome by emotion, to see these elderly, frail, sick, people at life's end, some were just mouthing thank you and wanting to touch me, to reach out. They would grab my hand and then they didn't want to let go.

So I went back to his room and put up my violin and told him I would leave early the next morning so would say good-bye at this time. I kissed him on the head several times — it struck me how the roles were now reversed. I went out to my car — I knew the nursing home well — so I went out a back way. I knew it was the last time I would see him. I sat in my car and cried.

Thomas D. Moore received his education at the University of Alabama and Eastman School of Music, University of Rochester. He has toured nationally and internationally with the Pro Arte String Quartet and has been concertmaster of major orchestras and ballet/opera orchestras in the U.S. and South Africa. He continues to perform in various chamber music groups and is Violin Professor at the New World School of the Arts in Miami, Florida.

☐ The Art of Survival
Lisa Wayman

My son Joe died of brain cancer in 1998 when he was 12. His illness and death was a pivotal experience in my life. I used art to process the experience and as a tool for survival. I am a nurse, but I am also an artist. I have created pieces in oil, acrylic, collage, and multimedia sculpture. When I speak about my experience of losing my son and share my art, I often hear comments such as, "Well, of course you use art, you are an artist. I could never use art for grief because I am not an artist."

There are two ways to approach art. Art may be viewed as something that professionals create and that adheres to rules of aesthetics and skill. Art can also be viewed as a tool for survival. Dissanayake (1992) is an interdisciplinary scholar who has studied art. She postulates that the reason every human culture makes art is that it has survival value. She speaks of art with a big "A" (the kind of art that hangs on museum walls) and art with a little "a" (the kind of art that all humans can create). Little "a" art contributes to human survival in several ways: providing expression for those experiences that are beyond everyday speech, expressing strong or socially undesirable emotion, and making the ordinary special.

I create both art with a big "A" and art with a little "a." I will share some of the ways that I have made art with a little "a" to help me survive and grow through the experience of grieving my son. The pieces that I created in my journals are pieces that would be easy for an untrained artist to create, but were still very healing for me. I hope through this example to demonstrate ways that art can be used to facilitate grieving, even with those individuals who are intimidated by art.

One of the experiences that will always exist beyond words is hearing a terrible diagnosis. A diagnosis of cancer was a paradigm shift for Joe, for me, and for our entire family. When I gave birth to Joe, I took for granted that I would see him graduate from high school, grow into a man, maybe have a family. The diagnosis of cancer meant that those things were no longer as certain as I thought they were. Hearing the awful word "cancer" was like being slammed against the wall. I felt unable to catch my breath or find solid ground. It is not a feeling that is easily conveyed. Here is how I drew it in my journal (Figure 19.1).

This drawing is reminiscent of Edvard Munch's painting "The Scream," but also has my thoughts from that time. I had to see how it felt, own the emotion, acknowledge that it was terrible, before I could really start to move beyond the shock. It still makes no sense to me. I still sometimes close my eyes and can't believe it happened, but this picture says what I cannot say, and somehow holds that experience for me so I don't have to continue to live in that moment.

It is also very hard for me to express what kind of mother I was. In a very real way I often feel like I have failed. What kind of mother cannot see her child to adulthood? I can logically think about that and convince myself that we fought long and hard against cancer, and in the end it was a terminal illness like it is for so many people. I know that. I am a nurse.

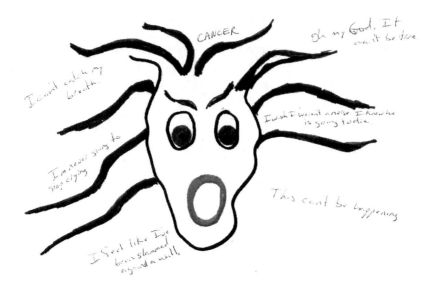

FIGURE 19.1 Reminiscent of Edvard Munch's "The Scream." (Photo courtesy of Lisa Wayman.)

I have certainly seen many good people die of cancer. I say that, but then my heart cries that I was a momma bear whose job it was to fiercely love and protect my children, and I failed. What kind of mother was I? What kind of life did Joe have? I made a small picture collage of Joe healthy and ill (he is the smiling little boy and the swollen ill kid in the center) and of our family; Charlie, Lisa, Joe and Katie (Figure 19.2).

When I look at this picture I do see Joe ill. I also see him well. This picture does not encompass all the experiences we had together, does not tell of Christmases and birthdays, and thousands of ordinary wonderful days, but it reminds me of the richness of our life. I can look at one small picture in the collage and think of a hundred different memories. My son did die, but he also lived. It does not totally ameliorate the feeling of failure, but it reminds me of the truth that I both failed and succeeded as a mother.

Joe's illness and death also engendered very strong feeling. One of those feelings was anger. I was not as angry that Joe got cancer, humans get cancer, as I was with the seemingly constant advice from friends, family, and even strangers. I was struggling to find my balance each and every day and much of the advice did not seem to be given out of concern for us, but out of an effort to convince the advisor that their life could not go like mine. One of my favorite quips of that time was, "I'm so glad everyone else is so good at my life because I am really having trouble figuring it out." I needed a way to vent my anger in a way that would not alienate my

FIGURE 19.2   Collage of Joe and his family. (Photo courtesy of Lisa Wayman.)

support network or poison the air around me with excess negative emotion. I turned to my journal.

This drawing puts all the hurtful things said to me on paper (Figure 19.3). When they are on paper they no longer need to be in my head, and they can no longer hurt me. I also could express how awful well meaning advice was. Truly the only helpful or soothing words were "I can't know how you are feeling, but I am here, I love you." Offers of real help were also appreciated. I had several friends who were gifted at giving of themselves. Margaret was often there for me with quiet and a cup of tea when I needed her.

Margaret

A clean soul
Restful to me
With her quiet
Listening
No judgment, no advice,
Just my worries
Washed by her clean tears.

FIGURE 19.3 Hurtful thoughts in a journal. (Photo courtesy of Lisa Wayman.)

This piece is not visual art, but poetry, and poetry makes words special. It distills and crystallizes words. I could have just said that Margaret was wonderful to me, but the poem is more expressive of what she means to me.

I also felt inadequate to the task of being a mother of an ill child, and annoyed at the expectations my community had. Joe went to school through the majority of his illness. He also went to scouts, church, and did activities with his friends. He was very visible, as was I. The pressure to be a good example and to show grace under fire was huge. It seemed as if everywhere I went people were watching me for my reaction, listening to my words to see if I was OK, and again offering advice, platitudes, even suggestions on how to pray. I can only be myself. I cannot change who I am. How is the mother of a dying son supposed to be? I still don't know. I had polite ways to say "go away." One of my favorites was "Thank you so much for thinking of us, please continue to pray for us, but we really can't have visitors over at this time." In my journal I was not so polite.

Fuck You

I pray how I pray.
I sing when I feel like singing.
I laugh.
I cry.
I love wildly.

I'm not sweet.
I'm not pretty.
My spirit is free.
I am beautiful.
I am who I am.

This poem is not only not polite, but shocking to those who know me since I don't swear, and generally try to be nice and get along. It was refreshing to say, even just to myself, that I could be just who I was. It became a reminder, and anthem for me to start living in ways that were good for me and to not worry so much about what others thought.

My family also used art to make special. Cancer is a big reminder that every day is a special event, that every breath is a wonderful gift. I journaled, I drew, I wrote poetry. My father created in wood. He asked to make the urn for Joe's ashes. (Figure 19.4)

The Urn

My father's hard hands
Caressed the cedar
As he measured the miter, and cut
To the shape of his
Practical art.
That board of cedar
Once stood on our land
In a fragrant forest
Where I walked the last days
Of my childhood,
Pulling leaves to release the scent.
The oak was tall and mighty,
And dead before we cut.
Hard and dry,
Planed to boards to sit,
Straight, next to the cedar.
The black walnut,
Bought from Pennsylvania,
Shoots up the center;
Together with the angles
Aims the soul to heaven.
Now they are joined
With seams so tight
I cannot find them
With finger or nail,
Sanded to satin.
I held it in my arms

> Inhaling the sweet smell of my youth,
> Until I had to let go of it,
> And the ashes it held.
> I laid my son in the rocky ground of Ouray
> Encased in the love
> My father couldn't put to words.

Joe's sister, Katie, also used art to work through grief. She is a talented flutist. When Joe was ill she often played for the comfort of the music. When we buried his urn (Figure 19.5), she played to honor him and express her grief. Creating music was an outlet for emotion. We could always tell what was in Katie's heart when she played the flute.

FIGURE 19.4 Joe's wooden urn on a table. (Photo courtesy of Lisa Wayman.)

FIGURE 19.5   Burying Joe's urn. (Photo courtesy of Lisa Wayman.)

Winter

His ashes lie
Under the Ouray snow.
My heart goes there.

Since Joe's death our lives have changed in a multitude of ways. I have used my experience to become a better nurse. Significant grief and loss has helped me to grow and change. The experience of grief in itself would not have helped me to become who I am today. In order to change I needed to be able to examine what had happened and explore the significance of the event. Art made my unconscious conscious and available for examination. It did enable me to express those experiences that are beyond everyday speech, to express strong or socially undesirable emotion, and make the ordinary special. I still miss Joe. I still have days when I am sad and grieving, but I also know joy and continue to live and love and grow. By using art I have been able to make my grief a part of my life rather than a focus of my life.

We all die, but we don't all live.
I want to take life with both hands
Eat it in big bites, juice running down my chin
Impolite and greedy for its sweetness.
Roll naked and unashamed on the grass,
Make wild love on clean sheets,
Let the rain soak me to the skin.
I choose joy!

Lisa Wayman is a nurse and an artist. She has used visual art to explore aspects of both her professional and personal life. She is interested in spirituality and in the nature of suffering and joy. Her art illustrates passages on her spiritual journey as well as speaking of things for which there are no words. She has exhibited art at the University of Colorado at Colorado Springs, and has published art in *The American Journal of Nursing*. Her thesis, *Self-Transcending through Suffering*, has been published in the *Journal of Hospice and Palliative Care Nursing*. Lisa works as a telemetry clinical nurse educator in an acute care hospital, and speaks and writes on the topics of self-transcending, healing through art, and the paradox of suffering and joy.

Resource

Dissanayake, E. (1992). *Homoaestheticus: Where art comes from and why*. New York: Free Press.

☐ Making an Art Connection in Residential Care*
Sandra M. Walsh

My friend and colleague Cathy and I were making several visits to an assisted living facility (ALF) where her mother had become a recent resident. We hoped our "art activities" would help her mother during this time of transition. Because I had found that some of our activities would not work for the hard of hearing, on this day I also brought my viola to play "familiar" tunes for people who could not participate in the activities we planned. I had previously made a "Ribbon Gem" for Cathy's mother Linda (for purposes of this narrative, names are fictitious), and sent it

---

*For purposes of this narrative, names are ficticious.

to her. Linda had said she wanted to learn how to make this item. We arranged this visit through the owner of the ALF and made our visit late one Friday afternoon.

As we entered the facility living room, Linda was sitting in her wheelchair in front of a small table with a paper protector on top of the table. Five residents were assembled and ready to make a "Ribbon Gem" for themselves. Two staff members and a high school student volunteer were present to help with today's art activities. Cathy and I looked like glorified bag ladies as we carried in our "bags" of supplies along with my viola — just in case some bed-bound people did not feel like doing the art. I also knew that the one blind resident might enjoy some "tunes." All of the residents appeared ready to begin but we soon learned that we would have to instruct by doing as two of the participants only spoke Spanish (and we were not bilingual). We demonstrated and began to proceed and found the language barrier was not a problem. Our activity, as requested by Cathy's mother Linda, consisted of taking small images (stencils), tracing the design on discarded watercolor paintings (any thick colorful paper would do such as old cards, thick magazine covers), and making "sandwiches" (back to back) images. We then glued these images back to back on a piece of ribbon with several images displayed down the piece of ribbon. A ribbon loop was added at the top end so the resident could use it for a wall decoration or hang it on a doorknob. Because I am also a watercolorist, I use my discarded paintings as thick paper for the Gems.

While this activity was proceeding I inquired about others not in attendance and was told that the blind man was at the doctor and that the one other patient, Andy, was sick in his room and couldn't attend. Residents also reported that Andy never talked anyway, and even if he were well would not likely want to participate.

In the meantime, I had played a few tunes for the group after they had settled in on completing their projects. I couldn't get any of the residents to identify any of the tunes I played, although I took them from a book of old favorites (from the '30s, '40s, and '50s). I was even more surprised when I played a special tune I specifically had prepared: "Somewhere over the Rainbow." Surely, I thought, everyone would know this tune because of *The Wizard of Oz* movie and knowledge of Judy Garland who had made the song famous. After playing it once, in desperation, I even tried to sing along with myself as I played (not an easy feat). Some of the residents then said, "Maybe they had heard that before." They weren't sure.

I still was interested in Andy and thought perhaps the music might help him or that I might even talk him into joining us for the "Ribbon Gem" construction. When I left to visit Andy, everyone was pretty quiet and intent on what they were doing — ALF staff were encouraging residents to choose designs and colors and glue the objects in place. Andy's room was quite spacious and well lit — window on the far wall, with a bed in the corner, and a chest of drawers opposite the bed. A wheelchair was beside the bed. Andy was fully clothed and resting in bed with his back to the door (facing the wall and window). I spoke his name when I entered and he turned his head slightly and said (it seemed with relief), "Oh, I thought for a minute that was a rifle and you had come to shoot me." I was taken aback and just said, "No, this is a viola, a musical instrument and I have come to play for you." He questioned me a little, we made small talk, I told him why I was there. I asked him what his profession had been — he had been a truck driver and never married, just drove trucks, had no family. He said he was born in 1922, so I did the math and said, so you are 84, and he said yes. By now, he had turned in bed and was facing me. I told him I was a viola student and had started studying the viola again after years of not playing the instrument. I asked him about any favorite tunes — I read him some names from an "Old Favorites" songbook — he said he hadn't heard any of them and couldn't think of any tunes ("I was just a truck driver"). I then talked about my song for the day, "Somewhere over the Rainbow."

I began to play, he was facing me, I was sitting down and playing, sitting on the corner of his bed. After I completed the song, he didn't say anything so I repeated my attempt and tried to sing along and he exclaimed, "I do know that song — you can't play it though — you need more lessons." Then he asked me to play those other songs and to sing along with them. He now said he recognized some of the tunes and said again, "Little lady, you cannot play." He was on a roll and I began to laugh and say I would tell my teacher that he said I needed more lessons. I had been in his room about 20 minutes so I said good-bye. I told him I would take more lessons. He said I should come back and try another time once I improved. That was all. He didn't say good-bye, thanks, or anything.

I reported these activities to the art group who were still working on their "Gems" in the living room. They couldn't believe that Andy had actually talked with me or listened to my music. They all got a big laugh out of his response to my efforts. Maybe they were in agreement. In a few minutes, I will take yet another viola lesson and get my teacher to help me again with my rendition of "Somewhere over the Rainbow."

Even if I cannot play, I learned that my attempt to make music seemed to help Andy temporarily. The music certainly provided the catalyst for my connection with him. He even mentioned I should return when I improved, which seems infinitely better than hoping for me to bring in a gun. I look forward to seeing Andy again. I remember that the Ribbon Gem activity seemed to be helpful as residents continue to display their creations and have made Ribbon Gems for new residents. Yet, my most pleasant and vivid recall of activities during that Friday afternoon is about my connection with Andy.

Sandra M. Walsh, RN, PhD, is a professor at the Barry University School of Nursing, Miami Shores, Florida. She was educated at Duke University, Wake Forest University, East Carolina University, and the University of South Carolina. Dr. Walsh is an artist and combines her passion for art with art interventions with vulnerable groups. She has received a number of international awards for her creative activities within the nursing professions. She is the author of numerous articles in art and nursing.

☐ Mr. Reid and the Day of the Dead: A Program for Teens and Grief
Penny Allport

In 1975 I am in Grade 7 at Maynard Public School in a small Southern Ontario town. Maynard has one gas station, a general store, a church, a large baseball diamond, and a public school that serves Kindergarten to Grade 8. The school is a melting pot for children from the neighboring towns whose schools only take them to Grade 5. I am bused in daily from another small town just north of Maynard. The Maynard School has bulged at the seams, creating the need for portables. I am in Mr. Reid's homeroom class in the furthest portable from the school and I love the feeling when the windows on both sides are open and an autumn crossbreeze blows through my hair and shuffles the papers on my desk.

Mr. Reid is also my science teacher and on a cool October day he instructs us to put on our coats and follow him outside. We walk into the track field behind the school where the winter chill is palpable in the air. Leaves from the large maples that border the property are changing into shades of goldenrod and crimson. As we walk behind the baseball field, wondering where we are going, the breeze stirs the leaves in the poplars above us. I follow one gold heart-shaped leaf as it journeys from its summer home on the branch and flutters slowly toward the ground. I track and interrupt this exhale from the tree, receive it in my hand, and allow a pause in its descent and ultimate dissolve. The freshness of this season and the gifts she offers holds all of my attention, until I hear Mr. Reid call us to a white metal gate that enters the back of the cemetery. He informs us we are taking Cemetery Study and invites us to spread out and pay attention to names, ages of the deceased, and anything else that interests us. I am enchanted and curious as I think of stories of ghosts and haunted graveyards.

I begin to notice the names — Robinson, Perrin, Polite, Jackson, and Throop. I recognize some of them as the last names of students in my class. There are no Allports here. My father's family is from North Gower, about an hour north. My father purchased a "plot" in the Maitland Cemetery, just 15 minutes south of Maynard where we are members of the St. James Anglican Church. "Room for six" my father tells people, like it's part of our asset base. I wonder how my parents, my brother, and I, and our future families will all fit.

I notice the gravestones dated from the 1800s to the present. Mr. Reid asks us to read the epitaphs. "Safely Home" and "Awaiting the Resurrection." "Jesus loves me, I am safe in his arms," and lengthy verses are carved into the stones which, through the tides of change, look like weathered rocks at the edge of the ocean.

I am curious about the stones with the short life spans and wonder how these young ones died. Mr. Reid instructs us to choose a family name that we will do further research on later in our study. I choose the Bass family whose tombstones date back as far as 1817. I discover this is not a one-day field trip and I am excited by the intrigue of further investigation of these souls' resting places.

Mr. Reid doesn't mention the word *soul* but I remember him referring to the now invisible people buried beneath us as "ancestors." After our return to the portable we discuss our findings and what we have noticed. I say that the young ones interested me. Others say they were called to the freshly dug gravesite or the last names that matched their own. One tells the story of her uncle who was recently buried there. I secretly wish some of my ancestors were here and make a mental note to ask my father about our plot, and where his grandparents are buried.

All of my grandparents are still alive. Two live in North Gower where my grandfather is a traveling salesman and my grandmother is a trained nurse who bakes, knits, and makes quilts. My mother's parents, whom we call Granny and Pop, live on the West Coast in British Columbia. I've met them a few times and we correspond by letter and reel-to-reel tapes. My mother makes my brother and I sit on her bed and, with a small microphone hooked up to the tape machine, we tell the stories of our day, details of our friends and our experiences. Sometimes months go by before we receive a return tape. We all gather again on my parents' bed and listen to Granny and Pop share their replies to our last correspondence, which we have all forgotten by now. We hear how they are and what the weather is like in the trailer park where they live on Vancouver Island. Pop usually shares what happens in the garden and always says we should live in "God's Country" like they do. We are deeply buried in snow when I hear his voice describe the purple crocuses and yellow daffodils at bloom in his garden. This beautiful and warm vision makes me dream of what it would be like to live there.

Mr. Reid's voice calls me back to our assignment for today. Design and draw tombstones of the future he says, maybe even your own. He gives us time to create and I draw one with a huge cut-out peace sign on it. I draw another one with a guitar and "This guy picked away." Another spells "LOVE" in round '60s lettering.

In a subsequent class, Mr. Reid reads *The Cremation of Sam McGee*. Riveted to my seat, I hang on every word. Mr. Reid's telling is alive and I feel the chill of the Northern air on his breath. I write the entire poem out in long hand and memorize all 15 verses.

> There are strange things done in the midnight
> sun by the men who moil for gold;
> The Arctic trails have their secret tales that
> would make your blood run cold;
> The Northern Lights have seen queer sights,
> but the queerest they ever did see
> Was the night on the marge of Lake Lebarge
> I cremated Sam McGee.

I tell my father about the poem, to which he replies, "We will not be cremated, and all of our family has been buried." I wonder if you can be cremated and still have a gravestone with your name engraved on it somewhere, but I don't ask.

Mr. Reid asks us to write a play for our Cemetery project. I write a short dialogue between an old man from the past and a young boy from the present. The elder is shocked at the amount of change on the planet and concerned for it and its people.

We make title pages for our projects which have turned into weeks of research and added assignments. My title page features a graveyard with several tombstones, including one with my teacher's name on it.

That night I am playing outside, making a snow sculpture for the Winter Carnival on Valentine's Weekend. I am creating a doghouse with Snoopy on top and work by the light of the front porch. My mother comes to the front door and calls me in. She sounds anxious and upset. "I need to finish a few things," I tell her. "Get in the house right away," she orders. At the back door I take off my toque, scarf, gloves, boots, and snowmobile suit. The temperature is minus 20.

I climb the steps and my mother meets me at the top of the stairs. She takes me to her bedroom where we sit on the bed. I know something is wrong by the strain in her face and the tightness of her jaw. She looks at the floor and says, "I have some bad news." I feel my heart pushing up through my throat as she finally says, "Your grandfather is dead." I see my Pop on Vancouver Island with his crocuses blooming, but then she says my father has left for my grandparents' home in North Gower and I realize it is Grandpa. She says it was a heart attack.

I later hear that he and my aunt, cousin, and grandmother had all spent the day shopping in the city for a new suit for grandpa, which was left at the tailors so they could fit it to his generous body. He always boasted that he had only worn a suit a handful of times in his life, at weddings or funerals. Upon their return, he puttered in his garage and came in short of breath, sat down on the kitchen chair and "dropped dead" right in front of my cousin and aunt. "No warning," everyone said. "Just quick, like that." "If you're going to go, that's the way to go," someone else said later.

I don't cry. I just stare into my parent's open closet at my father's cardigan — "Sunday sweater." At night I hear my mother's sniffling in the night as I lie in my own bed in the next room, curious about my new ancestor.

The days that follow fill with people, food, lots of tears, stories, and smells. The old funeral parlor smells musty and sterile at the same time and I want to get out of there. Instead, the wake lasts several days. People come to view his body between certain hours of the day and evening. Food comes in gross amounts to my grandmother's kitchen, where she continues to bake.

Grandpa looks pale and still, peaceful and fake. I know it isn't my grandfather anymore and I somehow feel he, the real him, has left. I don't quite know where he has gone and feel confused by my father's conviction that "you only live once." The Minister alludes to the same thing during the funeral and as I sit with my cousin I wonder if Grandpa can see us sitting and weeping for him. I secretly let him know that if he is around, that I know.

The ground is still frozen so we will have to wait until springtime to bury him. In the meantime, his body rests in the building at the back of the cemetery, where I visualize a stack of deceased people lying frozen on top of one another.

On my return to school, I am of interest to the rest of the class. They ask after my grandfather, give their condolences, and inquire about the funeral. I have missed several days of school but my Cemetery Study has entered the zone of my real life. The project takes on more meaning as we write what we would want to be remembered for. My grandfather is remembered for his sense of humor and love of food (especially Grandma's baking).

During the course of Cemetery Study I am intrigued by a subject spoken about briefly — the Day of the Dead. Mr. Reid tells us it is a custom in Mexico on Halloween where people gather in the graveyards to celebrate and commune with the dead. He doesn't have much information but he tells us that for one day people believe they can communicate with their departed loved ones and they make great preparations for the event. In Mexico and other traditional settings it is called All Souls' Day. He shows us a picture of skeletons and orange flowers, and although the introduction is brief in the scheme of the project, the image holds in my consciousness for many years.

In 2002, I awaken to church bells echoing in the distance. I look out the front window of the B&B my husband and I are staying in for the next 10 days in San Miguel de Allende, Mexico. Perched on the hill above the city, I feel as if I have awakened in a dream. The city spreads out in terra cotta, sunflower gold, greens, and other shades of painted stone. Rooftop gardens and church spires reach into the blue sky dotted with perfect white cumulus clouds. Fire crackers go off and I am startled, thinking it is gunfire.

It's November 1 and the Day of the Dead Celebrations are under way. We walk down the narrow cobblestone streets stepping on and off the narrower sidewalks to avoid collisions with the locals who are making their way up the hill. Some smile and greet us with *Buenos dias* while others quickly pass by with their heads bowed.

We arrive into the *jardin*, the garden courtyard in the center of town, and see altars everywhere. Large photos of people, famous in Mexico for artistic, cultural, or political reasons, are framed by rows of tightly packed marigolds. These vibrant and strong-scented flowers, which carry the smell of death and help to lead the deceased home, adorn the altars on tables or on wicker mats on the street itself. Some marigolds are formed into the shape of large crosses. Street vendors offer flowers, candles, and sugar statuary at the sugar market. Rows of stands, covered in plastic to keep the swarms of bees from descending, are filled with rams, snakes, roosters, skeleton heads in rainbow colors with bulging eyes, and coffins with skeletons that pop out when you pull a string. The women have spent days, and sometimes weeks, preparing these offerings. *Papel picado* or "picked paper," an Aztec custom, creates a curtained backdrop to the *ofrendas* or altars. Like paper dolls, the cut-outs reveal skeletons dancing, playing music, and smiling from their caskets. As we walk through town every merchant has an altar in their window with photos of their loved ones who have passed on. The town is alive with intention.

My new Spanish teacher invites me to come to the cemetery with her. The entrance to the cemetery is lined with merchants carrying still more flowers, long-stemmed roses, wine-colored carnations, and baby's breath for *ninos,* the children. Her family has gathered at her grandmother's grave, and some have been in the cemetery preparing all day. Her mother, now the matriarch, sits and tells stories as the family comes with food and other treats the grandmother loved. The *pan de muertos,* a rich egg bread shaped into animals or bearing the names of the deceased, is a special offering. When the spirit has feasted, which is believed to be through their sense of smell, it is then shared by those who have come to gather.

My senses are overwhelmed with sights, smells, sounds, and the masses of people who continue to file through the entrance gates. Some families are still painting and manicuring the gravestones. Some even bring the family pets, dogs, pigs, and roosters, as well as boom boxes to entertain the spirits all night. Copal incense burns and creates a woody aroma that is also expected to guide the dead home. The falling rain creates a mud walkway filled with a never ending stream of people. There seems no limit to how many souls this place can hold. My ears are filled with the overlapping rapid dialogue of greetings, storytelling, instructions being given, and more greetings.

Occasionally I see an orphan grave that no one has attended and I place one of my roses on it. I also walk to the gringo cemetery, and read the names and leave flowers on the graves of those who have their remains buried here. San Miguel is full of artists, expatriates, a colorful and eclectic gathering of Canadians and Americans who have been drawn by the rich culture, beauty, and relaxed way of life.

I return several years in a row. Each time I take in more of the ritual. I bring my ancestors' photos and create altars in my room. I spend time in the *jardin* immersed in the sensuality of the celebration. There are skeletons everywhere and *Caterina* or Lady Death, a grinning skeleton woman dressed in fancy clothes and a wide brimmed hat, seems the perfect image for our Western minds, that somehow still believe that she or he with the most toys (or hats and shoes) wins.

I take a group on retreat. I have contacted Maria Teresa Valenzuela (2005, pp. 7–11), a Mexican Indigenous woman who I have prearranged to support us in creating an altar and a deeper experience of the ritual of this culture that knows the art of dancing with death. Maria Teresa says frankly, "We are all indigenous."

We spend the day making the altar together. Upon completion, we bring photos of our ancestors. Each woman shares a story of what this ancestor means to her. The stories are rich and sweet — fathers, mothers, husbands and lovers, children and aunts. Maria Theresa invites us to sit with our ancestors during the coming days. I have brought Mr. Reid this year to give thanks as I feel he planted the seeds of my relationship with death, dying, and letting go in that Grade 7 portable (he'd died of leukemia when I was in high school). I am in a deep time of letting go and change in my life.

My last remaining grandmother is 85 and failing. I visit her the day before my departure and she asks if I will take her son David, who died at only a few months old, with me to the Day of the Dead. In the early morning hours of October 31, the day of the *Angelitos*, the souls of children who have died in infancy but have been baptized and are thus free of sin, Maria Theresa creates a healing ritual for me in the cemetery at an "orphan grave." I find myself gently weeping for the uncle I never knew, for the loss of his gifts in our lives, and for the pain my grandmother held all these years. The *angelitos* arrive by noon and then must be gone by noon on the 1st of November as the church bells sound and the firecrackers pop to mark the arrival of the elder spirits.

I wonder what it would have been like if we had a ritual of grieving and celebration once a year to honor our ancestors. I recall the *Achuar* in Ecuador whose dead are buried beneath the sand floor of the family home and whose spirits live on with the family in their daily life.

I return to my community in British Columbia, the place my grandfather called "God's Country." I create a *Dia de Muertos* with the teen girls I have been gathered with for several years. I ask each to bring a photo of a loved one who has passed on. We gather and begin to make our altar with the *papel picado* I have brought home with me. We cover cardboard boxes and stack them on top of each other to create the foundation of the *ofrendas*. I bring out the pink sugar coffin with the skeleton that sits up when you pull the string. The girls love it and I bring out smaller ones in rainbow colors for each of them to place with their loved one's photo when the time comes. We place the salt, for purification, a glass of water to satisfy their thirst, and finally the washcloth, towel, soap, with a basin of water and a mirror for the ancestors to wash up after their long journey from *Mictlan*, the Aztec underworld. It's difficult to find marigolds in October in Canada so we use yellow mums and red roses. I show them my photos and they linger over the images of skeletons, Lady Death (Figures 19.6 through 19.8), and the public altars in the center of town. They are awed.

When the altar is complete, we sit in a semicircle before it. Each shares the name and story of what this ancestor means to her. She places the photo on the altar with her sugar coffin and lights a candle. One brings her cousin who only a year ago committed suicide. I recall Maria Teresa saying that you don't call on departed loved ones for at least 40 days after they have passed on as they are making their journey through the underworld. One of the girls brings a photo of her dog and another brings one of her cat. One tells of a grandmother who died several years ago and how she was "her favorite." One doesn't have a photo but writes her grandfather's name on a piece of paper and tells us he died of cancer a short time after her birth. I bring Mr. Reid, as he seems to be with me these days. I tell them how he was my Grade 7 teacher and how he taught me cemetery study. I tell them that he died of leukemia when I was in high school.

They ask all kinds of questions about Mexico, "Did you get to go at night to the cemetery? " Do you think there really are ghosts?" "Do you think our ancestors can see us?" I tell them there is a belief in many shamanic

FIGURE 19.6 Sculpture of a woman in a hat. (Photo courtesy of Penny Allport).

FIGURE 19.7 Altar. (Photo courtesy of Penny Allport).

FIGURE 19.8 Three-tiered altar. (Photo courtesy of Penny Allport).

traditions that we each have a male ancestor standing behind us on the right and a female ancestor standing behind us on the left. I tell them that ancestors can be from our biological family, special people in our lives, animals, or even famous people in history with whom we have a strong resonance, like Gandhi or Mother Teresa. I say we can call on them when we need them to support us and that there is an old European ancestral song, passed down through an oral tradition that goes:

"Oh, may this be the one who will bring forward the good, true, and beautiful in our family lineage; Oh, may this be the one who will break the harmful family patterns or harmful nation patterns." I tell them, "We are the ones."

They are enchanted, alive, and engaged. It is difficult to draw the afternoon to a close. We sit in silence by the altar lit with candles. We take a few minutes to give thanks for those who have gone before us. We give thanks for the blessings of this sweet life. We listen in the silence and I hear Mr. Reid whispering in my ear "Thank you for listening, thank you for receiving, thank you for passing the gifts on."

Penny Allport is the creator of Swara Inspiration in Richmond, British Columbia. She leads teen programs in yoga, creativity, and painting from the inside out. She is trained both as a yoga teacher and Continuum Movement leader.

Resources

Arrien, A.. (1993). *The four fold way*. San Francisco: HarperCollins.
Valenzuela, M.T.. (2005, November) *Dia de Muertos ... a uniquely Mexican fiesta*. Punto de VISTA, San Miguel de Allende.

CHAPTER **20**   J. Earl Rogers

Conclusion

What an amazing life's work we therapists have chosen. To accompany fellow human beings to the depths of their suffering, for as long as it takes, until they find their own way back to an inner balance, a sense of oneness with themselves.

— **Sandra Bertman**, *Grief and the Healing Arts*

There are many forms of art and we have dealt with just a few. Art is not limited to the traditional forms of painting, sculpting, or writing. It is whatever form we use to express the unique creative process that lies within each of us. Studies have shown that the use of the creative process can be healing in many areas, including grief, chronic illness, emotional trauma, and physical injury (Bertman, 1999; Liebmann, 1986; Malchiodi, 1998; Mitchell & Friedman, 1994). Art done with an "exquisite witness" enhances the healing qualities of the creative process (Jeffreys, 2005, p. 22).

The only gift we have to offer is the quality of our attention; to be with our clients, patients, or group members with full attention. Our job then becomes to keep the intention to be with them in their deepest intuition and to create the vessel of safety and follow them into their deepest truth. Art, of every form, allows the healing of the unconscious and creates the conditions for self-healing through the creative process.

The art forms used in this book, and other creative forms, provide us with tools to use after the group has ended in a way that just talking does not. Expressive arts allow healing at different levels. In the group process, their use also allows bonding of the group and the opportunity to see others moving into a new life. Creative expression bypasses the intellect to allow a range of emotions that may be difficult in just talking.

Art therapy is a specific form of therapy that takes training and experience. This book was not designed for art therapy but to be used with a grief support group or process. For group members who are in need of additional support or therapy it is recommended that a referral be made to a qualified therapist or art therapist. Sandplay, painting, writing, music, and drama are all potential forms of art therapy that can be used to deepen the experience and assist in moving through complicated mourning. For art therapists this grief course may be of additional assistance as a workbook for your clients and groups.

☐ Notes to the Caregivers

While we as facilitators, counselors, ministers, teachers, therapists, and health care workers are offered the opportunity to walk with clients and patients in their journey through grief and loss, we are often forgetful of the fact that we too meet with loss and grief as we do our work. Sandra Bertman, in her book *Grief and the Healing Arts*, offers the book to "refuel" the caregivers. By allowing the artist within us we can become more creative and inspire our own work (Bertman, 1999). The story of Hernando Mispireta at the end of this chapter shows the value of taking a moment for ourselves to engage the creative soul we all have, and how this work does not feel like work.

Many of us in caregiving roles or situations find enormous fulfillment and a great sense of purpose in offering comfort to the sick, the dying, and accompanying people through illness, death, grief, and life transitions. But what of those times when we, as the caregivers, do not feel inspired, cannot be present in the moment, or do not feel life-directed to be of service in the arena of offering comfort and care to others? What happens when we are just plain worn out?

Nurturing ourselves during these times of low energy and low output is a must. Learning how to monitor our "output" as well as our "input" helps us to be wiser, healthier, and more effective caregivers. A physical practice, such as the one offered in session 4, and the use of creative activities in our daily lives, offers us the ability to nurture ourselves and prevent burnout. As burnout strikes we may see some of these common symptoms:

- depleted energy levels
- headaches
- muscle soreness — body aches and pains
- neglect of exercise routines
- unfocused thinking
- critical self-talk and depression or lethargy
- resentments toward other caregivers and clients
- indulging patterns of addictions or rationalizing unhealthy behaviors

On a normal day we may find that our output of energy often outweighs the input of energy. Personal practices such as yoga, art, meditation, or other activities that replenish our mental, physical, and spiritual parts of ourselves can enhance and add to our energy levels. By ignoring the signals of our body, mind, and spirit, we are sometimes our own worst enemy when it comes to caring for, nurturing, or loving ourselves.

Taking time for yourself:

- Can mean deeply looking at yourself and your focus on life.
- Might bring forward a set of needs that you have no idea how to fulfill.
- Might challenge the status quo of your life, family, and coworkers.
- Requires an act of deep self-love. It says "I matter" and "I will nurture myself and my body/mind/spirit in order to serve myself so that I may in turn serve, honor, and care for others."

We all know that self-care is important. We teach our clients, patients, and students the importance of self-care if they are to avoid burnout. Yet we often forget our own teachings. Art can be a fulfilling way to self-nurture and bring forth the creative juices that increase health and enjoyment in our lives. The expressive arts in this book can be used as a personal practice to increase our creativity, support our bodies, and nurture our spirit. It takes stamina and presence to attend to the process of the people in grief or health crisis. We cannot do that without self-care. The very fact of leading a grief group means that we are exposed to multiple losses and grief. Art and personal practice of physical and mental forms can rejuvenate us and reinspire our practice with those who suffer.

May the art forms you lead in this grief course also support your practice and life. Thank you for your willingness to be with those who suffer from loss and other life transitions.

☐ The Value of Art Making in Releasing Work-Related Stress
Hernando A. Mispireta

It was one of those days when stress reaches its peak. One of those days we have all experienced at least once in our lives, strong enough to undermine our strongest convictions; an experience capable of altering our breathing patterns and leaving a noticeable mark in our vital signs.

On just such a day I manage to leave the intensive care unit and go down to the cafeteria for a quick lunch. To my surprise there was a table set up at the cafeteria offering watercolor painting for any interested passerby.

I figured there was no way I could possibly find the time, even though it tickled my curiosity. As my mind was rising with the many concerns, and the preoccupation of my patients left in the hands of a colleague, I knew I must eat fast and go back to work.

As I sat down to have my lunch I realized there was no waiting line at the watercolor table, so I rushed my meal, and found myself sitting there being assisted by a kind lady who gave me a few brushes, an empty 5 × 7 blank card, watercolors, and half a glass of water to rinse my brushes. I embarked on the adventure.

By the time I finished painting a card with flowers I realized my lunchtime was over, yet time had passed so quickly as if I had been in a dream. The card in front of me was beautiful. It gave me a sense of accomplishment and pride. I simply had no idea I could paint. Furthermore it was Valentine's Day and I had no card to take home, and now I had no need to stop by a store and buy one, since I had just made my own.

Time had elapsed during this experience, taking over me, transcending all stressors, and placing me in a state of bliss. I was relaxed, no worries had intruded, and I instantly knew I wanted to repeat this experience again. No conversation with any colleague during lunch had ever offered as strong a focus and such a relaxing outcome as the simple fact of sitting down with some creative tools and making a simple watercolor card. No other attempts at relaxing have since equaled this day, no deep breathing, no casual chat.

There is undoubtedly a power to the creative moment that goes beyond any other efforts to overcome one's racing mind. Creativity may be a power untapped in our profession, one that I wish to bring back to my life and that of others experiencing a life of high stress such as mine.

Hernando Mispireta, BSN, RN, is an MSN student at Barry University and a nurse at the intensive care unit at South Miami Hospital. The painting session he participated in was part of the "Arts in Healthcare Program" at South Miami Hospital created by Dr. Sandra Walsh and Pat Collins. He says, "I work as a nurse in South Miami Hospital at CCU. It is a stressful job and yet it doesn't feel like a job, but more like life. I consider myself a very spiritual individual and look for the positive in all events that touch my life and that of others close to me."

Closing Words by Earl Rogers

Presented here are programs, art forms, and stories of healing and art. The common ingredient in each is the creative urge of the people involved. It is not so much what we do, but that we do. I submit that the creative process is not only healing, but is the very essence of our souls. The curriculum offered in this book is designed for each individual to touch the creative process and to allow that act of creating to heal the wounds of grief. Steven Levine wrote of *Unattended Sorrow* (2005), all those little griefs that we avoid, fail to realize the extent of the loss, or it is just too much for us to deal with. Art can work to heal those unattended sorrows and both consciously and unconsciously, slowly and gently bring us to a place of wholeness in a new world. As did Hernando, we can stop for a moment and create a piece of art; for our own healing and the healing of our clients and patients. Blessings, Earl Rogers

REFERENCES

Albert, I., & Keithley, Z. (2003). *Write your self well ... journal your self to health.* Whitefish, MT: Mountains Greenery Press.

Allende, I. (1995). *Paula.* New York: HarperCollins.

American Cancer Society. (2006). Retrieved September 16, 2006, from http://www.cancer.org/docroot/PRO/content/PRO11CancerStatistics2006presentation.asp?

Arrien, A. (1993). *The four fold way.* San Francisco: HarperCollins.

Art of Asia: Mandala teacher's guide. (n.d.). Retrieved July 15, 2005, from http://www.artsmia.org.

Attig, T. (1996). *How we grieve: Relearning the world.* New York: Oxford University Press.

Attig, T. (2000). *The heart of grief: Death and the search for lasting love.* New York: Oxford University Press.

Bayles, D., & Orland, T. (1993). *Art and fear: observations on the perils (and rewards) of art making.* Santa Barbara, CA: Capra Press.

Bennett, H. Z. (1995). *Write from the heart: Unleashing the power of your creativity.* Mill Valley, CA: Nataraj.

Bertman, S. (1991). *Facing death: Images, insights and interventions.* New York: Brunner-Routledge.

Bertman, S. (Ed.). (1999). *Grief and the healing arts: Creativity as therapy.* New York: Baywood.

Blackburn, L. B. (1991). *The class in room 44: When a classmate dies.* Omaha, NE: Centering.

Bizou, B. (1999). *The joy of ritual.* New York: Golden Books.

Boal, A. (1995). *The rainbow of desire.* New York: Routledge.

Boal, A. (2002). *Games for actors and non-actors* (2nd ed.). New York: Routledge.

Bolen, J. S. (1996). *Close to the bone.* New York: Scribner.

Bourgault, L. 2003. *Playing for life: Performance in Africa in the Age of AIDS.* Durham, NC: Carolina Academic Press pp. 169–170.

Buscaglia, L. (1982). *The fall of Freddie the leaf: A story of life for all ages.* Thorofore, NJ: Slack.

Cameron, J. (1992). *The artist's way.* New York: G.P. Putnam's Sons.

Capacchione, L. (2000). *Visioning: Ten steps to designing the life of your dreams.* New York: Tarcher.

Collie, K., Bottorff, J., Long, B., & Conati, C. (2006). Distance art groups for women with breast cancer: Guidelines and recommendations. *Support Care Cancer, 14*(8), 849–858.

Copony, H. (1989). *Mystery of mandalas.* (Theosophical Publishing House Trans.). Wheaton, IL: Quest Books.

Corr, C. A., Nabe, C. M., & Corr, D. M. (2000). *Death and dying, Life and living* (3rd ed.). Belmont, CA: Wadsworth.

Cossa, M. (2005). *Rebels with a cause: Working with adolescents using action techniques.* London, England: Jessica Kingsley.

Cummings, R., Michalski, J. H., Mishna, F., & Worthington, C. (2003). A multimethod impact evaluation of a therapeutic summer camp program. *Child and Adolescent Social Work Journal, 20*(1), 53–76.

Curtis, A. (2001). *Circles of life: A creative curriculum for healing traumatic loss in childhood.* Author.

Curtis, A. M. (1999). Communicating with bereaved children: A drama therapy approach. *Illness, Crisis, and Loss, 7*(2), 183–190.

Davis, C. (1994). *Celtic mandalas.* London: Blandford.

Decker, J., & Komando, V., (n.d.). Animal symbolism — Many cultures. Retrieved September 7, 2006, from http://www.princetonol.com/groups/iad/lessons/middle/animals2.htm.

De Mong, S. A. (1997). Provision of recreational activities in hospices in the US. *The Hospice Journal, 12*(41), 57.

De Spelder, L., & Strickland, A. (2002). *The last dance: Encountering death and dying* (6th ed.). San Francisco: McGraw-Hill.

Didion, J. (2005). *The year of magical thinking.* New York: Alfred A Knopf.

Doka, K. (Ed.). (1989). *Disenfranchised grief.* Lexington, MA: Lexington Books.

Dougy Center for Grieving Children. (1998). *Helping the Grieving Student: A Guide For Teachers.* Portland, OR: Author.

Dougy Center for Grieving Children. (1999a). *Helping Teens Cope with Death.* Portland, OR: Author.

Dougy Center for Grieving Children. (1999b). *Thirty-five ways to help a grieving child.* Portland, OR: Author.

Dougy Center for Grieving Children. (2000). *When death impacts your school: A guide for school administrators.* Portland, OR: Author.

Emunah, R. (1994). *Acting for real: Drama therapy, process, technique, and performance.* New York: Brunner/Mazel.

Erikson, E. H. (1959). *Identity and the life cycle.* New York: International Universities Press.

Ferszt, G., Massotti, E., Williams, J., & Miller, J. (2000). The impact of an art program on an inpatient oncology unit. *Illness, Crisis, and Loss, 8*(2), 189–199.

Furth, G. (1988). *The secret world of drawings: A Jungian approach to healing through art.* Boston, MA: Sigo Press.

Goldman, L. (2000). *Life and loss* (2nd ed.). Philadelphia: Taylor & Francis.

Gootman, M. (Ed.). (1994). *When a friend dies: A book for teens about grieving and healing.* Minneapolis, MN: Free Spirit.

Greenspan, M. (2004). *Healing through the dark emotions: The wisdom of grief, fear and despair.* Boston, MA: Shambhala.

Grollman, E. A. (Ed.). (1995). *Bereaved children and teens.* Boston, MA: Beacon Press Books.

Heegaard, M. E. (1992). *Facilitator guide for drawing out feelings*. Minneapolis, MN: Woodland Press.

Heegaard, M., Johns Clark, E., Zambelli, G. C. (1989). Art therapy for bereaved children. In H. Wadeson, J. Durkin, & D. Perach (Eds.), *Advances in art therapy* (pp. 60–80). New York: Wiley.

Hrenko, K. D. (2005). Remembering Camp Dreamcatcher: Art therapy with children whose lives have been touched by HIV/AIDS. *Art Therapy: Journal of the American Art Therapy Association, 22*(1), 39–43.

How does music therapy work? Music therapy in palliative care. (n.d.). Retrieved July 9, 2005, from http://www.mtabc.com/index.htm.

Iyengar, B. K. S. (1979). *Light on yoga*. New York: Schocken.

Jeffreys, J. S. (2005). *Helping grieving people — When tears are not enough*. New York: Brunner-Routledge.

Kabat-Zinn, J. (1990). *Full catastrophe of living: Using the wisdom of your body and mind to face stress, pain and illness*. New York: Delta.

Kabat-Zinn, J., Lipworth, L., Burney, R., & Sellers, W. (1987). Four year follow-up of a meditation-based program for the self-regulation of chronic pain: Treatment, outcomes and compliance. *The Clinical Journal of Pain, 2*, 159–173.

Kabat-Zinn, J., Massion, A.,O., Kristeller, J., Peterson, L., Fletcher, K., Pbert, L., et al. (1992). Effectiveness of a meditation-based stress reduction program in the treatment of anxiety disorders. *American Journal of Psychiatry, 149*(7), 936–943.

Kaye, R. (1991). *Spinning straw into gold: Your emotional recovery from breast cancer*. New York: Simon & Schuster.

Kennedy, A. (1991). *Losing a parent*. San Francisco: Harper.

Kidder, B. (2001). *ImaginACTION: Activities that allow students to get up on their feet and moving!* (2nd ed.). Fort Collins, CO: Cottonwood Press.

Klass, D. (1996). The deceased child in the psychic and social worlds of bereaved parents during the resolution of grief. In D. Klass, P. R. Silverman, & S. I. Nickman (Eds.), *Continuing bonds: New understandings of grief* (pp. 199–215). Washington, D.C.: Taylor & Francis.

Klass, D. (1999). *Spiritual lives of bereaved parents*. Philadelphia: Brunner-Mazel.

Kübler-Ross, E. (1983). *On children and death*. New York: Touchstone.

Landy, R. (2005). Introduction. In A.M. Weber & C. Haen (Eds.), *Clinical applications in drama therapy in child and adolescent treatment* (pp. xxi–xxvii). New York: Brunner-Routledge.

Lasater, J. (1995). *Relax and renew*. Berkeley, CA: Rodmill Press.

Liebmann, M. (1986). *Art therapy for groups: A handbook of themes, games and exercises*. Cambridge, MA: Brookline Books.

Lepore, S., & Smyth, J. (2002). *The writing cure: How expressive writing promotes health and well-being*. Washington, DC: American Psychological Association.

Levine, S. (2005). *Unattended sorrow*. Emmaus, PA: Rodale.

Lewin, M. (Ed.). (2005). *Buddhist reflections on death, dying and bereavement*. Newport, Isle of Wight: Buddhist Hospice Trust.

Luzzato, P., & Gabriel, B. (2000). The creative journey: A model for short-term group art therapy with post-treatment cancer patients. *Art Therapy: Journal of the American Art Therapy Association, 17*(4), 265–269.

Malchiodi, C. A. (1992). Art and loss. *Art Therapy: Journal of the American Art Therapy Association, 9*, 114–118.

Malchiodi, C. A. (1998). *The art therapy sourcebook*. Lincolnwood, IL:

Malchiodi, C. (1999). *Medical art therapy with adults*. London: Jessica Kingsley.Lowell House.

McColly, M. (2006). *The after-death room: Journey into spiritual activism*. Cambridge, MA: Soft Skull Press, 244, 247.

McNiff, S. (1992). *Art as medicine: Creating a therapy of the imagination*. Boston: Shambhala.

McNiff, S. (2004). *Art heals: How creativity cures the soul*. Boston: Shambhala.

Miller, J., Fletcher, K., & Kabat-Zinn, J. (1995). Three year follow up and clinical implications of mindfulness meditation-based stress reduction intervention in treatment of anxiety disorders. *General Hospital Psychiatry, 17,* 192–200.

Mitchell, R. R. & Friedman, H. (1994). SNADPLAY: Past, present, and future. New York: Routledge.

Monk, G. (1997). How narrative therapy works. In G. Monk, J. Winslade, K. Crocket, & D. Epston (Eds.), *Narrative therapy in practice: The archaeology of hope* (pp. 3–31). San Francisco: Jossey-Bass.

Nainis, N., Paice, J., Ratner, J., Wirth, J., Lai, J., & Shott, S. (2006). Relieving symptoms in cancer: Innovative use of art therapy. *Journal of Pain and Symptom Management, 31*(2), 162–169.

Neimeyer, R. A. (2000). *Lessons of loss: A guide to coping*. Keystone Heights, FL: Psychoeducational Resources.

Öster, I., Svensk, A., Magnusson, E., Thyme, K., Sjödin, M., & Åström, S. (2006). Art therapy improves coping resources: A randomized, controlled study among women with breast cancer. *Palliative and Supportive Care, 4,* 57–64.

Piccirillo, E. (1999). Hide and seek, the art of living with HIV/AIDS. In C. Malchiodi (Ed.), *Medical art therapy with children* (pp. 113–132). London: Jessica Kingsley.

Pucucci, M. (2005). *Ritual as resource*. Berkeley, CA: North Atlantic Books.

Rando, T. (1984). *Grief, dying and death: Clinical interventions for caregivers*. Champaign, IL: Research Press.

Rando, T. (1988). *How to go on living when someone you love dies*. New York: Bantam Books.

Rando, T. (1993). *Treatment of complicated mourning*. Champaign, IL: Research Press.

Rando, T. (2000). Clinical dimensions of anticipatory mourning. Champaign, IL: Research Press.

Rich, P. (1999). *The healing journey through grief: Your journal for reflection and recovery*. New York: Wiley.

Rohd, M. (1998). *Theatre for community, conflict and dialogue: The hope is vital training manual*. Portsmouth, NH: Heinemann.

Ross, B. (2002). *How to haiku: A writer's guide to haiku and related forms*. Boston: Tuttle.

Rozman, D. (1994). *Meditating with children: The art of concentration and centering*. Boulder Creek, CA: Planetary.

Saint-Exupéry, A. (1943). *The little prince*. Orlando, FL: Harcourt Brace Javanovich.

Saltzman, J. (1993). *If you can talk, you can write*. New York: Warner Books.

Saraswati, S. K. (1986). *Yogic management of common diseases*. Munger, India: Bihar School of Yoga.

Schuurman, D. (2003). *Never the same: Coming to terms with the death of a parent*. New York: St. Martin's Press.

Serlin, I., Classen, C., Frances, B., & Angell, K. (2000). Symposium: Support groups for women with breast cancer: Traditional and alternative expressive approaches. *The Arts in Psychotherapy, 27*(2), 123–138.

Some, M. P. (1993). *Ritual*. Portland, OR: Swan/Raven.

Stein, S. B. (1974). *About dying: An open family book for parents and children together*. New York: Walker.

Stewart, M., & Phillips, K. (1992). *Yoga for children*. New York: Simon & Schuster.

Stoyva, J., & Anderson, C. (1982). A coping-rest model of relaxation and stress management. In L. Goldberger & S. Breznitz (Eds.), *Handbook of stress — Theoretical and clinical aspects* (p. 745). London: Collier Macmillan.

Targ, E., & Levine, E. (2002). The efficacy of mind-body-spirit group for women with breast cancer: A randomized controlled trial. *General Hospital Psychiatry, 24*(2002), 238–248.

Valenzuela, M. T. *Dia de Muertos … a uniquely Mexican Fiesta* (2005, November) Punto de VISTA, San Miguel de Allende.

Webb, N. B. (2003). Play and expressive therapies to help bereaved children: Individual, family, and group treatment. *Smith College Studies in Social Work, 73*(3), 405–422.

Wheeler, W. (1998). *Path through the fire*. Northford, CT: Author.

Wolfelt, A. (1983). *Helping children cope with grief*. Bristol, PA: Accelerated Development.

Wolfelt, A. (1997). *The journey through grief: Reflections on healing*. Fort Collins, CO: Companion Press.

Wolfelt, A. (2001). *Healing your grieving heart for teens: 100 practical ideas*. Fort Collins, CO: Companion Press.

Worden, J. W. (1996). *Children and grief: When a parent dies*. New York: Guilford.

Worden, J. W. (2001). *Grief counseling and grief therapy* (3rd ed.). New York: Springer.

Wright, R. K. (n.d.). Totem Poles: Heraldic columns of the northwest coast. Retrieved September 20, 2006, from http://content.lib.washington.edu/aipnw/wright.html.

Zegan, L. (1982). Stress and the development of somatic disorders. In L. Goldberger & S. Breznitz (Eds.), *Handbook of stress: Theoretical and clinical aspects* (p.134). New York: The Free Press.

Zonnebelt-Smeenge, S. J., & De Vries, R. C. (2001). *The empty chair: Handling grief on holidays and special occasions*. Grand Rapids, MI: Baker Books.

INDEX

A

ActALIVE, 239–42, 247, 250–51
Acting for Real (Emunah), 117
Active music making, 108–12
Adewusi, Richie, 243
After-Death Room: Journey into Spiritual Activism, The (McColly), 245
Albert, Ina, 55, 57
Allende, Isabel, 60
Allport, Penny, 31, 259, 271, 278–79
Alternative art forms, 239–40
Arbogast, Marsha Roach, 174
Archetypes, 3
Artist's Way, The (Cameron), 61
Arts for Global Development, 247
Arts in Healthcare Project, 213, 223
Art therapy, 3–4, 6–7, 40; *See also*
        Alternative art forms; Expressive
        arts; Touch Drawing
  bereaved children, 231
  color with feelings and emotions, 184
  color and mark making, 183–85
  in grief process, 28–29, 281
  group painting experience, 176–81
  in hospice, 205–12
  a mother's narrative of survival, 260–68
  music and, 107–08
  painting though the pain, 182–87
  in residential care, 268–71
  work-related stress and, 284–85
Art Therapy for Groups (Liebmann), 6
Assisted living facility (ALF), 268
Attachment Theory (Bowlby), 25
Attig, Thomas, 26

B

Baker, Sara, 64, 189
Baughman, Sandra, 36, 227
Bennett, Hal Zina, 61

Bereavement groups, 9–10, 21, 36, 211
Bertman, Sandra, 6, 39, 281–82
Biographies, 62–63
Blauer, Shemaya, 172
Boal, Augusto, 122
Body awareness, 85–89
"Body Maps," 249
Bolen, Jean Shinoda, 133
Bon dance, 202
Bottorff, J., 213
Bourgault, Louise, 243
Bovee, Jaclyn, 124
Bowlby, John, 25
Bram Bharati Samiti, 241
Braque, Georges, 95
Breathing exercises, 89–90
Broomberg, Lola, 115, 119
Browning, Elizabeth Barrett, 101
Burgess, Nicole, 44, 64, 101, 112
Burnout symptoms, 283

C

Cameron, Julia, 61
Camp environment for children, 231–36
Cancer support groups, 212–13
Capacchione, Lucia, 98, 158
Caregivers, notes for, 282–83
Chandler, Lauren, 7, 39, 42, 45, 64, 92, 115
Chanting, 111–12
Chappell, Carol, 171
Check-in routine, 15
Children and teens
    ages 2 years and under, 34
    ages 3 to 5, 34–35
    ages 5 to 8, 35
    ages 9 to 12, 35–36
    bereavement workshop, 207
    camp programs for, 231–36
    children's songs, 113
    collage, 99
    creating a family mark, 232–36

creative arts and, 227–29
creative writing, 64–65
Day of the Dead program, 271–80
developmental levels, 34–36
drama and theater, 125
early and late teens, 36
grief and loss, 31–34
life review through song, 102
peer group, 118
physical movement, 93
rituals and, 146–48
sandtray and, 76
writing/journaling, 53
Circles of Life: A Creative Curriculum for Healing Traumatic Loss in Childhood (Curtis), 125
Clay mask, 222–23
Close to the Bone: Life Threatening Illness and the Search for Meaning (Bolen), 133
Cofacilitator, 11
Collaborative mural, 221–22
Collage, 6, 44, 95–100, 218–21, 263
   activities, 96
   children and teens, 99
   creating a vision, 98–99
   full-body painting, 220–21
   introduction to, 95–96
   materials needed, 96–97
   pictures of opposites, 98
   story of loss, 97
   types of, 97–99
Collie, K., 213
Community action, HIV/AIDS-related projects, 245–48
Compassionate Friends, 10
Complicated mourning, 27–28
Conati, C., 213
Counsel Process, 42, 145
Courageous Kids Theater Troupe, 115, 118–20, 124, 126
Creative writing, 42, 59–67
   activities, 60
   biographies, 62–63
   children and teens, 53, 64–65
   exercise for, 61–62
   fierce writing workshops, 195–97
   Haiku, 63–64
   HIV/AIDS-related projects, 244–45
   jump-off lines, 61–62
   materials needed, 60
   poetry, 63–64, 191–95
   Touch Drawing reflections and, 167–68

woven dialog workshops, 189–95
Curtis, Anne, 125

D

Dagara tradition, 130
Daily exercises, 83–90
Dance, 93, 168, 201–02; *See also* Physical movement
Dangerous situations, 18–19
Day of the Dead ritual, 31, 131, 271–80
Didion, Joan, 59–60
Dorph, Dough, 191
Dougy Center, Portland, Oregon, 33
Dow, Dona, 85–89
Drama and theater, 7, 45, 64, 115–27
   blind circle activity, 122
   challenges in grief support groups, 117–18
   children and, 125
   Courageous Kids Theater Troupe, 115, 118–20, 124, 126
   cover the space activity, 122
   curriculum, 120–25
   either-or activity, 123
   foundation of theory, 116–18
   HIV/AIDS-related projects, 242–44
   introduction to, 115–16
   materials needed, 121
   paths of grief activity, 124
   performance, 125–26
   sharing/closing, 125
   significant place tour activity, 123–24
Drug/alcohol abuse, 18
Drum improvisation, 109–11
Dual process model (Strolbe), 26

E

Emunah, Renee, 117
Erikson, E. H., 118
Expectations and ground rules, 13–14
Expressive arts, 3, 201–05; *See also* "Finding the Creative Fire" program
   Bon dance, 201–02
   for cancer patients, 212–23
   caring hands remembered, 210–11
   clay mask, 222–23

collaborative mural, 221–22
collage, 218–19
examples of, 209–12
full-body painting/collage, 220–21
hachimaki and fans, 201–02
healing stone, 220
kamidana, 201
mandalas, 209–10, 214–18
mask making, 252–56
puppet performance, 248
scribble drawing, 219–20
teens and creative arts, 227–29
toro-nagashi, 200, 203–05
"Exquisite Witness," 5, 50, 281

F

Facilitators, 3–5, 12–18, 40, 234
Family mark, 232–36
Family Therapy Center of Virginia Tech, 213
Feldman, Janet, 239–40
Fierce writing workshops, 195–97
"Finding the Creative Fire" program, 213, 223
    clay mask, 222–23
    collaborative mural, 221–22
    collage, 218–19
    creative arts experiences of, 214–23
    format of sessions, 214
    full-body painting/collage, 220–21
    healing stone, 220
    introduction to, 212–13
    mandalas, 214–18
    project participants, 214–15
    scribble drawing, 219–20
Four tasks of mourning (Worden), 25
Friedman, Gary, 248
Friedman, Harriet, 69, 72
Frost, Robert, 195
Full-body painting/collage, 220–21

G

Gary Friedman Productions, 248
Goldman, Linda, 32–33, 64
Grief facilitators, 3–5, 12–18, 40, 234

Grief and the Healing Arts: Creativity as Therapy (Bertman), 6, 282
Grief and loss
    basics of, 21–23
    challenges of mourning, 117
    children and teens, 31–34, 229–37
    complicated mourning, 27–28
    factors affecting, 23–24
    family therapies, 199–205
    long-term grief, 22
    lost relationship, 23
    modern day rituals (examples of), 133–39
    mother's narrative of survival, 260–68
    as normal emotional response, 21
    personal stories of, 259–79
    physical symptoms of, 82
    psychological characteristics of griever, 27–28
    ritual and art in, 28–29
    spiritual process of, 22
    various tradition of, 130–31
Grief Observed, A (Lewis), 60
Grief support groups; *See also* Group challenges; Leadership roles: Support group curriculum
    bereaved children and, 231
    cofacilitator, 11
    expectations and ground rules, 13–14
    group members, 13
    group sessions, 41–42
    individual sessions, 42–45
    leadership of, 9–11
    materials, 13
    opening/closing rituals, 15
    physical setting, 12
    preplanning and organization, 12–14
    purpose and structure of, 12
    session plans, 19–20
    setting up the group, 10–11
    situations during sessions, 15–18
Grief theories, 25–26
    Attig's relearning the world, 26
    Bowlby's attachment theory, 25
    Neimeyer's meaning reconstruction, 26
    Rando's six R's, 25–26
    Strolbe's dual process model, 26
    Worden's four tasks of mourning, 25
Ground rules, 13–14
Group challenges
    the challenger, 17

comparison grieving, 15–16
faith, 16
should, must, have to, 16
small talk (idle chitchat), 17
speaking for the group, 17–18
spontaneous nonrequested advice
    giver, 16
the talker/interrupter, 16–17
Group leadership, 11, 40
Group members, 13
Group painting experience, 176–82
Group session format
    check-in, 41
    closing, 41
    main activity, 41
    opening, 41
    ritual, 42
    sample format for, 41–42
Group singing, 112
Group work, 7

H

Hachimaki and fans, 201–02
Haiku, 63–64
Halifax, Joan, 69
"Hands Project, The," 240
Healing stone, 220
*Helping Grieving People: When Tears Are Not
    Enough* (Jeffreys), 22
HIV/AIDS-related grief, 239–40
    international projects, 240–44
    theater and music, 242–44
    visual arts and, 240–42
HIV/AIDS-related projects
    ActALIVE, 250–51
    community actions and personal
        expressions, 245–48
    Memory Project, 249–50
    puppet performance, 248
Horne, Kathleen, 157
Hospice, 10
    arts in, 205–12
    Keystone's experiences, 207–08
    music experiences in, 206
    staff support, 208
How to Haiku (Ross), 63
Hrenko, K. D., 231

I

"If You Can Talk, You Can Write"
    (Saltzman), 61
Intermodal expressive therapy, 4
International arts coalition, 239
International Peace Tiles Project, 241
International project, 242–44
Introductions, 49–50
Iyengar, B. K. S., 82

J

Jeffreys, J. Shep, 5, 22
Journaling, 5, 39, 42, 53–57, 59
    children and teens, 35–36, 53
    example of, 55–57
JUMP (Juveniles Using Media Power), 243
Jump-off lines, 61–62
Jung, Carl, 3

K

Kabat-Zinn, Jon, 82
Kalff, Dora, 72
Kamidana, 201
Kanji, 202–03
Keithley, Zoe, 57
Keystone's Therapeutic Arts program, 206
    coping with holidays, 207–08
    group examples, 207–08
    legacy of caring for staff, 208
Kinasewich, Kathleen and Alex, 133–39
Kiser, Laura, 36, 227, 229
Klass, Dennis, 26
Koeleman, Judith, 44, 153, 182, 184–87
Koff-Chapin, Deborah, 44, 153–54, 157,
    159–61, 163–64, 167, 169–70,
    172–74, 176
Kübler-Ross, Elisabeth, 26, 31
Kyle, Brian, 186–87

L

Lasater, Judith, 82
Leadership roles, 14–18

alerts for referral, 18–19
   dangerous situations, 18–19
Lee, Justine, 126
Lessons of Loss (Neimeyer), 63
Levine, Stephen, 3, 285
Lewis, C. S., 60
Liebmann, Marian, 6
Lifehome Center, 240
Life and Loss (Goldman), 64
Long, B., 213
Lowenfeld, Margaret, 72

life review through song, 102
making instruments, 110
materials needed, 103
personal narrative on grief, 259–60
for relaxation, 104–05
sample relaxation script, 106–07
song, 101–04
song writing, 103–04
Touch Drawing and, 162
well-known songs, 112–13
Music-guided relaxation, 211

M

McCarney, Valerie, 155–56
McColly, Michael, 245
McIntyre, Carol, 44, 153, 175–76, 178–80, 182
McNamee, Carole M., 199, 209–10, 212, 216–22
McNiff, Shaun, 205
Malchiodi, Cathy, 234
Mandala, 99, 107–08, 214–18
   exercise for, 107–08
   mandala quilt, 209–10
Mask making, 252–56
Meaning reconstruction (Neimeyer), 26
Meditation, 90–91, 145–46
Memorial float, 137–39
Memory Books, 249–50
Memory Project, 249–50
Mier, Debra, 199, 203–04
Mind maps, 215n
Miró, Joan, 95
Mispireta, Hernando, 282, 284
Monk, Gerald, 117
Moore, Thomas D., 259
Morgan, Jonathan, 249
Mourning, 6, 10, 117
Movement to music, 93, 168
Munch, E., 261–62
Mural, 221–22
Music, 44, 101–13
   active music making, 108–12
   art and, 107–08
   chanting, 111–12
   children's songs, 113
   drumming affirmations, 111
   drumming and leading a group, 109–10
   group singing, 112
   HIV/AIDS-related projects, 242–44

N

Narrative therapy, 117
Narrative Therapy in Practice: The
   Archaeology of Hope (Monk), 117
National Association of Drama Therapy, 116
National Community of Women Living
   with AIDS (NAC-WOLA), 249
Neimeyer, Robert, 26, 49, 54, 63, 117–18
Newman, Sara, 107–08
Nichols, Darcy, 74

O

O Bon festival (Festival of Lights), 200–201, 205
Odhiambo, Ron, 243
One World Beat, 244
Oral history, 49
   activities for, 50–51
   oral stories, 3–4, 42, 52–53
Ostaseski, Frank, 69

P

Paula (Allende), 60
Peace tiles, 241
Personal expressions, HIV/AIDS-related
   projects, 245–48
Phillips, Sara Spaulding, 64
Physical movement, 43, 81–93
   activities, 83
   alternative exercises, 92–93

centering with breath, 89–90
children and teens, 93
dance and movement to music, 93, 168, 201–02
introduction to, 81–83
meditation and visualization, 90–91
relaxation, 91–92
simple daily exercises, 83–90
starting the energy moving, 84
stretching and body awareness, 85–89
Physical setting, 12
Picasso, Pablo, 95
Piercy, Janyt, 156
"Playing for Life: Performance in Africa in the Age of AIDS" (Bourgault), 243
Poetry, 63–64, 191–95
Preplanning and organization, 12–14
Printaking brayer, 160
Puppet performance, 248

R

Raine, L., 252
Rando, Therese A., 25, 27, 40
Referrals, 18–19
Relationships, 23
Relaxation, 91–92
music for, 104–05
sample script for, 106–07
Relearning the world (Attig), 26
Remen, Rachel Naomi, 74, 189
Rituals, 3, 5, 40, 45, 129–48
artful expressions, 143
children and, 146–47
closing/opening ritual, 141–44
collective ritual, 134–35
council process or talking stick, 145
creating sacred space, 141–42
curriculum, 140–41
defined, 131–32
entering into, 142
facilitator notes, 140–41
grief and loss traditions, , 28–29, 130–31
in group sessions, 42, 51–52
how rituals help, 132–33
introduction to, 129–30
materials needed, 130
memorial float, 137–39
modern day examples, 133–39

personal rituals, 135
preparation checklist, 144
teens, 147–48
Tibetan prayer flags, 136
walking meditation, 145–46
Rogers, Janet Shaw, 40, 42, 45, 99, 129
Rogers, J. Earl, 3, 21, 31, 39, 49, 59, 69, 72–73, 81, 95, 239, 252–55, 281, 285
Rohd, Michael, 123
Ross, Bruce, 63

S

"Sacred" witness, 6, 50
Saltzman, Joel, 61
Sandplay, 71–74
Sandplay Therapists of America, 72
Sandtray, 6, 43, 67, 69–78
activities, 70
alternative forms, 74–75
children and teens, 76
historical perspective on, 69
materials needed, 71
process of using objects, 75
sandplay and, 71–74
selection and purchase of pieces, 76–78
Saraswati, Swami Karmananda, 82
Save the Children, 249
Schlumberger, Barbara, 176
Schwitters, Kurt, 95
Scribble drawing, 219–20
Session plans, 19–20
Shiva, 131
Shoro Nagashi (memorial float ritual, 131, 137–39
Silva, Shirley, 168
Six R's (Rando), 25–26
SOLID (Salt Spring Organization for Life Improvement and Development), 246
Song writing, 103–04
Spaulding-Phillips, Sara, 189, 195
Storytelling, 3
Stress, 82, 284–85
Stretching and body awareness, 85–89
Strolbe, Margaret, 26
Suicide risk factors, 19
Support group curriculum, 42–45
art of collage, 44, 95–100
drama and theater, 45, 115–27

introduction and oral history, 42, 49–57
music, 44, 101–13
physical movement, 43, 81–93
ritual, 45, 129–48
sandtray, 43, 69–78
written word, 42–43, 59–67

T

Talking stick ritual, 145
Teens. *See* Children and teens
"Ten Millions Memory Project," 249
Theater group, 39
Thich Nhat Hanh, 145
Thomae, Laura, 199, 205
Thoreau, Henry David, 98
Through the Veil, 159
Tibetan prayer flags, 136–37
"Time to Deliver," 245–46
Timmons, Tinky, 154, 156
Toro-nagashi, 200, 203–05
Torres, Lars Hasselblad, 241
Totem, 232
Touch Drawing: A Guided Experience, 159, 162
Touch Drawing, 153–75
    beginning to draw, 163
    closure of session, 169
    cloud gazing, 165
    drawing what you feel, 163–64
    ending drawing session, 166–67
    grief work examples, 153–59, 170–75
    imaginal body, 165
    inner body sensation, 165
    inner face, 164–65
    instructions for, 159–75
    materials, 160–61
    musical support, 162
    offering suggestions, 162
    physical set-up for sharing, 166
    preparing the board, 161
    privacy needed, 161–62
    relationship or situation, 165
    sharing images with group, 169
    technique, 160
    turning inward, 162–63
    using movement and sound, 168
    viewing drawings, 166
    witnessing the images, 166–67

writing reflections, 167–68
Touch Drawing Facilitator Workbook, 159
Tuvako, Stan, 243

U

Unattended Sorrow (Levine), 285

V

Valenzuela, Maria Teresa, 276
Visioning (Capacchione), 98
Visual arts, 240–42
Visualization, 90–91

W

Walking meditation, 145–46
Walsh, Sandra M., 259, 268
Warm-up phase, 15
Wayman, Lisa, 259–60, 264
Weber, Marion, 74
Wellens, Margaret, 170
Willow House, 199–205
Wilson, Christina, 158
Wolfelt, Alan, 9, 21, 26, 32, 230
Worden, William, 25, 40
World AIDS Day, 241–42, 248, 251
World Technique (Lowenfeld), 72
Worley, Robin, 243
Woven dialog workshops, 189–95
    group session examples, 191–95
    listening and observing, 190–91
"Write from the Heart" (Bennett), 61
*Write Your Self Well... Journal Your Self to
    Health* (Albert and Keithley), 57
Writing. *See* Creative writing

Y

Year of Magical Thinking, The (Didion), 60
Yoga, 82–83, 245
YouthAid Projects, 243